DELIMITATIONS OF
LATIN AMERICAN
PHILOSOPHY

WORLD PHILOSOPHIES

Bret W. Davis, D. A. Masolo, and
Alejandro Vallega, editors

DELIMITATIONS OF LATIN AMERICAN PHILOSOPHY

Beyond Redemption

—ɯ—

OMAR RIVERA

INDIANA UNIVERSITY PRESS

This book is a publication of

Indiana University Press
Office of Scholarly Publishing
Herman B Wells Library 350
1320 East 10th Street
Bloomington, Indiana 47405 USA

iupress.indiana.edu

Manufactured in the United States of America

Cagtaloging information is available from the Library of Congress.

ISBN 978-0-253-04484-6 (hdbk.)
ISBN 978-0-253-04485-3 (pbk.)
ISBN 978-0-253-04486-0 (web PDF)

1 2 3 4 5 24 23 22 21 20 19

Para Miguel y Violeta

CONTENTS

ACKNOWLEDGMENTS

IT'S BEEN DIFFICULT to write a book that is not rooted in my formal philosophical education but, rather, in a set of pressing questions that emerged while growing up in Lima, Peru, and becoming an adult as a Latino in the United States. For this reason, the encouragement of philosophers that I deeply admire, including Alejandro Vallega, Daniela Vallega-Neu, Charles Scott, Nancy Tuana, Linda Martín Alcoff, Eduardo Mendieta, and Ofelia Schutte, has been invaluable for the completion of this project. I am grateful to have been able to teach classes in Latin American philosophy at the University of Wisconsin–La Crosse and Southwestern University when such courses were almost unheard of in philosophy departments. This provided me the opportunity to learn with my students. In terms of this book, I want to thank Aaron Jimenez and Cat Kelly, both Southwestern students, who helped me with editing and research. I have been fortunate to receive grants and other kinds of support that have helped me finish this work. In particular, UW–L awarded me a Faculty Research Grant and an International Development Grant, and Southwestern granted me a Junior Sabbatical. I made the final revisions while being an ACLS-Burkhardt Fellow at LLILAS Benson Latin American Studies and Collections at the University of Texas at Austin.

I am especially thankful to Alejandro, who has been a defining presence during my philosophical trajectory since graduating college as well as an incredible friend. And I am above all thankful to Christina. Without her infinite patience, encouragement, and companionship I would not have been able to embark on this philosophical path.

DELIMITATIONS OF LATIN AMERICAN PHILOSOPHY

—⟋⟍—

INTRODUCTION

Pachakuti

THE INTERPRETATIONS of seminal texts on social and political liberation woven together by this book open paths toward the study of Latin American philosophy. Several core themes of this philosophical tradition guide my interpretations: the political and philosophical significance of "America," the social implications of legacies of colonialism, the epistemological consequences of rejecting universalism and Eurocentrism, the undoing of philosophies of liberation by racism, and the relationship between aesthetics and liberation, among others. I frame the themes in this book through two related problematics. The first is the possibility of articulating philosophies of liberation beyond redemption, that is, without positing a coming, definitive, and comprehensive event that would undo the oppression of a demarcated group and redeem their suffering. The second is the difficulty of envisioning liberatory programs from the critical positionality of the oppressed without essentializing their identities and those of other groups. The two problematics are connected because redemptive projects can essentialize oppressed identities. Exploring possibilities of liberation beyond redemption is an attempt to avoid falling into such essentializations.

Reading texts by Simón Bolívar, José Martí, and José Carlos Mariátegui in particular, and focusing on the way redemptive commitments shape their philosophical positions, I began to notice that three interrelated delimitations of Latin American philosophy became more apparent. I am referring to a contextual delimitation (emphasizing the situatedness of philosophy rather than its universality, and the character of oppressed identities as hermeneutic critical foci), a transcultural delimitation (denoting the embeddedness of philosophical

1

reflection in the crossings between cultural lineages and practices especially across power differentials), and an aesthetic delimitation (where philosophy engages the present in its liberatory, transformative potency, and at the level of embodied sensibilities, like memory, nostalgia, and other prereflective temporalizations, as they are elicited by artistic and festive cultural events). In my discussion these three overlapping delimitations reflect the work of Linda Martín Alcoff, Ofelia Schutte, and Gloria Anzaldúa, respectively.

In my analyses the problematic of redemption appears in relation to these three delimitations of Latin American philosophy. In the contextual delimitation, identities as critical foci can be constructed, fixed, and essentialized in the process of articulating the future liberation of oppressed peoples (see mainly chaps. 1, 2, and 3). In the transcultural delimitation, a commitment to the redemption of the oppressed can enforce projects of cultural recovery that not only essentialize identities but also override and curtail the critical capacity of liberatory philosophies positioned in between cultures in postcolonial contexts (see chap. 4). In the aesthetic delimitation, redemptive proclivities can yield a representative aesthetics of the oppressed submitted to the interests of lettered ideologies, one that suppresses aesthetic engagements formative of liberatory agencies at the level of embodiment and sensibility (see chaps. 5 and 6 and the conclusion). My interpretive perspective "beyond redemption" seeks to release both seminal texts in Latin American philosophy and the philosophical delimitations just laid out from the hold redemption can have in the articulation of liberatory programs.

This book, then, renders interpretive perspectives on key themes, texts, and figures in Latin American philosophy, and traces some of its delimitations, as two integrated projects. This introduction approaches the problematics of embodied sensibilities of and beyond redemption and of the essentialization of identities in liberatory projects and ends with a summary of the book's chapters.[1]

CÉSAR VALLEJO'S ROUNDED DIE

Vallejo's poetry is embedded in a Latin American aesthetic lineage that delves into the plight of the oppressed. Enrique Dussel touches on this lineage when he discusses the "tremendist Christs" of Latin America. He writes, "These Christs have deep wounds, enormous clots of blood, infinite sadness in their big eyes, great thorns, and a realism which is shocking in the pain portrayed.... [I]n Latin America he [Christ] is the suffering Christ of the oppressed classes."[2] Especially on the basis of Mariátegui's reading, I see Vallejo as also working with religious imagery and themes to explore the suffering of the excluded. His "The Black Heralds" begins thus:

> There are blows in life, so powerful . . . I don't know!
> Blows as from the hatred of God; as if, facing them,
> The undertow of everything suffered
> Welled up in the soul . . . I don't know!

The hatred of God names a consuming, exhaustive, and excluding form of oppression. The suffering it yields paralyzes. It appears that there is nothing one can do about it; one falls into a state of resignation trapped by a negating world. The poem ends

> And man . . . Poor . . . poor! He turns his eyes, as
> when a slap on the shoulder summons us;
> turns his crazed eyes and everything lived
> wells up, like a pool of guilt in his look.[3]

Oppression, "the hatred of God," is internalized by the oppressed as a kind of guilt that permeates the totality of life. Through this guilt, the oppressed carries the burden of her oppression. Yet her guilt can also express a longing to be loved by God, to be liberated, to find redemption in the embrace of a world to come in which her exclusion is definitively undone.

In "The Eternal Dice" Vallejo evokes a different oppressed sensibility:

> My God, in this deaf, gloomy night,
> You will not be able to gamble, for the Earth
> Is a worn die now rounded from
> Rolling at random,
> ˙˙˙ but in a hollow,
> ˙ nmense tomb.[4]

ınded die, does not stop rolling until it falls into the abyss of ettle into a definite arrangement. For the oppressed (the one the poem), this means that her oppression cannot be framed d. Thus, the hatred of God and the guilt it effects are never is sense, the suffering of the oppressed includes the aware- ce of comprehensive sense in a world that excludes her and in at would redeem her. This yields a second order of paralysis, und by fixed worlds and does not seek redemption. n here is not that all oppressed groups share these sensibili- r options to understand liberation as it manifests itself at an affective level. The "second order of paralysis" in particular withdraws from redemptive investments. In this withdrawal, it also undermines attachments to essentialized identities that articulate themselves in terms of totalizing exclusionary and redemptive worlds.

THE "PACHAKUTI SENSIBILITY"

Similarly, María Lugones describes two modes of stasis of the oppressed. Germinative stasis, which she connects with the possibility of resistance, does not fit within a modern Western conception of agency that "presupposes ready-made hierarchical worlds of sense in which individuals form intentions, make choices, and carry out actions in the ready-made terms of those worlds." Instead, it involves an "active subjectivity" that "has no such presuppositions, no ready-made sense within which our actions and intentions can be made congruent with our domination."[5] Resistant praxis emerges here out of an absence of "ready-made sense," out of an attunement to the turns of the rolling earth in Vallejo's poem, one could say. I underscore that active subjectivity does not even presuppose worlds of sense that are to come; in particular, it does not draw sense from a redemptive future. Germinative stasis, or what appeared earlier as a "second order of paralysis," faces the terror of "not belonging anywhere," but it also shelters the possibility of a nonredemptive liberation.[6]

It is possible to draw a connection between Vallejo's poetry, Lugones's theories of resistance, and Andean cosmologies. For Rodolfo Kusch, Andean indigenous sensibilities reach past objective, ready-made orders that define a world and approach a background of the sheer happenings of things beyond the purview of ready-made orders, happenings of things in their "así" (or in their "this is it"). The "así" is experienced through a "complete availability and openness of the subject, which leads one to suspect a constant fear in the face of the upturn or the fluctuation of the así of the world." Through these fluctuations or turns, the world (or "pacha") never fully settles with overarching sense. It appears always on the verge of undergoing a turn or "kuti."[7]

A "pachakuti sensibility" (pachakuti meaning "the turning of the world upside down") situates itself in the turn between worlds. It can sustain forms of resistance because it affirms happenings of life in excess of an oppressive world, yet this excess is not geared toward crystallizing itself within another world—which is what it means to be a sensibility of the turn or kuti. In the turn, past worlds and worlds to come are held at the same time, and their differentiation is not reducible to sequential logics: one world does not follow another. Especially through the notion of estar, Kusch shows that in constant upturns there is a moment in which worlds are not yet set but nevertheless appear without closure. He finds community and embodied affirmation of life as it is (that is, not subjected to overarching, objective orders of meaning) in this germinative state.

EXILIC MEMORY, EXILIC LOVE

A pivotal aspect of José Carlos Mariátegui's work is his elucidation of the relationship between aesthetics and decolonizing liberation that appears in his seminal text *Seven Essays for the Interpretation of Peruvian Reality*. There he interprets the nostalgia that characterizes Vallejo's poetry: "His nostalgia is a sentimental protest or a metaphysical protest. Nostalgia of exile; nostalgia of absence." Nostalgia is a kind of memory, a kind of attachment to and dwelling in the past, and Vallejo modulates it through an exilic state, which is a spatialization that enforces distance as a form of absence. I am interested in how this specific spacing of memory and time results in a sensibility of resistance beyond redemption that amounts to a metaphysical protest and in its connection to what I call a "pachakuti sensibility."[8]

"Exilic memory" means here the awareness that something is happening somewhere else and that our memory is our only access to it. It is a mode of the spatialization of time. Accessing an absent present through this kind of memory releases the present into the sphere of the possible as *what it could have been* rather than as *what it could be*, emphasizing the past as possibility rather than the future. This particular spatio-temporality of exile can inform a resistant sensibility in relation to an oppressive and excluding world. Through it the past can potentialize the transformative possibilities of the present. Exilically, the past is elusive, disseminated, creative. It is "heterogeneous and contradictory." It is a field of shifts and turns (or *kuti*) between worlds configuring a heterogeneous present and is disengaged from the redemptive draw of the future.[9]

Exilic memory echoes Mariátegui's account of a memorial revolutionary sensibility. He writes, "The ability to think about history and the ability to make it or create it come to be identified with one another. *Perhaps the revolutionary has an image of the past that is somewhat subjective, but it is animated and alive....* Revolutionaries incarnate the will of society of not becoming petrified within a stage."[10]

Here the present does not appear as a closed and definitive reality (with entrenched social, cultural, political, and economic forms, for example) but, rather, as always open to transformation by being accessed memorially. In this case, the image of the past cannot be exhausted in a totalized present; it is alive, obtruding the present's closure. The emphasis is on the present as open, as not petrified, and on the past that modulates it as fluid and elusive. The future is a "toward" that remains indeterminate and does not constitute a definitive temporal framing of revolutionary praxis. Like the exilic temporality of *what could have been*, this revolutionary memory does not belong to an actual or actualizable world; it holds itself back, remaining in the turns between worlds.[11]

Following Mariátegui's reading of Vallejo in the *Seven Essays*, exilic memory appears to be connected to the sensibilities of the excluded poor, especially the colonized. It is as if they are never in their place. Their relationship to the systems that exclude them is exilic, they can "remember" what their world was, and more important, *what it could have been,* and let this memorial eventuation disrupt the petrification of an oppressive present. Perhaps no other lines in Vallejo's poetry are as evocative of this disruptive, spatialized temporality as these:

> All of my bones are someone else's;
> Maybe I stole them!
> I have been given what perhaps
> was assigned to someone else;
> and I think that if I had not been born,
> another poor one would drink this coffee!
> I am a bad thief.... Where can I go!ary[12]

Excluded from the present, yet deeply connected to it, it is as if one's body could have been someone else's. This is a dissociation of the self of the colonized and it sheds light on resistant sensibilities. Perhaps it is also the human condition Vallejo reaches through his poetry. A kind of radical exilic memory of the "could have been" is the thread that connects us to others and to ourselves, like the love one can feel toward others who stayed in the place one is from, who stayed and suffered, or the love one feels for those who had to leave, whose place we are now occupying, or the love one feels toward versions of ourselves, toward who we could have been if we had stayed or left. These are inextricable dimensions of love made manifest by exilic memory, and they are also a love of the excluded. A love of those who are here but do not belong, of the excluded poor, of the racialized and colonized. This is the love that Mariátegui finds in Vallejo. He describes it as "tenderness and charity" and seems deeply entangled with his revolutionary sensibility. An exilic nostalgia exposes us and others as always already displaced by current social and political orders, yet as exilically connected in a temporality of what could have been. This sensibility lets historical forms appear without closure, open to transformation sustained by a liberatory memory, by exilic love.[13]

IDENTITY, MYTH, AND AESTHETICS IN MARIÁTEGUI

Mariátegui's notion of myth can shed light on liberatory sensibilities beyond redemption (like the pachakuti sensibility) and on the essentialization of identities by philosophies of liberation. He maintains that all genuine liberatory philosophies have to be myths. That is, they must effect a shift at the level of sensibilities that sustains the possibility of revolutionary praxis. *Myth* for Mariátegui has a specific meaning that does not coincide with common uses of the term and opens up the field of an aesthetics of liberation (see chap. 6). At the same time, echoing Marx's analysis of the proletariat, myths in Mariátegui's sense can acquire a specific redemptive form. They can define a population as an identity with a critical perspective that reveals systematic structures of oppression and also represent this identity, allowing for processes of recognition that elicit commitment to a particular political project tied to its redemption.[14]

I understand such redemptive myths to be fractured by opposing tendencies. On the one hand, they approach oppressed identities as hermeneutic foci that make possible critical interpretations of oppressive systems. In this hermeneutic role, identities cannot be fixed because they issue critiques that are attentive to various geographic and historical contexts and to sociopolitical changes. On the other hand, myths can engage in an aesthetic representation of identities in order to set forth clearly defined futural political projects on the basis of processes of recognition that gather the oppressed as a resistant collective. This latter tendency leads to a representation of identities as fixed and to articulate redemptive liberatory philosophies that essentialize oppressed identities. Such philosophies can form exclusionary and marginalizing political movements. In other words, myths can be fractured between hermeneutic and essentializing representative tendencies in relation to identities, and the latter aesthetic tendency can align itself with redemptive projects.[15]

This fracture can be healed beyond redemptive investments through aesthetic movements that constitute sensibilities that engage identities toward liberatory projects without reifying them and without assuming representative functions. The pachakuti sensibility just discussed expresses such an aesthetic movement. A kind of pachakuti sensibility also appears in Mariátegui's works through aesthetic phenomena informed by *indigenismo* and surrealism, specifically in an aesthetics of invisibilities and in the discipline of multitudes in festivals (see chaps. 5 and 6). This book culminates in interpretations of Mariátegui's texts and of some of his main readers by focusing on logics of redemption, especially in relation to aesthetic and redemptive aspects of his configuration of an Indian identity. There is a liberatory aesthetic turn at stake here (one developed in chaps. 5 and 6 and in the conclusion), a turn that allows for an aesthetic delimitation of Latin American philosophy beyond redemption.

THE ITINERARY: DELIMITATIONS OF
LATIN AMERICAN PHILOSOPHY

The pachakuti sensibility, in its connection to exilic memory and love, is a resistant sensibility withdrawn from a redemptive future. I explore it at the outset because it determines this book's general approach to Latin American philosophies of liberation and to the role of cultural identities within them. In the chapters that follow, this sensibility implicitly guides my interpretations of some of the central texts of the Latin American philosophical tradition. It also allows me to articulate interrelated contextual, transcultural, and aesthetic delimitations of Latin American philosophy.

Martín Alcoff interprets Simón Bolívar's emblematic Latin American political thought as contextually revealing the humanity and capacity for self-determination of Americans and their integrity and political future as a distinct people, rather than capitulating to political and epistemic European dominance. Chapter 1 preserves and critically develops this contextual delimitation of Latin American philosophy, yet it pursues a different interpretive angle on Bolívar's texts. Unpacking redemptive claims in the "Jamaica Letter" and the "Angostura Address" shows that Bolívar's political philosophy articulates the redemption of Americans, configuring this identity in its revolutionary and political potential. This implies the parallel construction of an Indian identity, the racialization of indigenous peoples as passive, and the explicit rejection of their ability to articulate their own projects of liberation. Chapter 1 also makes explicit an important futural aspect of Bolívar's vision, one that sustains an American identity with historical purpose and continues to justify its exclusions and political failures for the sake of an American redemption. The chapter ends by analyzing the redemptive implications of Bolívar's political thought through the works of Leopoldo Zea, Rebecca Earle, Anthony Pagden, and Mariátegui.

Chapter 2 turns to José Martí's text "Our America." It continues to build on Martín Alcoff's contextual delimitation of Latin American philosophy and heeds her important point: "Martí no doubt developed the most radical position: eschewing the need for racial or ethnic improvement of any kind, and rejecting any form of race-based superiority, he instead argued for a political culture that would embrace, include and come to an understanding of its own peoples, in all their variety and diverse histories."[16] On this basis, Martí, like

Bolívar, in this text interprets an overarching American identity and puts forward a liberatory horizon of redemption. There are, however, important differences between them.

In "Our America," Martí makes a devastating critique of the lettered and political class populated by white creoles, demoting them as agents of resistance against colonialism and imperialism and envisioning collective liberatory agencies in alignment with the demands of those most oppressed by dominant systems, a grouping of diverse marginalized peoples (including Indians and blacks) that anchor a new, recentered sense of an American identity. The recentering goes beyond Bolívar, especially since it brings with it a delinking from European knowledge production that Bolívar did not pursue, one that relates to the oppressed as a rich source of local histories, knowledges, and epistemologies, as well as of discernment of good government.[17]

This is where Martín Alcoff's quote just above is suggestive, especially her interpretation of Martí as "eschewing the need for racial or ethnic improvement of any kind." That is, Martí's configuration of an American identity anchored in the oppressed attends to them in their rich cultural forms, their liberation being a matter of extending their cultural forms with attention to their specific geopolitical realities, rather than projecting a future, different reality where their oppression would be redeemed. In my view, this disengagement from the future informs the whole text of "Our America," appealing to spatial sensibilities in the formation of peoples, rather than temporal ones. Approached in this way, Martí's text can open ways of thinking of Americans beyond redemption. As a result, Martí splits between its Bolivarian commitments, and a "transamerican" dimension. Ultimately, in chapter 2 "Our America" appears as a fractured, impossible text. The chapter ends with a discussion of the transamerican dimension of "Our America" in the work of Juan Flores and Boaventura de Sousa Santos.[18]

Chapter 3 retains a contextual philosophical delimitation, focuses on the essay "The Problem of the Indian" in the Seven Essays and lays out Mariátegui's development of an indigenous socialism in terms of an "indigenista logic of redemption." Mariátegui's logic appears opposed to a colonial logic of redemption that, even though directed toward the redemption of Indians, is operative as the support for a white creole economic and political leadership embedded in colonial structures. The analysis of these conflicting logics is the basis for understanding fractures in Mariátegui's texts that point to aspects of his thought in which the difference between the indigenista logic of redemption and the colonial one is blurred, but it also suggests ways of reading Mariátegui beyond redemption.

Chapter 4 deepens the exploration of tensions between strains in Mariáte-gui's texts, as well as aspects of them that are not defined by logics of redemp-tion and the essentialization of oppressed identities. It consists of a critical reading of Ofelia Schutte's interpretation of Mariátegui that uncovers a libera-tory philosophical perspective on cultural identities, making explicit a trans-cultural delimitation of Latin American philosophy.

Chapter 5 continues tracing nonredemptive aspects of Mariátegui's social-ism, focusing on his relationship with indigenismo. It connects Jorge Coro-nado's and Luis Alberto Sanchez's critiques of Mariátegui's indigenismo as an ideological construction of an artificial Indian identity. It also shows resources in Mariátegui's own works to respond to their critiques by positing an aesthet-ics of invisibilities emerging out of his approach to indigenismo, to the work of Enrique López Albújar in particular. The critical response puts Mariátegui in dialogue with María Lugones's work and brings forth a spatial, liminal sensibil-ity as a way of articulating oppressed liberatory agencies in excess of represen-tative demands. This chapter marks a turn toward an aesthetic delimitation of Latin American philosophy.

Chapter 6, through readings of the conflicting interpretations of Mariátegui by Aníbal Quijano and Alberto Flores Galindo, and by focusing on the latter's account of utopias, uncovers an aesthetic axis in Mariátegui's thought. It the-matizes a nonredemptive sensibility that is connected to a surrealist discipline and that supports the permanence of revolutionary wills, especially as a com-munal ethos expressed in festivals and other community-making events. This project offers an elucidation of an aesthetics of liberation.

The conclusion turns to Mariátegui's delimitation of philosophy as it appears in his reading of José Vasconcelos. It includes an approach to the role of cultural identities in philosophies of liberation that is different from Martín Alcoff's and Schutte's, one that resists configuring them in terms of futural projections for the sake of liberatory ends, and engages, rather, a utopic present. A brief encounter with Gloria Anzaldúa's essay "Border Arte" at this juncture shows the possibility for a community of the oppressed to become a collective agent of liberation in excess of fixations of identities. This community, with a spatial and border sensibility, is engaged in processes of resistance and renewal that take form beyond redemption. Bringing Mariátegui and Anzaldúa together in this way yields an aesthetic delimitation of Latin American philosophy.[19]

Reflecting back on this itinerary, I notice that my own positionality emerges as a guiding factor throughout the analyses in this book. Having grown up in the '80s and '90s in Lima, Peru, and being a male of European descent from the upper middle class, I developed an outsider's enthusiasm for socialist projects of liberation inspired by redemptive visions. Concurrently, I cultivated a fetishistic and uninformed interest in indigenous peoples in the Andes, and projected onto them ideological positions and resistant potencies. A narrow, and too simplistic, reading of Mariátegui's *Seven Essays* shaped my political positions at the time. After moving to the United States I was socially categorized as a Latino, both facing a second-class citizen status and becoming part of heterogeneous communities with robust histories of resistance. In this context I learned about the complexity of practices of resistance at the intersection of oppressed identities and cultures, and my investment in redemptive liberatory projects began to recede. This double positionality fractured between experiences in the north and the south informs the critical perspective through which I wrote this book. It explains my attentiveness to and deconstruction of logics and sensibilities of redemption within seminal texts in Latin American philosophy that I think partially informed my early political inclinations, and my resorting to Latina and Chicana feminist scholars in order to reflect on these texts with a view to articulating delimitations of Latin American philosophy that I now find compelling, especially in their ability to overcome redemptive tendencies. Each chapter and the conclusion of this book, then, do not aspire to provide definitive interpretations of texts. They, rather, express a fragmented positionality exposing its limits and overcomings in order to signal a path of philosophical education.

NOTES

1. For a collection of primary sources in Latin American philosophy (including the ones discussed in this book), see Gracia and Elizabeth Millán-Zaibert, *Latin American Philosophy*. Other readers and companions to the study of Latin American philosophy include Mendieta, *Latin America*; Mendieta, *Latin American Philosophy*; Nuccetelli, *Latin American Thought*; Nuccetelli and Seay, *Latin American Philosophy*; Nuccetelli, Schutte, and Bueno, *Companion to Latin American Philosophy*; Rivera Berruz and Kalmanson, *Comparative Studies*. My analysis of aesthetics and liberation intersects with Mignolo's works on decolonial aesthetics. See Mignolo, "Aisthesis decolonial." My approach is closer to Vallega's work on an aesthetics of liberation. See Vallega, "Exordio/Exordium," and Vallega, "Out of Latin American Thought." My analyses complement Linda Martín Alcoff's understanding of oppressed identities as experiential and hermeneutic. See Martín Alcoff, *Visible Identities*. An important reader for the relationship between identity and politics that I explore here is Martín Alcoff, Hames-García, Mohanty, and Moya, *Identity Politics*. My attempt to conceive of liberation without essentializing identities is also in dialogue with the work of Chela Sandoval. See Sandoval, *Methodology of the Oppressed*. (The translations of texts in Spanish are mine.)

2. Dussel, "Christian Art," 47.

3. Vallejo, *Complete Poetry*, 25.

4. Vallejo, *Complete Poetry*, 135.

5. Lugones, "From within Germinative Stasis," 86. See also the related essay, Lugones, "Motion, Stasis, and Resistance."

6. Lugones, "From within Germinative Stasis," 90.

7. A key text here is Lugones and Price's translator's introduction to Kusch, *Indigenous and Popular Thinking*. I also use as resources for my understanding of Andean cosmologies Estermann, *Filosofía Andina*; and D'Altroy, *Incas*. Kusch, *Indigenous and Popular Thinking*, 43. In this discussion of *pachakuti*, I draw from Mignolo, *Darker Side of Western Modernity*, 156–58.

8. Mariátegui, *7 Ensayos*, 303. Translation mine.

9. Mariátegui, "Heterodoxia," 407. Translation mine.

10. Ibid., 408; italics mine.

11. The relationship between revolutionary praxis and hope becomes problematic. Dussel may be of help here in Dussel, *Philosophy of Liberation*, 64–66, and Dussel, *Ethics of Liberation*, 334–41. For the relationship between Mariátegui's revolutionary socialism and religion, see Tirres, "At the Crossroads."

12. Vallejo, *Complete Poetry*, 308.

13. I am echoing here Dussel's use of the term *poor* in *Philosophy of Liberation*. Here I mean to evoke the meaning of "radical exteriority" in Vallega's work. See Vallega, "Radical Intelligibility." There is a connection between my account of exilic memory here and memory as it appears in Lugones's notion of "world-traveling." See Lugones, *Pilgrimages/Peregrinajes*, 89.

14. In relation to Mariátegui and myth, see Díaz, "Mariátegui's Myth" and Jaime Hanneken, "José Carlos Mariátegui and the Time of Myth." Mariátegui, *Siete Ensayos*, 308.

15. See Martín Alcoff, *Visible Identities*, 94–102, for identities as hermeneutic foci.

16. Martín Alcoff, "Educating," 9.

17. I am borrowing the term *delinking* from Walter Mignolo. See, for example, Mignolo, "De-linking."

18. Martín Alcoff, "Educating," 9.

19. This book sets up the stage for a number of dialogues that remain implicit in it. It can be the source of critical engagements with Castro-Gómez, *Crítica*, esp. chap. 3, 5, and 6; with Mignolo, *Darker Side of Western Modernity*, esp. the introduction and chap. 1 and 4; and with Dussel's notion of transmodernity in Dussel, "World System." See also Martín Alcoff, "Enrique Dussel's Transmodernism."

ONE

—◊—

RAPTURE

A "Contextual" and Redemptive
Reading of Bolívar

IDENTITY IN LATIN AMERICAN PHILOSOPHY: BEGINNING WITH MARTÍN ALCOFF

Linda Martín Alcoff approaches Latin American philosophy in terms of the complex processes of identity formation in the Americas.[1] The complexity is due not only to the diversity of peoples that come to be exposed to one another but also to the conditions in which these exposures happen, namely, colonial and postcolonial economic, social, and political conditions. She writes, "New identities have been continually foregrounded, exhaustively catalogued, hierarchically organized, and often instrumentalized in Latin American political thought and discourse but rarely ignored. Their existence demanded new narratives of identity, history, progress, national unity, aesthetic beauty, and the possibility of universality."[2]

In particular, Martín Alcoff draws attention to the investment of Latin American political philosophy in emerging identities and suggests that it recasts, or even renews and re-creates, these identities for the sake of liberatory political projects. Following her, I focus on the ways Latin American liberatory philosophical thought intersects with, and attempts to elucidate and influence, processes of identity formation in the context of coloniality, specifically with respect to the identities "Indian" and "American." In this sense, I am interested in tracing constructions of a "we" in identity narratives within Latin American philosophy; that is, in constructions of collective identities that confer senses of moral and historical purpose and elicit affective and ideological commitments to liberatory goals. In particular, this book turns to political liberatory philosophies—Bolívar's, Martí's, and Mariátegui's—in which the elucidation

13

of identities is the condition for the articulation and enactment of projects of social and political liberation.[3]

This first chapter delves into Martín Alcoff's identity-based, contextual delimitation of Latin American philosophy, complements it with Mariátegui's notion of myth, and pursues it as the basis for an interpretation of Bolívar's "Jamaica Letter" and "Angostura Address." It reveals redemptive dimensions of Bolívar's political project tied to the construction of the identities "American" and "Indian." The chapter ends with a discussion of the legacy of Bolívar's redemptive investments in the work of Leopoldo Zea and its racial, ethnic, and temporal implications as laid out in the work of Earle, Pagden, and Mariátegui.

MARTÍN ALCOFF'S CONTEXTUAL DELIMITATION OF LATIN AMERICAN PHILOSOPHY

In the text "Educating with a [De]Colonial Consciousness," Martín Alcoff identifies a "running thread of colonial self-consciousness" within the Latin American philosophical tradition, which, within its geohistorical frames, can become defensive of its integrity, abilities, and accomplishments in the face of Anglo and European philosophy. Yet Martín Alcoff sees a philosophically productive facet of such defensiveness: "This required defense, and concomitant defensiveness, has had the beneficial result of making visible the context in which knowledge occurs, and of disabling the usual pretensions, still found in European influenced philosophical traditions, of being able to make transcendent abstractions removed from all concrete realities. Hence a general approach to knowledge has emerged that renders it self-conscious and reflective about its context and social location."

There are two important interrelated aspects of Latin American philosophy exposed here. First, the defense of its validity in the face of a universal Eurocentered philosophy implies foregrounding the contexts in which Latin American philosophy takes place, showing that it philosophizes from a distinct set of experiences and geohistorical realities. Second, Latin American philosophy's defensiveness informs a particular way of doing philosophy, one in which all knowledge and knowledge production is taken as contextual, so that philosophical thinking cannot avoid including a questioning of the social, political, economic, and geographic determinants that condition it. In this way, Eurocentered philosophies' aspirations to universality, and their assumption of a universal locus of enunciation, can be challenged. Latin American philosophy, then, turns its defensiveness into a body of philosophical thought that must be studied in its own right.[4]

Martín Alcoff shows how this affects philosophies concerned with the possibility of social and political liberation. Eurocentered liberatory philosophies tend to turn local truths into universal ones, and "As a result, liberatory theories, including the truly rich resources of the Marxist tradition, developed no theory of race, no conceptualization of xenophobia, no critique of Eurocentrism, no concept of indigeneity, no understanding of the link between colonialism and culture, and no analysis of the ways in which geographical hierarchies affects the making of theory itself." In contexts not defined by histories of colonialism, or where such histories are denied or deemed secondary, oppression in terms of culture, race, and knowledge production, among others, is not readily considered central to the articulation of liberatory theories. It is interesting to recall here that in orthodox Marxism even class differences are understood as the distillation of all others and that cultural determinations are derivative. Hinting at the inefficacy and dangers of imposing such Eurocentered liberatory theories on colonial and postcolonial environments, Martín Alcoff evokes the contextual insights of Latin American philosophy: "theories of justice, of progress, of liberation or of oppression emerge within specific contexts, and . . . in fact these contexts play a constitutive role in the formulation of theoretical tasks and projects, setting the agenda but also affecting how reasons and arguments were judged in regard to their plausibility, adequacy and even intelligibility."[5]

In colonial and postcolonial contexts, for example, liberatory theories need to address the denial of the humanity of certain racialized populations, a denial tied to the formation of their identities within coloniality. Since it is the liberation of these populations that is primarily at stake, the structures that deny their humanity, whether economic, social, political, or ideological ones, have to be the primary target of liberatory theory and praxis. Rigorous attention to the complex processes of identity formation of the colonized is, then, necessary in anticolonial, liberatory philosophies. At the same time, through such philosophies, identities that are instantiated to further oppression can be reconfigured for the sake of resistance and liberation.[6]

In this sense, Martín Alcoff gives a contextual delimitation of Latin American philosophy and traces its lineage back to the debate between Juan Ginés de Sepúlveda and Bartolomé de las Casas. She notes that Sepúlveda denies the humanity of the colonized "on the basis of the specific cultural and social *identities* of the Indians."[7] Retroactively engaging de las Casas as an example of a Latin American contextual philosopher, she states, "He allowed that the Indians might look brutish to the Spanish, as Sepúlveda claimed, but this was only because the conventions within which their practices were embedded were strange and unknown to the Spaniards. The context of the judgment was here brought into relief."

Consistent with the delimitation of Latin American philosophy Martín Alcoff describes, de las Casas's argument for the humanity of the "Indians" is contextual, localizing the frames within which it has to be assessed rather than appealing to universal ones, and, thus, seeks to overturn the racist determinations of this identity by generating a new elucidation of it. The role of philosophy here is to engage particular contexts so that the humanity of colonized peoples comes through in a way that is not apparent to a "universal" perspective. This indicates that a strain of Latin American liberatory philosophy contextually challenges the racist framings of coloniality through elucidations of the identity of the oppressed on the basis of their specific historical, geographic, ethnic, and cultural determinations. Martín Alcoff states that this becomes "a general exploration of the relationship between thought and identity, cultural location and philosophy."[8]

Elucidations of identities such as de las Casas's, however, can continue to relate to foreign contexts. Moreover, Latin American philosophy, even when contextual, is always in danger of elucidating identities within entrenched dynamics of racism that continue to inform it. Martín Alcoff seems attentive to this when she notes that in "the nineteenth and early twentieth centuries, much of the discussions turned on the various methods of advancing, or repairing, the cultural context so that it might 'deserve' self-determination." Following this train of thought, one could delve deeper into the ways in which liberatory philosophies in the context of coloniality, by having to elucidate the identities of the oppressed, can themselves become racist mechanisms.[9]

Martín Alcoff maintains that Latin American political philosophy has contextually brought forth a Latin American identity in two ways. First, Alberdí, Sarmiento and Rodó "emphasized in various ways the dominance of the European lineage of Latin American culture, and proposed highlighting or expanding this dominance as a means to solve Latin America's inferior status." Martín Alcoff's point is that this call for the expansion of European dominance was argued for through contextual claims about specific characteristics, including historical and geopolitical determinations, of Latin American peoples. It, however, did not intend the liberation of "Latin Americans" as such because this particular elucidation of this identity affirmed the dependence on European and Anglo peoples. Second, she mentions a different, "non-capitulationist" lineage: Bolívar, Martí, Mariátegui, and Haya de la Torre. Her argument is that they followed the same philosophical contextual approach, but in their case the elucidation of a Latin American identity took them to contrasting views. They affirmed the humanity of Latin Americans as a group—their capacity for self-determination, their belonging to a distinct civilization, their potential to make contributions to world history—and, therefore, they proposed thwarting the expansion of European dominance and dismantling remaining colonial structures.[10]

The noncapitulationist political philosophers found, within their specific contexts, sources to argue for the cultural integrity, social and political viability, and historical purpose of Latin Americans as a distinct people, showcasing an identity characterized by a diversity and *mestizaje* that demand a distinct philosophical approach, one that eludes Eurocentered epistemic frames and challenges Anglo-European claims to political and philosophical dominance. Here I touch on an earlier point, in which Latin American philosophy, according to Martín Alcoff, appears to take root in the relationship between emerging determinations and formations of peoples and projects of political liberation in the Americas.

THE POSSIBLE CONVERGENCE OF THE CONTEXTUAL DELIMITATION OF LATIN AMERICAN PHILOSOPHY AND MYTH

This book hinges on three contextual noncapitulationist philosophers identified by Martín Alcoff: Bolívar, Martí, and Mariátegui. These three figures find themselves in revolutionary junctures and are invested in elucidating an identity in order to both reveal the humanity of the oppressed and galvanize collective agents that would endorse their specific liberatory projects. "Americans" for Bolívar and Martí and "Indian" socialist revolutionaries for Mariátegui, are identities argued for, and made manifest, through the articulation of their liberatory philosophies. In them, the conditions for the possibility and efficacy of alternative political options are at stake.[11]

These three liberatory philosophies can posit the overturning of oppressive structures as implicated in the affirmation of the humanity of a specific identity, something that appears possible only within the scope and aims of their particular revolutionary goals. Their approach elucidates a demarcated oppressed identity as a critical position that can make apparent both an oppressive structural totality and the structural transformation that would overturn it. In this way, the affirmation of the humanity of the oppressed gathered under an identity appears to be at issue in a coming comprehensive and liberatory event. The oppressed are thus oriented to a single liberatory futural horizon. In my terms, this is the mythical horizon of "redemption."

I am approximating here an aspect of the term *myth* in Mariátegui's work and relating it to Martín Alcoff's contextual delimitation of Latin American philosophy, even if she does not fall into redemptive commitments in the elucidation of her philosophical position. In Mariátegui's lexicon, the term "myth" can be seen as implicitly linked both to the lineage of Bolívar and to that of Martí as Latin American contextual philosophers of liberation, as well as to Marx's discovery of the proletariat as a revolutionary agent. In terms of socialism as myth, Mariátegui states,

> Marx appears as the discoverer and, I would say, the creator of the proletariat; he has, effectively, not only given the proletariat the conscience of its nature, of its legitimacy and historical necessity, of its inner law, and of the ultimate instance toward which it moves, and has, thus, conferred upon the proletariat that consciousness that they lacked; he has also created, one could say, the very notion and, supporting the notion, the reality of the proletariat as an essential class opposed to the bourgeoisie, the true and only bearer of the revolutionary spirit in modern industrial society.[12]

This quote gives the most important insight into Mariátegui's Marxism and aligns socialism with a philosophical approach to the elucidation of identities in view of redemptive liberatory horizons.

Following Marx's treatment of the proletariat, Mariátegui's liberatory project is invested in the elucidation of the identity "Indian." As Augusto Castro states, "Mariátegui concludes that Marx's exceptional merit consists in having, in this sense, invented the proletariat. The revolution demands a subject and, in this case, it is the proletariat that, as object of analysis and discovery, Marx converts into the leader of the social revolution. Not too much later, Mariátegui himself, in order to construct the Peruvian social myth, would invent—in Marx's style—the Indian that he would call socialist, in charge of the social transformation and revolution in Peru."[13]

In the Peruvian context, Mariátegui envisions socialism as myth, as projecting a liberatory horizon in which the redemption at stake is that of "Indians." In this sense, Mariátegui's approach to the identity "Indian" is both mythical and fits within Martín Alcoff's contextual delimitation of Latin American philosophy. This convergence of Mariátegui's and Martín Alcoff's thinking yields an interpretive approach to texts by Latin American noncapitulationist philosophers that reveals their redemptive strains. The case of Simón Bolívar's "Jamaica Letter" and "Angostura Address" is an example.[14]

FRAMING THE AMERICAN IDENTITY IN
BOLÍVAR'S "JAMAICA LETTER"

> The hatred we feel for the Peninsula is greater than the sea separating us
> from it. . . . The veil has been rent, and now we can see the light, now she
> [Spain] wants to return us to darkness. The chains have been broken, we've
> been liberated, and now our enemies [Spain] want to make us slaves.[15]

When Bolívar invokes a "we" or an "us" in the Jamaica Letter, he is not appealing to a formed people that would without question feel addressed by this
revolutionary text. Rather, Bolívar's "we" is elucidated in his very text. As it is
well known, the Jamaica Letter addresses the political difficulties facing the
new states liberated from Spanish colonialism. Yet it is also a reflection on the
defining characteristics of an emerging people. In this respect, Bolívar's "we"
is the revolutionary agent of the wars of independence from Spain that also
constitutes, for him, a burgeoning American people. If one reads the Jamaica
Letter together with the Angostura Address, the ethnic, political, and moral
characteristics of Americans appear as developing toward a future consolidation of a proper American people liberated from colonialism and its effects.
Bolívar's liberatory project, then, does not end with the defeat of Spain but
exceeds it so that Americans are caught in a mode of being toward liberation.[16]

The Jamaica Letter is an indispensable text in Latin American political
thought because it is written from the experience of the collapse of the colonies' commitment to Spain and gives expression to a people originating in that
historical fissure. On this unstable ground, the text gives shape to an American
identity as part of the articulation of a liberatory project. Its success depends
on the way it rewrites the colonial past and posits a redemptive future from
a constructed American perspective. This retroactive operation recognizes
Americans as victims of Spain, a recognition that defines an American identity
and subsumes an Indian identity under it. In this way, the letter makes explicit
to Americans the conditions for their own historical trajectory, signifying their
liberatory and redemptive destiny.

At the beginning of the Jamaica Letter, Bolívar's "we" is configured retro-
spectively in opposition to the Spanish conquistadors, whose actions "seem to
transcend the limits of human perversity." In this way, Bolívar redetermines
the corresponding civilized/barbaric, Spanish/Indian dualities at the core of
Spanish colonialism. He brings to light an alternative set of dualities: civilized/
barbaric, humanity/Spanish, according to which *Spanish* corresponds to "barbaric" and is opposed to "humanity." But this rearrangement is not a simple

reversal of the Spanish/Indian polarity. It, rather, inserts a third element, a new people who are civilized and who represent humanity. The new oppositional dualities are, then, Americans/barbaric, and Americans/Spanish. Moreover, with the emergence of Americans as a third position, the Indian referent loses efficacy. In particular, the association of Indians with barbarism is not explicitly challenged. It is simply shoved to the background. This demotion of the Indian polarity, together with the unchallenged correspondence between Indians and barbarism, is definitive in the determination of Bolívar's "we" as signifying an American identity.[17]

The text links this third, American people with the figure of Bartolomé de las Casas, who witnessed and denounced the "depraved acts of bloodfest"[18] that the Spanish inflicted on indigenous peoples. The evocation of this figure shows Bolívar's complex stance. De las Casas appears as embodying the perspective of humanity in his condemnation of the Spanish colonization and in his defense of the Indians. This perspective does not, however, engage one that would correspond to that of indigenous peoples. Rather, de las Casas speaks for the Indians even if he contextualizes his critique attending to indigenous cultural and political characteristics. In this way, he excludes an indigenous critical perspective in the very gesture of caring and fighting for Indians. The content of de las Casas's defense does not contradict the exclusionary character of its enunciation.[19]

De las Casas, in Bolívar's narrative, anticipates Bolívar's "we" and, to an extent, is the first American. There is, however, one important difference between de las Casas's stance and Bolívar's in the Jamaica Letter. While de las Casas stands as witness to and accuser of the Spanish treatment of indigenous peoples, Bolívar presents Americans as witnesses, accusers, victims, and judges of the Spanish atrocities. In doing so, an indigenous historical and critical position disappears at the same time that the complex identity Indian is brought into play as denoting a people in need of redemption from the atrocities inflicted upon them. In a move that is fundamental in the configuration of the American identity, Bolívar aligns the plight of Americans with that of the Indians during the conquest. This alignment not only subsumes Indians under the identity Americans, but also makes all Americans equal victims of Spanish colonialism. Bolívar describes, for example, the revolutionary resistance to Spanish forces as driving "back into the sea those savages insatiable for blood and crime and who rival the first monsters who obliterated the primitive tribes of America."[20] Later in the Jamaica Letter, he anachronistically differentiates the treatment of European vanquished kings from American ones (like the Inka, for example), showing the lack of respect for the dignity of Americans that characterized Spanish colonial practices. Throughout the letter, Bolívar speaks of the efforts of American revolutionaries as facing a second conquest.[21]

This alignment of Americans with Indians must be qualified. Bolívar affirms it only insofar as they both have been victims of Spanish atrocities, both deemed subhuman by the Spanish. The other dimension of the American identity, the one that embodies a perspective as witness, accuser, and judge of Spanish colonizing practices cannot be shared with indigenous peoples because it considerably exceeds their capacities. Indigenous peoples on their own can be victims but are not allowed to assume the critical position of witnesses, accusers, and judges of their own victimization. But when Indians are included within Americans, the whole group can frame their victimization as an issue of justice and, thereby, understand the moral and political implications of their own victimization. Indigenous peoples by themselves cannot even articulate the barbarism of their Spanish oppressors and, hence, their own association with barbarism is left indeterminate. Of course, these erasures are covered up with the emergence of Americans who appear in defense of the Indians. This elucidation of the American identity includes indigenous peoples as Indians in order to posit the need of an American redemption but excludes them at the same time. This is a tension that remains unresolved.[22]

ETHNICITY, MORALITY, POLITICS

The emergence of the new American identity occurs as a sudden geohistorical shift that makes possible a new destiny: "That wicked stepmother [Spain] is the source of all our suffering. The veil has been rent, and now we can see the light; now she wants to return us to darkness. The chains have been broken, we've been liberated, and now our enemies want to make us slaves." Earlier Bolívar had announced: "Success will crown our efforts because the destiny of America is irrevocably fixed; the tie that bound her to Spain is severed, for it was nothing but an illusion." Bolívar's "we," comes through in full force in the sentence "now we can see the light." His "we" is configured in the overcoming of darkness, in the rending of a veil, in the dissolution of an illusion. These three figures of concealment refer to the ties between Spain and its colonies, ties that have been broken. The shift is evident and irreversible. The sympathy that united the colonies to Spain, in fact, concealed suffering and enslavement. Any attempt to restore the Spanish colonial order after the emergence of an American identity would be a return to that dehumanizing plight. In Bolívar's writings, then, the American identity comes to be determined from the future.[23]

Bolívar lays out the characteristics of Americans in terms of ethnicity, morality, and politics. In the Jamaica Letter, intertwining ethnicity and politics, he writes, "We . . . who are moreover neither Indians nor Europeans, but a race halfway between the legitimate owners of the land and the Spanish usurpers—in short, being Americans by birth and endowed with rights from Europe—find ourselves forced to defend these rights against the natives while maintaining our position in the land against the intrusion of the invaders."[24] The notion of Americans as a race "halfway between" has been taken to be a culmination of Bolívar's genius that anticipates the socially and politically fruitful approach to Latin America in terms of mestizaje. I pursue another interpretive option that brings me back to the issue of mestizaje from another perspective.

In the quote just above, ethnicity and politics are related to birth. In the case of the Indians, birth in a particular territory automatically translates into rights: Indians are the "legitimate owners of the land."[25] At the same time, people of Spanish descent born in the colonies also have rights by birth, but theirs are not as legitimate as those of Indians. The fundamental difference between these two, which translates into a difference in legitimacy, is ethnic. In the case of Indians, their culture, history, and blood relations are embedded in their place and land. In the case of Americans, their ethnicity can be traced back to Europe, and their history is not one of belonging to the land as it is one of usurping the lands of others. Bolívar seems to suggest that in a colonial context where two peoples share the location of birth, the ones whose ethnicity is foreign (who trace their culture and history to a place that was disconnected from the one they now occupy) lack a legitimate right over the land. At this juncture, ethnicity and race, more than birth, are the definitive factors between competing rights to territory.

The issue becomes complicated in terms of the relationship between Americans and the Spanish. In this context, Americans are not usurpers. Born in America, they are not ethnically reducible to their Spanish predecessors. In this case, birthplace marks the difference between Americans and Spanish peoples. Having a status that does not fit neatly within ethnicity and birthplace as categories of identity and rights, Americans constitute a third people and, thus, cannot be fully defined by their opposition to Indians or to the Spanish. But even faced with this third, in-between, people, it would seem that the right thing to do would be to continue to respect the Indian's legitimate rights to the land. That is, however, not what Bolívar thinks.

The configuration of a third, in-between, American identity changes everything. Bolívar's reasoning is complex and implicit in the Jamaica Letter. He comes to see the problem of legitimate rights against the rights of usurpers to be defined only by the polarity Indian/Spanish, which does not include Americans. In his view, with the introduction of Americans as a third element, the problem must be reframed from the ground up, even to the extent that Indian rights are suspended. The introduction of a third identity changes the terms of the discussion of the legitimate rights to the land. The change comes to be justified by the consolidation of a new American identity, which absorbs an Indian one, a corresponding social and political order, and a destiny of redemption.

The Jamaica Letter does not fully clarify the implications of being a race "in-between." In their difference from indigenous peoples, Americans seem to not be the legitimate owners of the land; but in their difference from the Spanish, they are not the usurpers of land either, which calls for a reframing of our understanding of the rights of Americans as a different, third people. This indeterminacy is ultimately solved in the Angostura Address, where Bolívar writes, "Our people are not European, nor North American, but are closer to a blend of Africa and America than an emanation from Europe, for even Spain herself lacks European identity because of her African blood, her institutions and her character. It is impossible to say with certainty to which human family we belong. Most of the indigenous peoples have been annihilated. The European has mixed with the American and the African, and the African has mixed with the Indian and with the European." Here Bolívar understands Americans in terms of mestizaje, opening a way of reframing the dichotomy Indian/Spanish for the sake of forging an American identity. This mixture stands for an American people and constitutes a new ethnic formation that erases the polarity Spanish/Indian as relevant to the adjudication of rights. In this sense, a form of mestizaje is mobilized by Bolívar as a way of setting forth a new ethnic horizon within which Indians are gathered among others, discontinuing their ethnic-based legitimacy of rights and thus solving the ambivalence of the race "in-between" in the Jamaica Letter. This new ethnic era of mestizaje is evoked when Bolívar states that "All born in the womb of our common mother, our fathers, different in origin and blood, are foreigners, and all differ visibly in the color of their skin; this difference implies a bond and obligation of the greatest transcendence." In a move that responds to the complications that arise between the factors of birth, ethnicity, and rights in the letter, Bolívar returns to the issue of birth by positing the duality mother/father. In the letter, problems of competing rights arise because of the ethnic difference between peoples born in the same territory. Bolívar now ascribes that difference to a multiplicity of fathers. Underneath this multiplicity he posits a shared mother—America—as birthplace that dilutes the ethnic difference into a kind of mestizaje. Such an America needs to be unified by a sense of obligation beyond ethnic claims, that is, by a commitment to a political project. Thus, for Bolívar the mestizaje implied in the American identity inaugurates a new political field of rights and obligations. In this way, ethnicity is intertwined with, and superseded by, politics.[26]

This turn to the political field is apparent in an earlier statement in the "Address" that at first seems to be just a repetition of the Jamaica Letter: "we are not Europeans, nor Indians, but a species halfway between aboriginal and Spanish. Americans by birth and Europeans by law, we find ourselves contending with the natives for titles of ownership and at the same time trying to maintain our rights in our birth country against the opposition of the invaders; thus our case is most extraordinary and complex." Despite the similarities between the texts, there are some fundamental differences. First, Indians are no longer the legitimate owners of the land but appear to be in equal footing with Americans in their rights. This equalizing is the political implication of the figure of the shared mother and of mestizaje. Second, in a move that we have already seen, Bolívar aligns his people with indigenous peoples in their opposition to the Spanish usurpers, who violate American rights.[27]

What is this new political order that is intertwined with mestizaje and inaugurates an era in which Indians are on the same footing as other ethnicities? Bolívar is explicit about this: it is the application of the European enlightenment with its values of equality, individual rights, and freedom. The decision for this political program remains undisputed here, and its Eurocentrism is out in the open. Bolívar states, for example, "When we are at last strong... then the arts and sciences that were born in the Orient and that brought enlightenment to Europe will fly to a free Colombia, which will nourish and shelter them." By "arts and sciences" Bolívar means, above all, politics. From his perspective, indigenous peoples did not attain the science of politics of the enlightenment and, as a consequence, could not articulate a form of government based on equality, individual rights, and freedom. Once again, this is a juncture in Bolívar's thinking where an indigenous critical perspective seems not to be endowed with a political awareness that would allow indigenous peoples to understand themselves as having rights and to judge the Spanish for having usurped them. It is easy to see that, despite the mestizaje that Bolívar endorses as the ethnic form of America, Europe remains a guiding referent, especially in a political register.[28]

It is almost as if Bolívar made a mistake in the Jamaica Letter that he corrected in the Angostura Address. It seems that from the perspective of the latter, to state that Indians were the legitimate owners of the land is a projection of European political consciousness upon them, since they could not articulate this assessment for themselves. The Indians owe Europeans the possibility of this articulation, and the debt is paid for by their inclusion in an American identity in which the distinction of their ethnicity in its connection to their land is erased. Here the entry into political modernity corresponds to a process of mestizaje that leads to the consolidation of an American people.

Yet this entry into modernity is complex. According to Bolívar, the alienation of the ruling class during Spanish colonialism has had disastrous political consequences for the emerging independent states. He writes in the Jamaica Letter that "Americans have made their debut on the world stage suddenly and without prior knowledge or, to make matters worse, experience in public affairs, having to enact the eminent roles of legislators, magistrates, ministers of the treasury, diplomats, generals, and all the other supreme and subordinate authorities that make up the hierarchy of a well-organized state." One of the fundamental political problems for Americans is that they seem doomed to produce only an imitation, a false image, of a properly governed state. Bolívar's argument for such an assessment is well known: Americans by birth were not allowed to participate in the political organization of the colonies, being reduced to a state "lower than servitude." This lack of participation and practice in politics means that Americans have been "purely passive," and he adds "We were . . . lost, or worse, absent from the universe in all things relative to the science of government and administration of the state."[29]

Yet one of the central aspects of Bolívar's vision is that America as a mixed ethnic formation encompasses the possibility of political enlightenment. In fact, America, in his account, appears as the transition from a heterogeneous ethnic formation to a homogeneous political condition of citizenship: "The diversity of origins requires an infinitely firm and infinitely delicate touch to manage this heterogeneous society whose complex structure becomes dislocated, divided and dissolved at the slightest alteration." The point here is that America, and the formation of the American identity, constitute the possibility for "this heterogeneous society" to be firmly and delicately managed politically. America and the identity of its inhabitants make possible a political uniformization that sets the stage for a principle of equality that would affirm the humanity of all Americans. Bolívar explains this principle as: "all men are born with an equal right to the benefits of society. . . . All men are equally capable of aspiring to the highest attainments." But this principle has another political function: "We need equality in order to reconstitute the race of men, political opinion, and public customs." In this way, Bolívar articulates an American identity as an ethnic/political category, one that implies a process of unification of peoples through which ethnic heterogeneity is reconstituted so that politics (as the management of peoples under the principle of equality) can take hold. Through this process of reconstitution, Americans, including indigenous peoples, would be ultimately redeemed from colonialism.[30]

Above all, the management that America as an ethnic/political identity makes possible involves a moral aspect. As already noted, in Bolívar's view Americans find themselves not fitting in the political form they aspire to, the one that maximizes freedom, justice, and equality. In the Jamaica Letter, he writes "perfectly representative institutions are not appropriate to our character, our customs, and our current level of knowledge and experience.... Until our compatriots acquire the political skills and virtues that distinguish our brothers to the north, entirely popular systems ... will, I greatly fear, lead to our ruin. Unfortunately, the acquisition of these qualities to the necessary level would seem to be remote from us."

In the Angostura Address, he specifically addresses morality: "Our moral constitution did not yet possess the necessary consistency to receive the benefit of a completely representative government." Here the political lack of fit becomes a moral deficiency. The double root of this seems to be (1) that Spanish colonial rule did not foster the right moral constitution in its subjects that would allow them to thrive in conditions of political freedom and equality and (2) that indigenous habits and cultures cannot be taken as a source for the cultivation of political virtues. Americans, then, appear as people in the process of being morally educated in political virtue. What is this education in virtue? As Bolívar states in the "Address," "We endeavor in vain to show them that happiness consists in the practice of virtue, that the rule of law is more powerful than the rule of tyrants because the former is inflexible and everything must yield to its beneficent rigor, that good habits, not force, are the column of the law, and finally that the practice of justice is the practice of freedom."[31]

This moral education has two implications. First, the obvious one, is that Americans are in the process of aligning their wish for happiness and freedom with the demands that the law imposes on them and in the process of discovering that this alignment is the condition for genuine happiness and freedom. Second, Bolívar's "we" in this statement is split into a duality of "we/them," in which the "we" educates and the "them" is educated, yet both refer to the same people. This underscores the fact that Americans are in the process of moral self-education, with a futural orientation.[32]

The ethnic and political cohesion of America is at stake in this process of moral education. The recognition of this process informs Bolívar's vision of the adequate political forms for the newly emancipated states. He favors paternalistic governments that are not fully democratic, with a strong division of power between a congress and the executive in order to protect executive powers, and he supports the idea of a hereditary senate and a state-sanctioned "moral power" that would educate citizens in political virtues. The moral aspect of Bolívar's project overrides the ethnic and political aspects as a process of development, as a commitment of a people to a future that would morally redeem them from colonialism.[33]

BOLÍVAR'S RAPTURE AND FAILURE: FUTURAL REDEMPTION

Both the Jamaica Letter and the Angostura Address are characterized by a concern for the future. In the letter, Bolívar writes, "one can only offer imprecise conjectures, especially concerning the future successes and the true plans of the Americans," and a little later he proclaims, "the destiny of America is irrevocably fixed." The two statements are not contradictory. Bolívar is operating here on a destiny that is not tied to the practical realm, but rather a destiny that operates as a guide for political and liberatory praxis. This is the point of his reflections at the end of the "Address": "Flying from age to age, my imagination reflects on the centuries to come. . . . I feel a kind of rapture, as if this land stood at the very heart of the universe. . . . I see her as unifier, center, emporium for the human family. . . . I see her seated on the throne of liberty, grasping the scepter of justice, crowned by glory, and revealing to the old world the majesty of the modern world."

The issue here is the status of this vision. Because of Bolívar's skepticism about defining the actual future of America, this vision cannot be that of a realizable ideal. It is a kind of rapture. Even though the possibility of its actualization is suspended, in this suspension Bolívar's redemption of America inscribes itself in the present with a sense of urgency and futural projection.[34] The futural sense operative here resonates with one of Bolívar's fundamental insights: "I consider the current state of America to be similar to the circumstances surrounding the Fall of the Roman Empire, when each breakaway province formed a political system suitable to its interests and situation or allied itself to the particular interests of a few leaders, families, or corporations. There is, though, this notable difference, that those dispersed members reestablished their former nations."

For Bolívar, America does not have a past from which to reconstruct itself. It has, rather, to create itself with historical purpose from its destiny. This futural rapture is the dynamic basis constitutive of the identity "American" as an ethnic/political/moral phenomenon. America never quite catches up with itself.

It exists in a mode of "being-toward" that temporally configures an "American" identity.[35]

This sense of futurity emerges from an ambivalence toward the conquest and colonial order. On the one hand, Americans reject the barbarism of the Spanish colonial order. On the other hand, they affirm what it made possible, the emergence of America as an ethnic, political, and moral project. This ambivalence does not cause a standstill; it is resolved in the process of redeeming America. Disguised beneath a continental identity, one can find a creole avant-garde enraptured in a future that remains inconclusive but is sustained by a movement of redemption. The temporality at work here is a "redemptive time."

Redemptive time is futural, yet held in the suspension of an actualizable future, and final in its promise of the affirmation of the humanity of the oppressed. It determines the present as something to be overcome and transformed. Through it Americans are always on the way to fulfill their destiny and historical calling in a continuous movement of redemption. Bolívar as a figure of rapture, as caught in constant struggle, becomes inscribed in this redemptive movement as one of its main symbolic sources. Leopoldo Zea writes: "Bolívar, like the biblical Moses on the peak of Mount Sinai, could see in the distance the promised land, but without being able to reach it, without living it, without experiencing it."[36]

ZEA'S BOLIVARIANISM: FRAMING
A LATIN AMERICAN IDENTITY

Bolivar's redemptive politics not only constitutes an identity for a nineteenth-century people, it also is at the basis of later philosophical articulations of the meaning and political implications of being Latin American (as it is the case for Martí, Rodó, Sandino, García Belaúnde, Roig, and others). In this section, I will briefly focus on Zea's Bolivarianism, as it appears in his *Simón Bolívar, Integración en la Libertad*. I approach Zea's Bolivarianism in terms of the problem it addresses and the solution it prescribes.

The problems are servitude, inauthenticity, and dependence. Faithful to Bolívar's assessment, Zea underscores that the Spanish colonial rule resulted in habits of servitude. He sees those habits as a fundamental Latin American problem. The problem unfolds in this way: First, as Bolívar already concluded, habits of servitude lead, after independence, to the inability of Latin Americans to live up to the standards of political functions, being doomed to improvise or simulate those functions. Second, now adding to Bolívar's account, Latin Americans are caught in inauthenticity, the condition of impersonating what they are not. Third, inauthenticity traps Latin Americans in a dependence with clear colonial roots. As Zea states it, "Improvisation, transformed into simulation and inauthenticity, will lead to other forms of colonial juxtaposition. Alien social, political and cultural forms will be imposed on top of a reality that remains untouched. In an attempt to overcome their orphanhood, Americans will impose on themselves or search for new forms of paternalism that will not be any different from the ones imposed by Spanish colonialism. Substitution of one colonialism for another. Substitution now made in the name of freedom."[37] Following Bolívar, Zea reveals a pathological pattern that defines Latin Americans, the pattern of dependence rooted in colonialism that persists, in his view and in his time, in the very attempt to enter modernity.

According to Zea, Bolivarianism presents the solution to the problem of dependence through a search for authenticity and identity. These last two conditions are interrelated in Zea, since inauthenticity is a state in which Latin Americans fail to be themselves, that is, in which they lack an identity. Following Bolívar's approach, *politically* authenticity and identity are sought in the proper form of management of Latin American peoples, and *ethnically* authenticity and identity are sought in the proper embrace of an integrated mestizaje as the condition for political equality. In Zea's words: "The diversity, that had been an element of stimulus and development in Europe, was presented by the Europeans in America as degradation and as justification of dependency. For this reason, the racial or cultural diversity of people that form this America, seen as negative, has to be overcome in a nation that is the expression of everyone; expression of what is held in common without negating its multiple and natural differences." *Morally*, authenticity and identity are sought in the readiness for freedom (understood as the capacity to govern oneself and as political participation). Moral authenticity and identity form the most complex aspect of Zea's thought. Zea writes: "the proper mode of being of free men does not emerge. The long lasting colonial order having been destroyed, the order of freedom does not replace it." Later he states, "The sought-after freedom was not ingrained in the habits and customs of these peoples, it was not something natural to them, even if the desire to reach it was."[38] The moral problem here, then, is the inability to exist in freedom. It is grounded in an existential split that affects all "Latin Americans": on the one hand, servitude, on the other, the desire for freedom. In Zea's view, this split is resolved in the process through which "Latin Americans" gain conscience of their servitude, which leads to their commitment to the struggle for freedom. Zea finds in Bolívar the articulation of this process of conscientization as the development of a "Latin American" identity and of a liberatory praxis: "the forces of freedom obligated to expel and annihilate their oppressors, they will have to, at the same time, invest themselves in saving, redeeming, this people in order to make them overcome servitude."[39]

Bolivarianism, in Zea's view, is a project of redemption, of the triumph of the desire for freedom over moral servitude. At this juncture, he inscribes the figure of Bolívar into Bolivarianism: "Simón Bolívar himself is the expression of this other identity." Bolívar, then, attests to the other, positive, side of being Latin American, becoming a figure of redemption. Zea's account takes a telling turn in this respect. He continues to ask about the source of Bolívar's desire for freedom, of his redeeming force. This is what he finds: "Bolívar, animated by the same fire that animated the conquistadors, the fire that animated the Cortés' and Pizarro's to impose their dominion in this América." Zea continues this idea by quoting Bello: "The native Spanish constancy has crashed against itself in the inherited constancy of the sons of Spain."[40]

In an intriguing twist, this Latin American redemption appears here as the redemption of the Spanish. Zea's Bolivarian redemption is the movement from servitude and inauthenticity to authenticity, identity, integration, and freedom. It is a movement guided morally by the Spanish character of the conquistadors.

READING REBECCA EARLE AND ANTHONY PAGDEN

The way Rebecca Earle situates her historical analysis in *The Return of the Native*, complements my interpretation of Bolívar's Jamaica Letter and Angostura Address. Her approach to the identity "Indian" in nineteenth-century Latin America is particularly helpful. She recognizes that this identity is fabricated, that it is a colonial and European projection upon heterogeneous peoples, and that it pervades both the early political programs of creoles seeking independence from Spain and later social and political movements such as *indigenismo*. For this reason, she notes, "The problematic nature of the very concept of the 'Indian' has led many scholars to substitute terms such as "Native American" or other less obviously European labels." Yet she adds that she is indeed concerned with "Indians," that is, with the "European concept encoded in the word." In other words, Earle maintains that the artificiality of the term "Indian" should not dissuade one from exploring the effective history of the term and its influence on articulating emancipatory and revolutionary projects in particular. Both the shifting meaning of the term and the loci from which it is enunciated can reveal fundamental aspects of such projects, like their justification, who is included in them as agents of liberation, and the specific political and social future they envision.[41]

Earle uses the concept of "indianesque nationalism" to express the way in which creoles included the "Indian" into the national imaginaries that justified their struggles for independence. In particular, "indianesque nationalism" implies a peculiar historical perspective that glorifies a pre-Columbian past and posits the creoles as the legitimate heirs of that past. In this way, as the emerging bourgeoisie assumed a leadership role socially, economically, and politically that alienated it from Spain, it generated a discourse of the "Indian" that legitimized its rebellion. Earle argues that this creole strategy was necessary in order for nascent independent nations to claim a past and to sever ties with Spain while retaining a sense of historical identity.[42]

Moreover, the destruction of pre-Columbian societies by colonialism could then be part of a legitimizing narrative for the struggles of independence, since it could allow for the positioning of the creoles as the restorers of ancient rights, as avengers, as historical agents of the redemption of the "Indians." In this sense, indianesque nationalism deemphasized racial differences between creoles and Indians and affirmed a historically based alliance between them. Thus, Earle reminds us that San Martín stated, "I too am an Indian," and that indigenous leaders that fought against the conquest came to be seen as "the true fathers of Spanish America." Yet indianesque nationalism is articulated from the perspective of the creoles, creating a narrative that could be either appropriated or rejected by the indigenous peoples themselves but which was not necessarily enunciated from an indigenous perspective. This is one of Earle's main points: indianesque nationalism was meant for creoles and articulated a creole liberatory project.[43]

Earle also notes that indianesque nationalism was defined by an irresolvable tension, since it was impossible to perfectly bring together the creole and the Indian. This inner tension is apparent in at least two ways. First, the confusion about when to mark the historical origin of the emerging Spanish American independent states was never resolved. There were three possibilities, all of which were operative in the articulation of national imaginaries: a pre-Columbian origin; 1492 as an origin; and, eventually, the continental movement for independence itself as an origin. Indianesque nationalism, then, as a historical perspective, was never able to fully coalesce, demonstrating the difficulty of establishing a national past through an evocation of pre-Columbian legacies.[44] Second, "indianesque nationalism" was a double discourse about the Indian. Earle writes, "although preconquest history might be welcomed into the national past, contemporary indigenous peoples were rarely accepted as part of the national present. Far from benefiting from positive appraisals of the pre-Columbian era, they were on the contrary perceived largely as a problem for the republican state, and were often declared incapable of participating in the political life of the nation."[45]

The double discourse is here split between glorifying pre-Columbian Indians (which is an anachronism) and dismissing contemporary Indians as citizens. The former, according to Earle, is a mythical appropriation of the Indian that supported the movement of independence and even the identity formation of creole elites in emerging independent states. The latter is the actual political, social, and racial disposition of creoles toward contemporary, living Indians. It was not unusual for creole writers to affirm both the glorious Inca past, for example, and the degeneration of the contemporary Indian who had lost touch with her own historical lineage. This double discourse allowed creoles to claim to be the true heirs of pre-Columbian civilizations and the ones charged with, in my terms, bringing about a future order in which the humanity of Indians would be redeemed. It also shows, however, the limits of indianesque nationalism. Earle states, "As a limited nationalist mythology, indianesque nationalism functioned best when no attempts were made to connect the preconquest past with the indigenous present."[46]

These fissures within indianesque nationalism provide a way of framing Bolívar's writings, one that Earle begins to explore. She suggests that the new identity "Americans" was an attempt to cover up the tension between Indians and creoles by configuring an identity that would refer to both groups. Bolívar was one of the main creators of this identity in texts like the Jamaica Letter. Earle writes, "Bolívar in his 'Jamaica Latter,' an eloquent denunciation of anticreole discrimination, described the victims of the conquistadors as 'we Americans.' By metonymy, the suffering Indians came to stand for the disgruntled creoles." The new identity "Americans" forged a "we" that allowed creoles to appropriate the identity "Indian" in ways that justified their emancipatory efforts, at the same time that it explicitly anchored the enunciation and leadership of these efforts in a creole, rather than indigenous, agency. "American" is, then, an identity configured by Bolívar that refers to a people (including Indians and creoles) whose humanity was denied by Spain and that are charged with their own liberation. This operation, however, does not resolve the double discourse of indianesque nationalism. It, rather, covers it up and surreptitiously enforces one dimension of it: the mobilization of an Indian pre-Columbian past while contemporary Indians come to be included and erased within the new American identity. In this complex way, the identity "American" continues the redemptive lineage of indianesque nationalism, but now Americans are both redeemers and redeemed. One of the effects of this demotion of the Indian within a new redemptive American narrative is that the marginalization of contemporary Indians can be bolstered. Earle states, "Civilizing the Indian was . . . simultaneously redemptive and purgative."[47]

In an emerging America, civilizing the Indians meant redeeming their colonial past through the agency of Americans, something that came to imply the devaluation of the economic, social, and cultural forms (if not the very lives) of contemporary Indians, as well as the erasure of their critical perspectives. One of the outcomes of the emergence of an American identity is both the exacerbation and concealment of the difference between creoles and contemporary Indians. Another connected subtle shift from indianesque nationalism apparent in the Jamaica Letter is the valuation of the future over the past. Even if the investment in the redemption of a pre-Columbian past remained, this redemption is not seen as a restoration of ancient rights, but as the opening of an era for the future development of an American people.

Along these lines, Anthony Pagden, in *Spanish Imperialism and the Political Imagination*, posits two creole identities. One is similar to Earle's indianesque nationalism in the sense that it understands itself to be in an explicit relationship to Indians as a restorer of their ancient rights. In this respect, he mentions the work of Clavigero and Viscardo. The second identity, also echoing Earle's analysis, is the creole identity as defined by the emerging American one. In Pagden's analysis, Bolívar is a transitional figure between these two identities. Pagden writes thus about this transition:

> Simón Bolívar, *El Libertador*, the leader, political and intellectual, of
> the southern Independence movements, had begun his carrier as one of
> Miranda's generals. We do not know how far, at the time, he shared Miranda's
> fantasy of a new, partially republicanized, partially Anglicized, Inca state.
> But by the time he came to draft his first political thesis in 1815—the
> famous *Jamaica Letter*—he had already, under the influence of a miscellany
> of Enlightenment authors, come to believe that any future independent
> Spanish-America state had to be a very different kind of political society to
> anything that then existed in Europe or had ever existed in America itself.

Pagden brings to light Bolívar's particular futural vision. His analysis also underscores Bolívar's dismissal of contemporary Indians: "For the most part Bolívar thought of the Indians, when at all, as an essentially docile unpoliticizable mass." For Bolívar, Indians lack in qualities that prepare them for citizenship and political leadership. In this line of thought, not only do the contemporary Indians fall short of their ancient greatness, but they also are unable to be historical and political agents in the forging of an American future. This is the case even if Bolívar's own discourse, the Jamaica Letter in particular, continues to operate within the task of the redemption of the Indian as belonging to an American redemption.[48]

MARIÁTEGUI'S "THE UNITY OF INDO-SPANISH AMERICA"

Mariátegui's "Unity of Indo-Spanish America" is important because it explicitly links the emergence of a continental identity to the legacies of colonialism. As to the generation of the independence, Mariátegui finds that "Hispanic Americans" emerge as peoples [pueblos] that move "in the same direction . . . [they] proceed from a single matrix [una matriz única]." Their bond is determined by a single historical beginning that sets them in a path toward a shared destiny. What is this origin, this "single matrix"?[49] Mariátegui writes, "The Spanish conquest, destroying the native cultures and communities, made uniform the ethnic, political and moral physiognomy of Hispanic America. . . . The methods of colonization solidified the destiny of its colonies."

The Spanish conquest and its methods of colonization are the "single matrix" out of which Americans are born. The relationship between them is clear: both are mechanisms of destruction and erasure of indigenous peoples. They become a single matrix and origin of an Hispanic American people through a destructive, yet homogenizing, process. Thus, according to Mariátegui, the development of a "Hispanic American" identity is built on the suppression of the historical trajectories and agencies of contemporary, living indigenous peoples. As noted in Earle's work, this operation coincides with the fabrication of the category "Indian." It is also important to underscore the three aspects of the "physiognomy of Hispanic America": ethnicity, morality, and politics. As the previous discussion of Bolívar shows, these three aspects are interrelated: in the term "Hispanic America," particular ethnic/racial formations become submitted to both political ideals and to senses of moral cultivation as part of processes that intend to forge a people emerging from the destruction of indigenous peoples and cultures.[50]

The methods of Spanish colonization formed a new people with a new historical purpose, one that was not intended by those who implemented those methods—a new people beyond the Spanish colonial imaginary. In Mariátegui's account, the generation of independence, including Bolívar, does not disavow colonizing methods and the destruction of indigenous peoples they carry out. Rather, it recognizes in them a necessary origin and fate and articulates sociopolitical programs out of this recognition. Such programs include redemptive liberatory projects. From Mariátegui's perspective, these programs signal the continuance of colonial social, political, economic, and cultural dynamics.

Mariátegui's perspective is informed by his notion of myth, emphasizing that Bolívar's Americans have an origin or single matrix that provides a sense of historical destiny. They "move in the same direction."[51] They are a being-toward; for them, the future has a more definitive significance than the past. They disengage from a destroyed indigenous past and disown the Spanish colonial past for the sake of a new futural determination, which is the draw of Bolívar's redemptive political project.

NOTES

1. See the bibliography for a list of works.
2. Martín Alcoff, "Educating," 10.
3. By "coloniality" here, I mean (following Quijano), the planetary racial and racist classification of peoples that accompanies the emergence of global capitalism and the rise of European modernity, one that benefits and enforces the cultural, political, social and economic dominant positioning of Anglo-European white males and creates the context for movements of liberation from within these structures of domination. See Quijano, "Coloniality of Power"; Maldonado Torres, "Coloniality of Being"; Mignolo, "Decolonizing"; and Mignolo, "Geopolitics."
4. Martín Alcoff, *"Educating,"* 6.
5. Martín Alcoff, *"Educating,"* 7. Ibid.
6. See *"Communist Manifesto,"* in Tucker, ed., *The Marx-Engels Reader.* 459–501.
7. Martín Alcoff, *"Educating,"* 7; italics mine.
8. Martín Alcoff, "Educating" 8. For a critique of Spanish colonizing practices, see de las Casas, *Short Account.* See the important contribution to this issue in Castro-Gómez, *Hybris del punto cero. DE,* 9.
9. See Mignolo's alternative interpretation of de las Casas in Mignolo, *Idea of Latin America. DE,* 9.
10. See Domingo Faustino Sarmiento, *Facundo,* and Rodó, *Ariel. Martín Alcoff, "Educating,"* 11.
11. Haya de la Torre was not only Mariátegui's interlocutor but also a continental leader and founder of the APRA (Alianza Popular Revolucionaria Americana). For his international relevance, see García-Bryce, *Haya de la Torre.*
12. Mariátegui, *Defensa del Marxismo,* 74.
13. A. Castro, *Filosofía y política.*
14. A. Castro, *Filosofía y política,* 111.
15. Bushnell, *Simón Bolívar el libertador,* 13.
16. Belaúnde writes about the Jamaica Letter: the letter is "an exact analysis of the situation of each country, of the state of the revolution and the attitude of Europe and America" (Belaúnde, *Bolívar,* 160).

17. Bushnell, *Simón Bolívar*, 13. Mignolo has a thorough reading of de las Casas's four classes of barbarians, and of the determination of the "Indians" in terms of those classes. As is evident in this discussion, the alignment of indigenous and barbarian is not undone by de las Casas and foreshadows Bolívar's relationship to indigenous peoples. See Mignolo, *Idea of Latin America*, 22.

18. Bushnell, *Simón Bolívar*, 13.

19. This reading conflicts with the way Dussel's philosophy of liberation aligns itself with de las Casas. See Dussel, "Anti-Cartesian Meditations," 11–52. For a historical approach to de las Casas, see D. Castro, *Another Face*.

20. Bushnell, *Simón Bolívar*, 15.

21. The idea of the "second conquest" is evident in statements like this one from the Jamaica Letter: "the madness of our enemy, to want to conquer America once again, without a navy, with no money in the treasury, almost without any soldiers!" (Bushnell, *Simón Bolívar*, 16). Bolívar writes, "However, there is such a difference between the fortunes of the Spanish kings and the American kings that no comparison is valid; the first were treated with dignity, allowed to live, and ultimately restored to freedom and power, while the latter suffered unimaginable torture and shameful abuse" (Bushnell, *Simón Bolívar*, 17).

22. Bushnell, *Simón Bolívar*, 17.

23. Bushnell, *Simón Bolívar*; italics mine.

24. Bushnell, *Simón Bolívar*, 18.

25. Ibid.

26. There are some important texts on race and mestizaje in Latin America that inform my discussion throughout this book. See Richard Graham, ed., *The Idea of Race*; Hooker, *Theorizing Race*; and Sanjinés, *Mestizaje*. Bushnell, *Simón Bolívar*, 39, 18. For the relationship between an ethnic unity and a political unity, and the related failure of Bolívar to forge a people, see also Aguilar Rivera, "Men or Citizens?" and Sergio Armando Gallegos-Ordorica, *The Racial Legacy of the Enlightenment in Simón Bolívar's Political Thought*.

27. Bushnell, *Simón Bolívar*, 33.

28. Bushnell, *Simón Bolívar*, 30. Transmodernity in Dussel, and Martín Alcoff's interpretation of it, are an alternative approach to the question of the way modernity and the enlightenment belong to a Latin American philosophical tradition. See Dussel, "World System"; and Martín Alcoff, "Enrique Dussel's Transmodernism."

29. Bushnell, *Simón Bolívar*, 21, 19, 20. Ibid.

30. Bushnell, *Simón Bolívar*, 39, 38, 40.

31. Bushnell, *Simón Bolívar*, 38.

32. For an alternative interpretation of morality in Bolívar, see Castro-Klaren, "Framing Panamericanism"; Bushnell, *Simón Bolívar*, 23.

33. See Bushnell, *Simón Bolívar*, 23, 45, 37, 43, 50.

34. Bushnell, *Simón Bolívar*, 12, 13, 53.

35. Bushnell, *Simón Bolívar*, 18, 33.

36. Bushnell, *Simón Bolívar*, 53.

37. Zea, *Simón Bolívar*, 52.

38. Zea, *Simón Bolívar*, 83, 57, 71.

39. Zea, *Simón Bolívar*, 57.

40. Zea, *Simón Bolívar*, 71, 56, 57.

41. Earle, *Return of the Native*.

42. See Earle, *Return of the Native*, 2.

43. Earle, *Return of the Native*, 26, 37. Earle helpfully reminds the reader that in colonial and nineteenth-century Latin America, race was not a strictly physical category, that it included social and cultural factors. See Earle, *Return of the Native*, 15–16. Quoted in Earle, *Return of the Native*, 38, 4.

44. Earle, *Return of the Native*, 7.

45. Earle, *Return of the Native*, 165.

45. Earle, *Return of the Native*.

46. Earle gives a thorough account of the different ways in which criollos understood the causes of this degeneration. Earle, *Return of the Native*, 169, 43.

47. Earle, *Return of the Native*, 43, 162.

48. In Pagden's analysis, Bolívar constitutes more of a break than in Earle's. Pagden, *Spanish Imperialism*, 133. In relation to Bolívar's relationship to Rousseau and Montesquieu, see Castro-Klaren, "Framing Pan-Americanism," 25–33. Pagden, *Spanish Imperialism*, 138.

49. This discussion is not an attempt to define the meaning of Latin America as a political project, but it is an account of it as a form of Bolivarianism. In order to see an anti-imperialist meaning of this political configuration, one that puts into question decolonial analyzes of it, see Gobat, "Invention of Latin America."Mariátegui, *Invitación a la Vida Heróica*, 270.

50. Mariátegui, *Invitación a la Vida Heróica*, 271. For Mariátegui, situated in Peru and witnessing indigenous revolts and movements of resistance, the destruction of indigenous peoples was not as definitive a process as Bolívar suggests in the Jamaica Letter. Helg makes explicit Bolívar's strange relationship to contemporary "Indians," as if denying their existence and agency. She states, "Two dominant images of Bolívar's "indios" emerged: either they had completely disappeared as a result of the conquest, or they formed scattered and peaceful families without ambition on the fringes of the nation" (Helg, "Simón Bolívar's Republic"). "Indian" has a double meaning, one for the past and one for the contemporary.

51. Mariátegui, *Invitación a la Vida Heróica*, 270.

TWO

—⚏—

DISPLACEMENT

Spatializing Martí's "Nuestra América"

Martí's profile of "nuestra América" still looms like a grid over the map of the entire continent, with the northern co-optation of the name America demanding special scrutiny and revision.

Juan Flores, *From Bomba to Hip-Hop:*
Puertorican Culture and Latino Identity

FLORES'S STATEMENT captures a spatial aspect in Martí's classic text, "Our América," which is the focus of this chapter. It is easy to point to the map of "nuestra América" as a continent, yet this spatial determination can be disrupted by others. Martí brings into play various and unsettling spatialities beyond strictly geographic ones, some of which are constitutive of the identity of American peoples. Through these spatialities, Martí approaches the North-South differential in a way that both fissures and refounds America and challenges its Bolivarian redemptive thrust. By paying attention to space in Martí's text in this way, this chapter reveals a different modality of Martín Alcoff's identity-based and contextual delimitation of Latin American philosophy,[1] one that comes to be released from the hold of redemption that I have noted in Bolívar's texts. The outcome of this reading is the articulation of two aspects in Martí's work, a redemptive one and a transamerican one. The chapter ends with tracing the transamerican aspect in texts by Juan Flores and Boaventura de Sousa Santos.[2]

VILLAGE SPACE/WORLD SPACE

Martí brings up a problem of space in the very first sentence of "Our América": "The conceited villager believes that the whole world is his village." The meaning of *village* (*aldea* in Spanish) here is spatial as it becomes manifest in relation to the whole world. The conceit of the villager is about space, it is the confusion of two kinds of space that cannot be reduced to each other: village and world. In particular, the villager attempts to reduce world space to village space, a conceit that reveals the villager's ignorance of the character of world spatiality.[3]

Martí sheds light on village space right away. It is inhabited with the certainty that the universal order is good. Martí gives examples of this: the villager can be the mayor of the village, he can count on an increase in his savings, and he can humiliate rivals that steal his lovers. The certainty that the universal order is good is, then, a feeling of security that is made possible by a spatial determination through which the world of the villager is circumscribed by the field of action that he sees as under his control. The village, in this case, is a modality of spatial awareness that sustains a particular kind of secure and dominant, though narrow, subjectivity.[4]

This awareness, according to Martí, is also a kind of ignorance: the villager "is unaware of those giants with seven-league boots who can crush him underfoot, or of the strife in the heavens between comets that streak through the drowsy air-devouring worlds." Village space sustains a dominant certainty that assumes that the whole world is a village, as if this spatiality could extend indefinitely. World space does not, however, imply the same modality of spatial awareness. Unbeknownst to the villager, world space is, in fact, volatile and encompasses him and implies the possibility of the sudden destruction of the village and of the villager's secure situation; a destruction coming, for example, from the projects of US imperialism. But the villager, entrenched in his spatial certainty, can be blind to even the destruction of his village; he can continue to act as a villager amid the ruins of it. The crux of Martí spatial insights here is the connection between a particular modality of spatial awareness, village space, and the securing of a domain of action that is effectively abstracted from and in denial of a world space defined by the political and economic forces of imperialism. One could recall here García Márquez's "Macondo" as a metaphor of the conflicting spatialities of "America."[5]

Martí states that "what remains of the village in America must rouse itself." With this phrase, he sets into play a constellation of meanings, all of which are relevant: that there are still conceited villagers in America, that all Americans are to some extent conceited villagers, that some aspect of village space remains definitive of America. There is also a slippage between America as something formed by villages and the whole of America as a village. All these alternatives reveal the tension between village space and world space as the key to what

America could be, to "our America." In this sense, Martí exhorts Americans—
including himself—to wake up and find a way to inhabit the tension between
village space and world space differently, even reframing the polarity. This new
wakeful existence involves finding new spatial determinations and alternative
modalities of spatial awareness.[6]

CONFLICTS IN THE VILLAGE

Martí inherits from Bolívar a deep concern for the fragmentation of the continental unity of America into battling groups. He addresses the conflicts that
Bolívar had experienced and predicted as a threat to his political, ethnic, and
moral configuration of an American identity. For Bolívar, these conflicts are
the result of emerging nations not yet being ready to take on the political ideals of freedom, liberty, and equality, a problem that he tried to resolve through
the recommendation of paternalistic, enlightenment-inspired, forms of government. This diagnosis also fuels Bolívar's redemptive project: the conflicts
are the result of emerging nations' being on the way toward an ideal harmony
(both internal and continental), and they are part of plights that will be futurally redeemed through the process of consolidation of an American people.
Martí, however, sees these conflicts differently.[7]

For Martí the source of the conflicts the emerging American nations find
themselves in is the villager's slumber, his lack of proper engagement with the
contested world space of imperialism and of the legacies of colonialism. Martí
presents these conflicts as village conflicts: those between jealous brothers, for
example, or those arising when the cottager envies the squire's mansion. Within
villages and across villages, the secure and dominant subjectivity of the villager
is bound to enter into conflict with others like it, and through this conflict
American peoples almost inadvertently engage in the kinds of violence and
antagonisms that support imperialism and colonialism or, in Martí's words,
they continue "the authority of a criminal tradition." In this respect, one could
point to economic and political structures such as the gamonales, as well as
exploitative social structures such as racism, that transcend the village as part
of global structures and that manifest themselves as village conflicts. In this
way, the particular spatial awareness of village space, and the dominant subjectivity that accompanies it, exist together with, and support, the colonial and
imperial realities of world space. The conflicts within the village are rooted in
world space, but the villager cannot see this.[8]

Like Bolívar, Martí calls for unity: fists need to become holding hands; a
sense of honor needs to overcome ambition and envy. An American identity,

however, is not brought about by becoming more enlightened (that is, ethnically homogeneous, politically manageable, morally upright, as in Bolívar's
project). In Martí's account, instead, this identity is formed through a sense of
shared threat: "Nations that do not know one another should quickly become
acquainted, as men who are to fight a common enemy." An American identity
is configured by a liberatory project. It is at stake in the tension between village space and world space and in the possibility of villagers waking up to the
structural and transnational realities behind that tension.[9]

Martí introduces an image to address the issue: "We can no longer be a
people of leaves living in the air, our foliage heavy with blooms and crackling
or humming at the whim of the Sun's caress, or buffeted by the storms." He
presents the villager's slumber as a kind of passivity. In the village's conflicts,
the dominant subjectivities of the villagers are tossed around, but the villagers continue to sleep. Their certainty is a manifestation of a lack of agency and
historical purpose that can be overcome only by waking up and unifying as
Americans against the threats of colonialism and imperialism. Martí states
that "The trees must form ranks to keep the giant with seven-league boots from
passing! It is the time of mobilization, of marching together, and we must go
forward in close order, like silver in the veins of the Andes."[10]

Here Martí differs from Bolívar once again. The emergence of an American
identity depends most of all on a different spatiality from that of the villager, one
anchored on a new geopolitical awareness of world space. For Martí, emerging
Americans as villagers are not "being-toward," they are, in fact, stuck sleeping
in village space. The stagnation is not redeemed in the forward movement of
history but is disrupted by a spatial, geopolitical redetermination. Martí seeks
an alternative spatiality, one that is not inhabited by sleeping, conceited villagers nor by giants with seven-league boots, but by true Americans. The rest of my
discussion of "Our America" will focus on alternative spatialities that imply a
departure from the temporal underpinnings of Bolivarianism. Martín Alcoff
sensed such a delinking from the future when she notes that Martí "developed
the most radical position: eschewing the need for racial and ethnic improvement of any kind."[11]

THE TRAVELER

In Martí's text, the traveler's space complements village space. This figure
explains the villager's slumber, his disengagement from the world space of
imperialism. It also reveals another way in which Martí shows a critical distance from Bolívar, since the traveler represents the lettered class, those who,

following European models, are responsible for civilizing the emerging Latin American nations. From the perspective of "Our America," Bolívar's call for a civilizing process can enable a creole class that blocks Americans from understanding their geopolitics and their vulnerable exposure to the "giants with seven-leagued boots."

Martí describes the lettered class: "Their puny arms--arms with bracelets and hands with painted nails, arms of Paris or Madrid--can hardly reach the bottom limb, and they claim the tall tree to be unclimbable. The ships should be loaded with those harmful insects that gnaw at the bone of the country that nourishes them. If they are Parisians or from Madrid, let them go to the Prado under lamplight, or to Tortoni's for a sherbet." Martí sees the lettered class as one of appearances, wanting to appear European. But this appearance is also cosmetic, it hides its inadequacy, its being out of place, its inability to embrace American roots. The dynamic of appearance/cosmetics is a trap for the lettered class; it is stuck not being able to be either European or American. Being American is a task the lettered cannot achieve with their "puny arms." Being European, for them, cannot be but a superficial engagement, like going to "Tortoni's for a sherbet." For Martí, this entrapped, in-between existence of the lettered class undermines the integrity of the emerging nations.[12]

In this respect, it appears that Martí mobilizes one of Bolívar's tropes against Bolívar's intent in the "Jamaica Letter." He writes, "Only those born prematurely are lacking in courage. Those without faith in their country are seventh-month weaklings." Bolívar infantilizes the emerging American nations, since they are not born ready and are unable to fulfill their political and moral duties. Specifically, for Bolívar, Americans are not ready to live up to the expectations of European models of government and to apply them correctly to the new American reality. This status as "not-yet-being-ready" is one of the axes of Bolívar's futural, redemptive project. Martí reengages this trope away from its Bolivarian intent and from futurity. For him those born prematurely are the lettered class in their attachment to Europe. In fact, the lettered class's not being ready for governing the emerging Latin American states is precisely the result of their desire to be Europeans. In this reengagement with Bolívar's trope, Martí shifts the discussion: the task to find the right government for American nations cannot have European models of government as its main referents, and the group that in Bolívar's view could bring redemption to America can be instead an obstacle for good government. In Martí's account, Americans are already set for self-determination and constituted as a people.[13]

Returning to the specific figure of the traveler, it opens a complex epistemological aspect of the text. Martí writes: "The arrogant man believes that the Earth was made to be his pedestal because he has a facile pen and colorful words, and he accuses his native republic of being incapable and irremediable, because its virgin jungles do not provide a way for him to travel around the world as a famous landowner [gamonal] driving Persian ponies and spilling champagne."[14] The lettered, arrogant man echoes the conceited villager. In fact, he is also defined by a secure and dominant subjectivity that is sustained by his writing, a subjectivity that insidiously thrives in its dependence on Europe. Writing provides an abstract spatiality for the lettered class, one that appears worldly but is, in fact, nothing more than an extension and modification of village space. One could point to Martín Alcoff's "capitulationist" philosophers (like Sarmiento) as part of this lettered class.

In the spatiality of writing, the lettered class projects itself as a world traveler. Martí is emphatic about this: the traveler wants to travel as a gamonal, that is, a tyrant landowner, the kind of tyrant that belongs to village space and its conflicts. Lettered travelers make the world into a village, a spatial extension through which they are secure to assert their power and dominance at the level of knowledge. Their Europeanization, their condemnation of their "native republic" as incapable of good governance, is nothing but a lettered strategy to assert dominance over the village. The villager and the traveler are complementary figures that seal the villager's slumber from the world space of imperialism. They define the fates of the emerging American nations and the ways in which power is controlled and exerted externally and internally. Martí's reference to the gamonal, the landowner who exploits indigenous labor and continues colonial economic and social structures, is essential. It is a reminder that village space is always already defined by world space, especially by the linkages between imperialism and internal colonialism. In their pernicious complementarity, the villagers and the travelers as political and lettered leaders allow these linkages to be effective. Martí states, "The colony lives on in the Republic"—even epistemologically.[15]

IDEAS AS WEAPONS

> These are not the times for sleeping in a nightcap, but with weapons for a pillow, like the warriors of Juan de Castellanos.[16]

"With weapons for a pillow," one does not withdraw into sleep; the cycle of day and night is continuously unsettled. The soldier does not sleep like the villager. Weapons hold the soldier in this interstice between sleep and wakefulness and remind him of an unrelenting threat. While previously Martí seems to call for "America" to wake up, now he qualifies his call by holding America at the threshold between sleep and wakefulness, or in a state of constant awakening. After mentioning Juan de Castellanos (a sixteenth-century poet, soldier, and priest), Martí reveals what the "weapons" are: "weapons of the mind, which conquer all others. Barricades of ideas are worth more than barricades of stone." The introduction of ideas as weapons is a powerful interpretive clue that Martí gives his readers, and it reflects the nature of his own text. It is an epistemological figure that will define a large portion of it and counters the knowledge of the traveler. Dominant Western epistemologies, at least since the Enlightenment and until the critical philosophies of the nineteenth century (Marx, Nietzsche, and Freud, among others), do not allow for ideas to be weapons because knowledge is seen as anchored in stable, universal structures of subjectivity, which suppresses contextualized mobilizations of knowledge. Martí's epistemology, instead, informs collective action in response to specific oppressive historical and political junctures. It resonates with Martín Alcoff's contextual delimitation of Latin American philosophy and with Mariátegui's mythical understanding of the power and truth of ideas. In Martí's "Our America," at least at first, one finds a contextualized epistemology of resistance. This is evident in the image of a "barricade of ideas" but also in the statement "There is no prow that can cut through a cloudbank of ideas. A powerful idea, waved before the world at the proper time, can stop a squadron of iron-clad ships."[17]

This epistemology of resistance seems to have at least two aspects. First, its ideas do not conquer anything, they, rather, neutralize the imperialist ideologies behind the actual, physical weapons that threaten American nations. These ideas are appropriate in their fitting time, and as they are timely they do not themselves turn into ideological foundations embedded in universality. Second, its defensive power resides in its capacity to dismantle colonizing and imperialist economic and political projects that are both internal and external to emerging nations. Its target, then, is twofold: imperialist ideologies and the lettered knowledge production within the nascent independent states. Hence Martí's preference for "the critical philosophy which in Europe has replaced the philosophy of guesswork and phalanstery that saturated the previous generation."[18] Ideas are for mobilization and resistance, and the text "Our America" can only be understood from this perspective.

THE EPISTEME OF THE NATURAL MAN

The natural man is perhaps the most important figure in "Our America." It makes visible tensions in the text that include those between resistant and affirmative epistemologies, reactive and self-assertive political praxis, world space and village space, and nature and politics. Amid these tensions, the natural man emerges as an authentic American and as a replacement for the villager and the traveler, yet not without fracturing the text.

The natural man appears in the context of Martí's critique of eurocentrism: "A decree by Hamilton does not halt the charge of the plainsman's horse. A phrase by Sieyes does nothing to quicken the stagnant blood of the Indian race. To govern well, one must see things as they are. And the able governor in America is not the one who knows how to govern the Germans or the French. . . . That is why the imported book has been conquered in America by the natural man. Natural men have conquered learned and artificial men." The introduction of the natural man brings about a shift that becomes more and more significant as the text unfolds. It reverses a Eurocentric perspective that is still operative in Bolívar's thought and implies the assumption of a new, American, identity. According to Martí, the failure in governing the emerging American nations is the result of the importation of European sciences of government to a non-European context. For Martí this critique goes further than recognizing that different geohistorical sites call for different theoretical approaches, something that one could argue Bolívar does. His complex insight, rather, is that when European knowledges, especially the sciences of government, are uprooted from their geohistorical sites and planted in others, they not only cease to be knowledge if left decontextualized but also continue to appear as knowledge regardless of their context, that is, as universal knowledge. This universal appearance is the essential significance of Eurocentrism and is effectively embedded in the material conditions of colonialism and imperialism. It both curbs the intent to contextualize European sciences and continues to deny the potential of local and indigenous knowledges. This double operation, which Bolívar did not foresee, enables the incompetent rule of "artificial men," or the lettered class, over American nations. The critique of Eurocentrism, then, hinges on acknowledging the danger of having political leaders trapped by the illusion of possessing universal knowledge, an illusion that stops them from engaging knowledges that emerge out of their own geopolitical sites.[19]

For Bolívar, Americans fall short of their political roles and need to be Europeanized in the sciences of government in order to apply these sciences to their own contexts. Bolívar, like Martí, recognizes the geopolitical factor in the science of politics, the need to understand knowledges in their particular sites. But Martí goes beyond Bolívar. He engages in a critique of Eurocentrism that understands the geopolitics of knowledge as a matter of thinking otherwise, nonuniversally, rather than applying European knowledges in foreign settings. This critique makes Martí turn to knowledges as they arise from and for America. This is why he calls for the study of pre-Columbian civilizations, for example. In this sense, *America* here names not only a new geopolitical site, but also an epistemological decolonial turn.[20]

At first it may seem that the natural man emerges simply as a reaction against Eurocentrism. Martí's language, however, gives a different picture. The natural man interrupts the dominance of the epistemic colonial/imperial perspective and posits an alternative. Martí writes, "The struggle is not between civilization and barbarity, but between false erudition and nature." From the colonial/imperial stance inhabited by the artificial, lettered men, anything that challenges their "civilized" knowledge, or any shortcoming in the application of it, appears as a symptom of barbarity. The natural man unsettles this by reversing the polarity civilized/barbarian. For the natural man, the Eurocentrism and false erudition of the artificial men are evident. The failure of false erudition is inherent because of its decontextualized universality, rather than being a symptom of the barbarity of others. At the same time, the natural man finds in the supposed barbarity the possibility for a natural epistemic disposition that generates local knowledge. Before going deeper into the meaning of *natural* here, it is important to note the reversal through which those who were civilized are now the ones lacking in the knowledge possessed precisely by those who were barbarians. The colonial/imperial perspective is, then, both undermined and reversed by the natural man, a reversal that is perhaps most apparent when the natural man appears reconfigured as the conqueror of the artificial man.[21]

The figure of the natural man defines Martí's epistemology as affirmative rather than simply reactive. America becomes the site for a new form of being with epistemological and political implications, one that is committed to anti-colonial and anti-imperialist projects of liberation. The relationship between the defensive epistemology that dismantles the ideologies of imperialism and internal colonialism, and non-Eurocentric, localized knowledge production as part of a comprehensive epistemological and political praxis is, however, not fully explored by Martí.[22]

THE POLITICS AND SPATIALITY OF THE "NATURAL MAN"

Martí posits a kind of political principle in order to develop the natural man as a figure of American being: "In nations composed of both cultured and uncultured elements, the uncultured will govern because it is their habit to attack and resolve doubts with their fists in cases where the cultured have failed in the art of governing. The uncultured masses are lazy and timid in the realm of intelligence, and they want to be governed well." Martí puts the question of knowledge, the knowledge of being governed well in particular, at the core of politics. Here, the distinction between cultured and uncultured elements provides the basis for understanding the political field. While the cultured possess the knowledge of how to govern, the uncultured have the knowledge to decide whether they are governed well and the power to overthrow the cultured. These two perspectives are not reducible to one another, and the cultured cannot be assumed to represent the perspectives and interests of the uncultured. The difference between them has nothing to do with a lack of knowledge in the uncultured masses. The political knowledge of the uncultured masses arises from their experience, while that of the cultured political leaders relies on established sciences of government. There are, thus, two kinds of knowledge at work here, but the knowledge of the masses is the most politically decisive. Specifically, for Martí, the masses can anchor the anti-imperialist and anticolonial critical philosophies in a vast array of experiences, knowledges, and histories that emerge from their contexts (which include a racial and ethnic diversity of peoples) in order to decide whether they are governed well. The masses are, then, engaged in critical knowledge production that constitutes collective agents moved by political projects of liberation, and they embody a perspective that is not fully accessible to the cultured political leaders.[23]

It is not surprising that at this juncture Martí brings up again those who "go out into the world wearing Yankee or French spectacles, hoping to govern a people they do not know." Martí, rather, is interested in the knowledge of the masses. The masses can critique the lettered sciences of government in at least two ways. First, they can engage in a critique based on geo-politics. That is, they can ask: is the science of government one that is sensitive to the geographic, historical, social, cultural and economic particularities of its context? And, second, they can ask: has the science of government grown from below, from knowledges that arise from the experiences, histories and cultures of the masses? This last question is decisive in "America," where the masses include non-western peoples with knowledges and experiences marginalized by a lettered class. Eurocentrism can be deconstructed when *both* questions are posed. In other words, Martí's significant epistemic shift implies mobilizing the knowledges of the masses, the knowledge of whether one is "governed well," and recognizing the gap between the perspectives of the those who govern and those who are governed as between two different foci of knowledge production. He departs, then, from the enlightenment political forms that assume a shared political horizon between governing and governed.[24]

Martí's productively fissured politics from below, however, is limited because of his investment in forging a definitive American identity through the figure of the natural man, who materializes from the masses. Martí's writes, "The natural man is good, and he respects and rewards superior intelligence as long as his humility is not turned against him, or he is not offended and disregarded." The natural man affirms the masses' power and their capacity to judge whether they are governed well. But he also has an understanding of the need for politics to be grounded not only in the judgment of the masses, but also in critical knowledges arising from particular natural and geopolitical contexts. The natural man, thus, appears as an ideal political leader: "he must know the elements that compose his own country, and how to bring together, using methods and institutions originating within the country, to reach the desirable state where each man can attain self-realization and all may enjoy the abundance that Nature has bestowed on everyone in the nation to enrich with their toil and defend with their lives." The natural man as a political leader supersedes the political split between cultured and uncultured, revealing the split to be a transitional phase toward a harmonic political ideal. Specifically, it is the cultured that are demoted, since the natural man rises from the masses to represent them in accordance with his knowledge of "Nature." Nature, then, is the harmonic, unifying referent for an American identity.[25]

Martí posits a knowledge of nature, rather than the knowledge of the lettered classes, that would comprehend the diverse experiences, knowledges, and histories of the masses. *Nature* here points to an epistemic ground that constitutes a different subjectivity than that of the villager or the traveler, a subjectivity that, instead of being reductively self-certain, is engaged with the historical, cultural, and geographic variations within ethnically and racially diverse peoples that articulate political demands. This turn to nature also opens a new, concrete spatiality that is different from both village space and world space because it is the setting for distinct geospecific political forms, each claiming power from below. Nature is a spatial determination that was hinted at since the beginning of "Our America," and it refocuses the basic determination of the American identity away from time (as in Bolívar) toward space and geopolitics.

Both cultured and uncultured peoples, drawn together by the natural man, say, "Let the world be grafted onto our republics, but the trunk must be our own." Martí makes explicit and identifies the force that attaches people to their land with shared commitment and historical purpose, an attachment that is the test of all sciences of politics, the basis for the judgment of good governance from below: nationalism. He states, "Nationalist statesmen must replace foreign statesmen." It is a commitment to one's own spatial and natural specificity and a discovery of the key dimension of space for the political articulation good governance. "Our America," while continental in scope, does not necessarily override spatial differences. It can indicate a collective disposition that, in resistance to the false erudition of a creole political leadership, returns Americans to the specificity of their spaces in order to generate nations guided by the localized political knowledge of the masses.[26]

The text, however, fractures here. There is an inner tension in the political determination of the natural man. I noted earlier that the gap between cultured and uncultured peoples could render and safeguard effective political mobilizations from below by destabilizing the claims of the science of government. The natural man, as a figure grounded in nature, could undermine this politics from below by positing organic, harmonized forms of government and knowledge, forms that may be at odds with disruptive liberatory movements. This facet of Martí is connected to a desire for a coherent configuration of an American identity. It is not difficult to see that this fracture has to do with Martí's evoking nature as a coherent, harmonic, affirmative ground for political projects. In this regard, Bruno Bosteels's critique of Martí is helpful for understanding this issue and the organic and harmonic strains of Martí's thought.[27]

THE FAILURE OF THE INDEPENDENCE MOVEMENT AND THE FRACTURES OF "OUR AMERICA"

Despite the fact that, according to Martí, "Venezuelans to the North and Argentinians to the south began building nations," "our America" as a political project does not culminate with these movements but, rather, reveals their failures. He states that "The bookworm *redeemers* failed to realize that the revolution succeeded because it came from the soul of the nation, they had to govern with that soul and not without it or against it. America began to suffer, and still suffers from the tiresome task of reconciling the hostile and discordant elements it inherited from a despotic and perverse colonizer and the imported methods and ideas which have been retarding logical government because they are lacking in local realities." In contrast with Bolívar, who found the independence movement forced and untimely, a reality for which the emerging nations were not ready, Martí thinks that the movement was an organic expression of the undeniable power of nationalism. In his view, nationalism—the attachment to principles of governance rooted in the geohistorical specificities of a people— was a process already in place. The "uncultured" mass had already exercised its judgment and fought for independence. But the independence movements failed because those who took up the political leadership over these multitudes were uprooted from their geopolitical specificity and therefore blind to the power and historical significance of the multitudes collectivized under an American identity. For that reason, Martí states, "The problem of independence did not lie in a change of forms but in a change of spirit," a nationalistic spirit that was stunted and did not unfold as appropriate political forms and practices.[28]

One may be tempted to interpret Martí to be in agreement with Bolívar. Both note that the colonizers had not allowed the colonized to participate in government (Martí writes about the colonized: "Thrown out of gear for three centuries by a power which denied men the use of their reason"). While for Bolívar this meant that the people in the emerging independent states could not govern themselves properly, for Martí the legacy of colonialism prevented emerging political leaders from understanding the knowledge that the multitudes already have. Americans for Martí, at least to this extent, are not caught in a futural "not yet." In his words: "the continent disregarded or closed its ears to the unlettered throngs that helped bring it to redemption." Leaving the meaning of *redemption* aside until later, the difference from Bolívar's assessment seems obvious once again, since Bolivarianism can bolster the leadership and "methods and ideas" of those Eurocentric "bookworm redeemers" who think that the problem of independence is one of political form rather than spirit.[29]

Martí expands on one more aspect of nationalism that reveals the legacy of colonialism in America. The knowledge of the multitudes is anchored in the critical position of the oppressed: "It was imperative to make common cause with the oppressed, in order to secure a new system opposed to the ambitions and governing habits of the oppressors." He establishes, then, a correspondence between the natural man, the uncultured and the oppressed that is the key to understanding Martí's take on the configuration of an American identity. These three elements, however, are in tension with one another and fracture our America. The natural man brings with him an investment in harmonies drawn from nature that is at odds with the disruptive power from below of the uncultured, and with the oppressed as including a multiplicity of critical foci that resist being subsumed under integrated political options.[30]

It is almost as if there are two versions of an American identity here. One is defined by homogenizing natural forces and harmonizing social and political horizons with a continental reach that resist global imperialism and colonialism. The other is heterogeneously differentiated by spatial disseminations of geopolitical and historical formations, yet horizontally interwoven by liberatory projects that not only resist imperialism and colonialism but also continuously disrupt political national and continental unities by preserving the tension between the masses from below and the governing classes. Further-more, this duality sets forth two meanings of nationalism: one that can com-pose a continental political ideal and another tied to the always disruptive power of the masses from below that eludes stable identities based on integra-tive political ideals (like Bolívar's). There are also two spatialities at play here: one is continental and the other transamerican.[31]

Martí further determines who the oppressed are in America: "The colony lives on in the republic, and Our America is saving itself from its enormous mistakes . . . because of the higher virtue, enriched with necessary blood, of a republic struggling against a colony." The oppressed are those who are system-atically exploited by imperialism, including British and US imperial designs, and persisting colonial structures. Martí's insight brings together colonialism and imperialism and sees their necessary connection to the failed governing lettered class. He also posits, as an oppositional force to this, a driven national-ist American multitude, guided by the figure of the natural man anchored in the critical position of the oppressed and led by a commitment to America. Yet, as I have noted, within this oppositional force, there is a deep ambivalence in the very configuration and sense of an American identity.[32]

DOUBLING MARTÍ

Martí points to the possibility of a social and political identity through which "peoples would live criticizing themselves, because criticism is health; but with one breast and one mind." The sway of nationalisms could sustain cri-tique (here meaning the critique of global capitalism and internal colonialism) because it would be supported by an organically configured continental Amer-ican identity unified and grounded in the harmony of nature. The power of this American identity is apparent in statements like "nations stand up and greet each other. How are we? [Como somos?] is the mutual question, and little and little they furnish answers." This dialogue between nations is made possible only by a stable continental identity that brings them together. Moreover, the question "How are we?" suggests that the American identity refers here to a process that unfolds little by little, an ongoing process that recalls the progres-sive temporality in Bolívar's "Letter" and "Angostura Address."[33]

At the same time, when Martí evokes the oppressed (which includes the "Indian," the "Negro," and the "peasant," among others), for whom the internal and external structures of colonialism/imperialism become explicit, he does not seem to identify them necessarily with a particular, stable and restrictive "we" that circumscribes the political force of the multitudes. The oppressed as a category can be open to determination and challenges the fixation of an American identity. Here Martí understands the oppressed as constituted by proliferating and contested foci for critique from below corresponding to specific localities. In this respect, the Americans affected by liberation movements, rather than constituting a unified identity, are better articulated through suggestive figures (such as the villager, the traveler, the natural man, and even the oppressed) that are in tension with one another. In this strain of Martí's thought, the figure of the natural man would be just another figure, not a unifying force that yields a continental identity. From this angle, the constitution of a definitive "we" would not be part of Martí's liberatory politics, nationalism would not be grounded in continentalism, and an overarching process of articulation of a unifying American identity would not sustain "our America."[34]

THE INDEPENDENCE THAT IS *NOT YET*, REDEMPTION, AND TRANSAMERICANITY IN MARTÍ

In the continental strain of "Our America," an American redemption is suggested through a progressively unfolding continental identity that gives direction to emerging nations. In this respect, the figure of the natural man can guide an anticolonial and anti-imperialist political impulse. The liberation of American states is a process through which this impulse expresses itself, beginning with the movement of independence influenced by Bolívar, a movement that, in Martí's view, is in need of restoration. Its culmination would be nationalist multitudes taking power unified under America as a liberatory political project supported by a cohesive identity. In other words, this strain of Martí's thought preserves Bolivarianism in a particular way: as a movement of return to its original impulse, a return that itself has to be understood as a futural projection in which the saving of the emerging American nations is at stake. This urgent return is the reason that, in Martí's view, emerging American nations still need to be saved or redeemed. In fact, one could see the liberatory project of "Our America" as a movement within Bolivarianism, one that brings it to its true intent, including its redemptive investments in an American identity.

On the other hand, there is a spatializing strain in "Our America," one that reveals a "transamerican" Martí. From this interpretive perspective, the text has a fundamental spatial, rather than temporal, character. Its liberatory project is a matter of reengaging conditions that are already at play, one that involves a geopolitical and spatial adjustment, implying differential and site-specific epistemologies. These reengagements mean that anticolonial and anti-imperialist movements do not necessarily involve a definitive futural projection through which an identity comes to be consolidated as the support for political liberation. The transamerican Martí dislodges coherent and unified senses of an American identity from projects of liberation and is attentive to America as a fluid spectrum of identities defined by a geopolitics of resistance from below against global capitalism. Can there be any redemption when an identity and a definitive futural horizon are not essential referents? Does the transamerican Martí go beyond redemption?

There is a further transamerican factor in the configuration of the oppressed, one that is operative from the very beginnings of the text and is informed by Martí's own experience. This factor begins to engage modes of being between identities, in border positionalities, that is an issue that will become central as this book progresses. As an exile from Cuba in the United States, that is, as an outsider to both, he engages in a double critique of the United States and the emerging states south of it. From this liminality, he is able to critique the North American culture of excess; its violent control of the masses through work and empty leisure; the joint illusions of unlimited wealth and control over nature; its colonial legacy of racism that insidiously continues to articulate economic, social, and power differentials; and its imperialism. This critique informs and is informed by the simultaneous critique of nations south of the US/Mexican border, where he sees the imitative, empty, Europhilic disposition of the lettered who become complicit through their passivity to imperialistic, specifically US, political and economic projects, and end up failing at their responsibility to govern on the basis of an appropriate understanding of their own historical and geopolitical determinants. One critique depends on the other and, from this liminal double critique, the expanse for "our America" as a transamerican differential field of critical positionalities in anticolonial and anti-imperialist resistance begins to appear. This spatiality is an alternative to village, world, and continental spatialities, one that crosses the border between North and South America. This crossing is, perhaps, the most important geopolitical displacement and spatialization that "Our America" reveals.[35]

This transamerican perspective is at stake at the end of the text. One especially needs to be attentive to the opposition between North and South. Martí writes, "But perhaps Our America is running another risk that does not come from itself but from the difference in origins, methods, and interests of the two halves of the continent, and the time is near at hand when an enterprising and vigorous people who scorn or ignore Our America will even approach it and demand a close relationship."[36]

At first, it seems that this statement emphasizes the North-South differential, denying a liminal transamerican perspective. The difference is so marked that the North would look at the South from the outside, unable to comprehend it. At this juncture, it is important to note the overarching movement of the text. It begins with the blindness of the villager, his inability to see the threat of the world space of imperialism. It ends with the blindness of imperialism to the emergence of America as a new spatiality, the one that is outlined in Martí's text. Through this development, blindness, and a lack of spatial sense, have been reversed. That is why the solution seems to be for "South" America to present itself to the "North" as a continental unity: "the pressing need of Our America is to show itself as it is, one in spirit and intent, swift conqueror of a suffocating past, stained only by the enriching blood drawn from hands that struggle to clear away the ruins, and from the scars left upon us by our masters." Facing the threat of the North, the continental spirit is called upon to show itself. A unifying past, and a movement of overcoming the past, a redemptive temporal movement, becomes essential for this showing. The need arises for America to affirm itself in the face of the North, that is, to define itself through its difference from the North and not as transamerican. At this point, redemption, the futural fulfilling of the "not yet" of the Bolivarianism, becomes essential to an image of America as seen from the North in order to elicit respect: "The scorn of our formidable neighbor who does not know us is Our America's greatest danger.... Once it does know us, it will remove its hands out of respect."[37]

The investment in the way the North sees the South makes Martí's text slip, with its transamerican dimension abandoned for a dimension that is entrenched in the unity of America and that is tangled up with Bolívar's redemptive project. The fragile, alternative, disseminative, transamerican spatiality of America that insinuates itself in this disruptive and disrupted text begins to fade. In this slippage, a temporal redemption that comes to imply a coherent American identity reveals a logic that affects the core of Martí's text. This redemption would even "save the Indian" and force the transamerican spatial redeterminations of the text traced out earlier into the background. Two senses of America manifest themselves.[38]

In this call for a futurally redemptive continental unity, Martí nevertheless states that North America's "madness and ambition" is still not definitive, but something "from which North America may be freed by the predominance of the purest elements in its blood, or on which it may be launched by its vindictive and sordid masses, its tradition of expansion or the ambitions of some powerful leader." Revealing an unresolved ambiguity in the text, Martí suggests that whether the North-South differential as seen from the perspective of the North is definitive of America remains undecided. Like the "South," "North" America is fractured by a series of political projects and dispositions defined by colonialism and imperialism and by resistances to them from below. Thus, the text suggests that the kind of spatiality and nationalist politics from below explored in it as transamerican can liberate the North as well. This could even dismantle the opposition of North and South.[39]

In the end, "Our America" sets into play a twofold movement, a double articulation. If North America is not defined by its purest elements, if it consolidates itself as an imperial power, an actual continental unity will have to be formed in the South, a continental identity forged in opposition to it; and an essentialist form of an American identity in its redemptive mission become necessary. This is a matter of forging an identity that commands respect in the affirmation of the homogeneity of lineages and traditions, and in a definitive futural horizon. This project is articulated from a perspective that owes much to Bolívar. This alternative is not, however, the only one. The other path could be that of a transamerican power from below, challenging colonialism and imperialism from within and without, undermining their structures and social forces, articulating America as a differential field of critical positionalities that is not defined by the North-South split but that acts as a motivating liberating political project that returns Americans to their own locality, in a moment that engages the specificities of natural and cultural settings, as well as the demands of the oppressed. This possibility gives a double register to Martí's famous text, making his writing fundamentally ambivalent, unresolved; but perhaps the fracture is its legacy.

JUAN FLORES'S APPROACH TO MARTÍ'S "OUR AMERICA"

In the important book *From Bomba to Hip-Hop: Puerto Rican Culture and Latino Identity,* Juan Flores invokes "Our America" as a critical framework for understanding the meaning and scope of the Latina/o identity, especially from the specificity of the colonial and diasporic history of Puerto Rico. Flores not only shows a nuanced understanding of Martí's text but also extends its critical impact in original ways.[40]

In the chapter "Pan-Latino/Trans-Latino," Flores struggles with the homogenizing force of the label *Latino* that could erase the specificities of the various populations that it signifies. Flores's concern is that not all Latinos share the same history with the United States, as it is evident in the case of Puerto Ricans' unique colonial condition. He finds that this label could very well erase the difference and, thus, misrepresent the plight of Puerto Ricans in the United States and continue their social, political, and economic marginalization and oppression. At the same time, Flores recognizes that the label "Latino," signaling a homogeneous identity, has an important political and social efficacy, empowering peoples designated by it, opening political options of critique and resistance that benefit even Puerto Ricans. Flores implicitly uses Martí's text "Our America" as a blueprint to help navigate this tension.

The first move in this respect is to connect the Latino population to the economic transnational space of US imperialism. Approaching New York City as a global city, Flores suggests, makes possible "to find a common thread in the intricate 'Latino' weave, or at least a framework in which to interpret the huge and diverse Latino presence in some more encompassing way." Flores applies the same geopolitical framework that Martí applied to the emerging American states below the North-South divide to the "Latino" presence of the immigrants of those same states within the United States. In other words, in Flores's view, the diaspora in the United States does not invalidate Martí's perspective but, rather, situates it within the United States, allowing for a critique of the internal ramifications of US imperialist designs.[41]

This translation of Martí's approach allows Flores to see the category "Latino" through productive critical lenses. First, it presents the demographic as one determined by transnational economic and political structures across the North-South divide that make it necessary to always see Latinas/os in relation to the countries from which they originate. In other words, attention to the transnational geopolitics of the particular countries where Latinos come from forms a critical perspective that stunts some of the dangerous homogenizing effects of the label "Latino." Part of this effort would be, for example, to emphasize the difference between recent immigrant populations and "more historically established communities of Chicanos and Puerto Ricans." One result would be that the internal differentiation of this demographic, and thus of the category "Latino," makes it a panethnicity, that is "a group formation that emerges out of the interaction or close historical congruence of two or more culturally related ethnicities."[42] Flores, then, following Martí, incorporates a productive principle of geopolitical, localized difference through which to understand Latinas/os.

Second, this differentiation marks the presence within Latinas/os of those with a history of direct US colonialism. As Flores explains: "Pan-ethnicity only stands up as a reliable group category if it is recognized that each group making up the aggregate is at the same time participating in a transnational community, the example of the Puerto Ricans, as colonial Latino immigrants, being the most salient case in point." Flores also indicates that this specific colonial history ultimately defines the economic, political, and social marginalization of all Latinos, even if in different ways and with different intensities. In other words, anticolonialism can constitute a galvanizing political perspective of critique and resistance that allows for the articulation of demands and needs of Latinas/os in the United States. Added to the transnational perspective, this anticolonial one is a second way in which Flores, in my view, appropriates insights from "Our America."[43]

The appropriation becomes explicit in Flores's text in his critique of a report by Fordham's Hispanic Research Center, *Nuestra America en Nueva York*. Flores notes its lack of attention to historical differences and states: "This conflation of "racial," national, and ethnic categories does not seem to concern the researchers, nor does the potential value of comparisons and contrasts with other groups, particularly African Americans and Asian Americans. And as for any resonances of the José Martí vision echoed in their title, *Nuestra America in Nueva York* is without an inkling of a hemispheric, transnational frame of analytical reference." This statement allows for a more general assessment of Flores's reliance on Martí: he thinks of Latinas/os from the liminal position that I noted in Martí's double critique across the North-South border. Thus, the conditions of internal coloniality that affect both the North and the South come to be articulated together with the transnational space of US imperial, economic, globalizing designs. He states, for example, "It is the directness of the colonial tie that thus places U.S. Puerto Ricans both inside and outside of U.S. domestic politics, with interests rooted equally in the struggles for justice and equality in the U.S. and in the struggles for sovereignty in the Caribbean and Latin America." Through this analysis of the Latina/o identity, Flores makes the transamerican dimension of Martí's "Our America" more explicit and definitive (freeing it from an essentialized American identity) and adapts it to the diasporic geopolitics at the end of the twentieth century. Martí reveals in his classic text the coming together across the North and the South of an anticolonial movement from below that could create alliances between Americans in the South and those who share a lineage of colonialism in the North, like Native Americans and African Americans, for example. Flores adds to this group Latinos in ways that Martí himself perhaps could not yet see, as well as Asian Americans. Thus, he extends and actualizes Martí's vision. It is not surprising, then, that he asks the reader to "embrace the trans-latino vision of 'nuestra América.'"[44]

The presence of Martí's "Our America" can also be felt in the chapter "The Latino Imaginary" of Flores's text. Flores conceives of "imaginary" as a community being "for-itself," that is, reflecting about its defining characteristics—a reflection that is a process without closure. He states, "The 'imaginary' in this sense does not signify the 'not real,' some make-believe realm oblivious to the

facts, but a projection beyond the 'real' as the immediately present and ration-
ally discernible. It is the 'community' represented 'for-itself,' a unity fashioned
creatively on the basis of shared memory and desire, congruent histories of
misery and struggle, and intertwining utopias." The imaginary is a fluid determination where differences are negotiated in the establishment of a shared
critical locus of the oppressed. This locus allows for solidarity across peoples
that come to form a community that is imagined yet politically effective. In
this way, Flores's text, echoing Martí, attempts to determine a Latino/a people
from the locus of the oppressed.[45]

The text "Our America" makes "Americans" explicit as a new spatial determination and appears to repeat Bolívar's gesture in the "Jamaica Letter." In this
respect, one could trace a lineage from Bolívar to Martí to Flores. But Flores
makes explicit the departure from Bolívar that Martí introduces. The issue here
is that the imagined community is complex, differentiated, and fluid, which
shows Martí's and Flores's critical attentiveness to the fragility and limits of any
community, but especially that of the oppressed, as a coherent identity. Flores
describes the complexity of the imagined community thus: "Beyond the issue
of names and labels, and even who is using them, there are different levels or
modes of meaning simultaneously at work in the very act of apprehending and
conceptualizing the 'community' and 'identity' in question."[46]

Flores envisions political organizations from below, gathering liberatory
movements in solidarity with the oppressed as constituted by diverse marginalized peoples such as blacks, Mestizos, Latinos/as, diasporic national group-
ings, and others. Exceeding Martí in the clarity of his political position, Flores
finds in this proliferation of identities a multiplicity of critical perspectives from
the oppressed that elude a single liberatory horizon. Moreover, he attends to
the dynamics between inside and outside perspectives in the determination
of the imagined community. For Flores, the community from below imagines
itself always in relation to the marginalizing and oppressive perspectives of those
from above. In fact, much of *From Bomba to Hip-Hop* is an account of the power
struggles for self-representation that occur within these dynamics and the possibilities of resistance to the perspectives from above. Martí's "Our America" is
not indifferent to this issue. In fact, my interpretation of it in terms of different
spatialities (world space, village space, continental space, and transamerican
space) implies conflicting perspectives from which to understand America.[47]

It seems that Flores deals more directly with the differential nature and
indeterminacy of his imagined community because he studies the Latina/o
community, one that does not correspond to Martí's Americans in its diasporic,
rather than nationalist or continental, character. Flores is explicit, however,

about the use of Martí's *Our America* as an important basis for his analysis, which indicates that Flores's appropriation of this text draws from its trans-american dimension. In this sense, Martí's text anticipates, and provides a theoretical frame for, the study of the configurations of Latina/o identities and their role within liberatory projects. In fact, if one follows Flores's directive that the diversity of the Latina/o population has to be understood from its specific migrant histories that point to specific nationalities below the North-South divide, "Our America" in its transnational spatiality prefigures a broad critical perspective that makes salient the intimate, coconstitutive relationship between "South" American nations and their diasporic lineages in the "North." Flores can be quite explicit about this: "the features of José Martí's 'nuestra America, do stand out in the Latino historical unconscious in that long narrative of Spanish and North American colonial conquest, the enslavement and subjugation of indigenous and African peoples, the troubled consolidation of nations under the thumb of international power, and the constant migratory movement of peoples, cultures, and things which has been attendant to all aspects of the Latino saga."[48]

There are at least three ways in which Martí's classic text anticipates Flores' treatment of the Latina/o imagined community. First, Martí's text engages in a double discourse that positions itself in the liminal space between North and South, articulating critiques that engage the North and South from within, which leads to a transnational point of view. This double critique seems operative in Flores's work. He states that "The Latino imaginary infuses the clamor for civil rights with a claim to sovereignty on an international scale; retribution involves reversing the history of conquest and subordination, including its inherent migratory imperative. A full century after its initial pronouncement, Martí's profile of 'nuestra América' still looms like a grid over the map of the entire continent, with the northern cooptation of the name America demanding special scrutiny and revision."

Second, Flores shares with Martí the desire to avoid presenting his imagined community as driven by reactive impulses. The natural man and the oppressed in Martí anticipate Flores's critical point: "But Latino memory and desire, though standing as a challenge to prevailing structures of power, are not just reactive. . . . It is important to recognize that the Latino imaginary, like that of other oppressed groups, harbors the elements of an alternative ethos, an ensemble of cultural values and practices created in its own right and to its own ends." This line of inquiry leads Flores to an insight that also defines "our America" (it is not surprising that he makes another explicit reference to Martí's text at this juncture): the need to invert the North-South divide so as to neutralize it.

Flores suggests this kind of geohistorical inversion in relation to Latinas/os: "if we add to that the Indian American and Afro-American dimensions of 'our America,' a full-scale revision or inversion, of the national history results, with the supposed 'core,' Anglo-Saxon culture appearing as the real intruder, the original illegal alien."[49]

Third, the implicit liminal perspective of Martí as an exile in New York is made explicit and thematic in Flores's analysis. In a way, Martí is configured by Flores as an emblematic Latino, a label that we can't be sure Martí himself would have adopted. In this gesture, however, Flores submits Martí's "Our America" to a movement that decenters and overcomes it, particularly in its attachment to nature as a harmonizing basis for geographically specific national formations. Instead, Flores works from a delocalized sensibility in his articulation of the Latino imaginary as migratory. He states, "For Latinos in the United States, the passage to, and from, 'el Norte' assumes such prominence in the social imaginary that migration is often confounded with life itself, and any fixity of the referential homeland gives way to an image of departure and arrival, the abandoned and the reencountered." In this way, Flores opens the possibility of a rereading of "Our America" from a Latina/o border identity, one that explodes the Bolivarian investment in an American identity. This would be a rereading that may retroactively free Martí's text from the homogenizing, continentalist strains that determine it, and even from the gaze of the North.[50]

ASPECTS OF BOAVENTURA DE SOUSA SANTOS'S
INTERPRETATION OF "OUR AMERICA"

In *Epistemologies of the South*, de Sousa Santos gives Martí's classic text a central role. He emphasizes the importance of "Our America" as a text that captures the political and epistemological vision of an alternative (and lesser known) twentieth century that is different from the one defined by US and European imperialism and colonialism. The latter is constituted by "societal fascism," that is, the marginalizing and exclusion of peoples in accordance with social and racial identities so that they cannot expect to be treated as humans in their everyday lives. He argues that the "Nuestra America" century, on the other hand, is directed by interests from below articulated from perspectives aligned with those most vulnerable to oppression that are organized locally and globally. De Sousa Santos notes "a new pattern of local, national, and transnational relations. Such a pattern entails a new transnational political culture embedded in new forms of sociability and subjectivity."[51] He is an acute reader of Martí and captures the broad implications of "Our America" beyond a reaction to the threat from the North, which allows him to make a geopolitical shift that unsettles the global axis of the regime of "societal fascism," and enunciate a different global order: "My analysis highlights some of the emancipatory potential of a new insurgent cosmopolitan politics, culture, and law based not on the ideas of European universalism but rather on the social and political culture of social groups whose everyday lives are energized by the need to transform survival strategies into sources of innovation, creativity, transgression and subversion." De Sousa Santos puts forward five founding ideas that he finds in "Our America." The rest of this chapter focuses on three of them, deferring a more thorough engagement with de Sousa Santos's analysis of this text.[52]

First, de Sousa Santos envisions "nuestra América" as the "antipode" of European America. He points to the indigenous lineage of resistance to Spain that, in his view, leads directly to Martí. He states that "Its deepest roots are the struggles of the Amerindian peoples against the invaders, where we find the true precursors of the Latin American *independistas*." In light of my analysis of the Bolivarian erasure of indigenous positionalities (an erasure implicit in the label "Indian") for the sake of an American identity, and of the way claiming an indigenous lineage of resistance can be used for this very purpose, one has to be somewhat careful with de Sousa Santos's claim here, especially because of the way "Our America" remains tethered to Bolívar's configuration of an American identity. de Sousa Santos quotes Martí: "Is it not evident that America itself was paralyzed by the same blow that paralyzed the Indian?" De Sousa Santos's uncritical reception of Martí's statement is problematic. In fact, it is not evident that the same blow paralyzed the Indian and America, since there was no America when that blow happened—and no Indian for that matter—and since the America evoked here is under construction through the same text that evokes it. That is, this very statement can be a symptom of the Bolivarian erasure of indigenous peoples for the sake of forging an American identity, which opens the complicated question of the meaning of the term "Indian" in Martí.[53]

Second, de Sousa Santos finds Martí's text to be attentive to the "mixed roots" and "infinite complexity" of America. This *mestizaje* interests him as a "universalism from below," and he finds indications of it in Martí's rejection of "race" as a divisive category of difference. His characterization of this mestizaje, however, is problematic since, perhaps inspired by the "baroque ethos," it uncritically promotes and overvalues practices of appropriation and assimilation. He refers to anthropophagy as "the American's capacity to devour all that was alien to him and to incorporate all so as to create a complex identity, a new, constantly changing identity." In this articulation, it is clear that the American identity both precedes the incorporation of others and is constituted by it at the same time, so this "new" fluid identity becomes, in fact, a dominant one. These processes of anthropophagy, even in their indeterminacy that eludes essentialist configurations of identities, are conceptualized from a specific and unique American identity. In this sense, anthropophagy can still constitute an erasure of oppressed peoples. One has to remain sensitive to the ways in which mestizaje, even if from below, does not occur outside of geopolitical referents that can eradicate others. There is a Bolivarian influence in de Sousa Santos's analysis here, one that he channels through Martí. Anthropophagy cannot be absolute, there are always those that remain outside of it, there is no incorporation of all, particularly in terms of the geohistorical differentials of oppressed peoples.[54]

Later in the text, de Sousa Santos seems aware of this problem, but he does not deal fully with its complexity. He critiques Martí's "Our America" for leaving "unexamined the social processes through which *mestizaje* came about. Untold violence and destruction of life were thereby swept under the façade of a benevolent *mestizaje*. The latter became the self-serving narrative of whites and mestizos. Not surprisingly this concept of *mestizaje* became a target of the indigenous peoples and Afro-descendent movements and struggles. The colonial *mestizaje* was to be strictly distinguished from a postcolonial or decolonial *mestizaje*, the white mestizo *mestizaje* from the dark mestizo *mestizaje*."

The question remains whether this critical analytic of white and dark mestizajes, one that ostensibly could guide the formation of proper alliances among the oppressed, is enough to salvage a notion of mestizaje without exclusions, whether the white-dark divide captures the complexity of power struggles and sedimentations and mobilizations of identities even for the sake of projects of liberation. De Sousa Santos may be too quick to endorse a dark, perhaps "pure," process of mestizaje. It seems that one can always ask about who enunciates, and benefits from, mestizaje.[55]

Finally, de Sousa Santos argues that the political thinking behind "Our America" "far from being nationalistic, is rather internationalistic and strengthened by an anticolonialist and anti-imperialist stance, aimed at Europe in the past and now at the United States." This is a bold interpretation in light of the explicit role that nationalism plays in Martí. It seems that de Sousa Santos sees nationalism and internationalism as opposites, while Martí sees them as complementary even if in a conflicted way. In fact, the tension and complementarity between nationalism and internationalism in "Our America" opens productive interpretive engagements with this text, tracing complex issues such as the reactive and affirming dimensions of it, the relationship between critical epistemologies of resistance and non-Eurocentered knowledge production, and even

the emergence of the natural man as a nationalistic leader within an anticolonial and anti-imperialist horizon. One could even say that, rather than moving
away from nationalism toward internationalism, Martí points to the need for a
redetermination of the meaning of both. The reason for de Sousa Santos's bold
interpretation is that he emphasizes the moments in "Our America" when the
threat of the North is deeply felt, eliciting a (South) American continental unity
in opposition to the United States and its global imperialist political and economic interests. That is, he endorses one of the poles of the ambivalence I have
revealed in Martí's text and does not explore its transamerican dimension sufficiently. The North-South divide does not appear to be rigorously questioned
in his reading of Martí.[56]

NOTES

1. See Martín Alcoff, "Power/Knowledges," 249–68, and Martín Alcoff,
"Epistemology."

2. The present essay is meant to be read in conjunction with Saldívar's
interpretation of Martí. In particular, I note Saldívar's emphasis on space,
on different senses of modernity, on migratory subjectivities in relation to
epistemologies and anti-imperialist politics, and on a notion of transamericanity
that is close to the one I develop in this essay. See José David Saldívar, *Trans-
Americanity*, 31–56.

3. The focus on space will limit the range of my interpretation. In view of my
overall argument, interpretations on Martí's aesthetics in relation to his politics
could be helpful here. Especially the classic study of Martí in Julio Ramos,
Divergent Modernities. See also Saldívar, *Trans-Americanity*, 47–49; Martí, "Our
América," 245.

4. See Martí, "Our América," 245. Ibid.

5. Martí, "Our América," 245. Macondo can be a metaphor for America as
a village surrounded by the space of imperialism. See the story of Macondo in
García Márquez, *Leafstorm*, and García Márquez, *Cien años*.

6. Martí, "Our América," 245.

7. Here I am going back to Zea's appropriation of the figure of Bolívar. See
my previous discussion of the "Jamaica letter" in chapter 1.

8. Martí, "Our América," 245.

9. Martí, "Our América," 245.

10. Ibid.

11. In this sense, Martí is a precursor to Mariátegui's notions of nationalism and
internationalism (Martí, "Our América," 245–46). See also Mariátegui, "Destino," 9.

12. See Ramos's discussion of the relationship between Martí and the *letrados*
in Ramos, *Divergent Modernities*. See also Martí, "Our América," 246.

13. Martí, "Our América," 246. The other axis being the erasure of indigenous positionality.

14. Ibid. I have modified this translation.

15. Martí, "Our América," 249. Martí anticipates the important critique of the relationship between knowledge and power in Salazar Bondy and Martín Alcoff. See Salazar Bondy, *Dominación y Liberación*; Martín Alcoff, "Power/ Knowledges"; and Martín Alcoff, "Epistemology."

16. Martí, "Our América," 245.

17. Martí, "Our América," 245. Here I note resonances between Martí's use of critical philosophy and Nietzsche's hammer. See the section "The Hammer Speaks" in Nietzsche, *Twilight of the Idols*. See also, Martín Alcoff "Educating"

18. Martí, "Our América," 249.

19. Martí, "Our América," 247. In this respect, I am in dialogue with Martín Alcoff, "Cuestión del eurocentrismo."

20. See Martín Alcoff's interpretation of Bolívar as a contextualist philosopher in "Educating."

21. Martí, "Our América," 247.

22. In my view, this problematic is taken up in Enrique Dussel's notion of transmodernity.

23. Martí, "Our América," 247.

24. Martí, "Our América," 247.

25. Martí, "Our América," 247.

26. Martí, "Our América," 248.

27. See Bosteels's account of claims for the notions "natural" and "organic" in Martí, ones that commit him to conservative, even antirevolutionary positions, in Bosteels, *Marx and Freud*, 29–36.

28. Martí, "Our América," 248, 249. Italics mine.

29. Martí, "Our América," 249.

30. Martí, "Our América," 249.

31. This term is meant to echo Saldívar's determination of it in *Trans-Americanity*.

32. Martí, "Our América," 248.

33. Martí, "Our América," 248. I have modified the translations.

34. This point challenges the very sense of modernity. For Martí's relationship to Native Americans and its impact on "Our America," see chap. 6, "Native Americans and Nuestra America," in Fountain, *José Martí*. See also Ramos's interpretation of Martí in Ramos, *Divergent Modernities*.

35. For the theme of exile in Martí's work, see Rotker, "(Political) Exile Gaze." See Martí's essay "Coney Island," for example.

36. Martí, "Our América," 251.

37. Ibid.

38. Ibid.

39. Martí, "Our América," 251. Ibid.

40. Other texts that bear on this discussion are Lomas, *Translating Empire*, and Silva Gruesz, *Ambassadors of Culture*.

41. Flores, *From Bomba to Hip Hop*, 145.

42. Flores, *Bomba to Hip Hop*, 150.

43. Ibid. Flores, *Bomba to Hip Hop*, 156.

44. Flores, *Bomba to Hip Hop*, 158, 163, 165.

45. "The logic is that solidarity can be posited only when the lines of social differentiation are fully in view, but the goal, nevertheless, is solidarity" (Flores, *Bomba to Hip Hop*, 198).

46. Flores, *Bomba to Hip Hop*, 193.

47. Flores, *Bomba to Hip Hop*, 193–94. This lineage could include many others engaged in a similar project, like Vasconcelos and Zea.

48. Flores, *Bomba to Hip Hop*, 198. Here Flores echoes the epistemic implications of Saldívar's discussion in *Trans-Americanity*.

49. Flores, *Bomba to Hip Hop*, 200–201.

50. He characterizes Latinos as a "delocalized transnation." Flores, *Bomba to Hip Hop* 200, 198–99.

51. See de Sousa Santos, *Epistemologies*, 49. See also 48.

52. This could lead to a conception of Americanity in relation to coloniality. See Quijano and Wallerstein, "Americanity as a Concept," and de Sousa Santos, *Epistemologies*, 51. The remaining two founding ideas coincide with my own interpretation: situated knowledge and the critique of the Europeanized class in America. Beyond his founding ideas, de Sousa Santos's analysis includes the relationship of Martí to the baroque ethos, a critique of "Our America" that reveals its limits, as well as suggestions on how to build upon it.

53. De Sousa Santos, *Epistemologies*, 51, 52. See chap. 1. SECLIT.

54. De Sousa Santos, *Epistemologies*, 52. De Sousa Santos's complex explanation of Martí's relationship to the baroque ethos sheds light on the scope of Martí's text in its proposal of an alternative sensibility that values the formation of fluid marginal identities for the sake of counterhegemonic practices. Such a discussion is too extensive to engage fully here. But even though it deepens the meaning of mestizaje in his argument and interpretation of Martí, it does not resolve the problems with it that become apparent from my foregoing discussion. In relation to the concept of anthropophagy, he relies on Oswald de Andrade's determination of it. See de Andrade, *Escritos Antropófagos*.

55. De Sousa Santos, *Epistemologies*, 65.

56. De Sousa Santos, *Epistemologies*, 54.

THREE

—∿∿—

DISSEMINATION

Logics of Redemption in Mariátegui's
Seven Essays

In this epoch, with the coming forth of a new ideology that translates
the interests and aspirations of the masses—which gradually acquires a
class conscience and spirit—, a national current or tendency emerges that
feels itself to be in solidarity with the fate of the Indian. . . . The problem
of the Indian ceases to be . . . a secondary or adjectival theme. It begins to
represent the main theme.

José Carlos Mariátegui

THIS CHAPTER continues to trace the disruption of redemptive philosophies
of liberation, now in terms of Mariátegui's understanding of nationalism, internationalism, and the "problem of the Indian." This interpretive perspective on
his *Seven Essays* reveals a "colonial logic of redemption" and an "indigenista logic
of redemption" that can become dangerously tangled up with one another. Yet
it also points to a practical political and transcultural dimension of Mariátegui's socialism that is not defined by redemptive liberatory investments and
the essentialization of identities that they imply. The pursuit of this dimension
marks a transition from a contextual delimitation of Latin American philosophy to a transcultural one in my discussion (a transition elucidated in the next
chapter).

NATIONALISM, INTERNATIONALISM

Taking fascism as a cue, Mariátegui dismisses an outmoded nationalism
invested in fixed cultural identities and rejects the fabrication of an embel-
lished past that seeks to define a people's present and future: "Fascism, in its

66

theoreticians' own words, assumes a medieval and Catholic sensibility; they imagine themselves representing the Spirit of the Counterreformation.... But all attempts to revive olden myths are destined to immediate failure. Every era wishes its own sense of the world. Nothing is more sterile than to try to revive an extinct myth." Following this critique, Mariátegui redefines the meaning of nationalism in relation to internationalism.[1]

For Mariátegui, internationalism at his historical juncture appears as a "superior reality." This superiority consists in that nationalism (even if at first appears to be the most immediate) is derivative of internationalism: "the internationalists do not contradict every nationalist theory. They recognize that it corresponds to reality, but only in its first approximation. Nationalism apprehends a part of reality, but only a part. Reality is much more ample, less finite." Nationalism is a "first approximation" and a "part" of the reality of internationalism. It has to be situated within it. From an internationalist stance, nations, and identities supported by nationalism, are not only temporal projections (in terms of historical trajectories that appeal to senses of collective memory and joint purpose) but are also localities within a geopolitical field. Temporal projections can never fully absorb or neutralize the proliferation of these localities. In internationalism, space exceeds time as the matrix from which peoples understand themselves and acquire collective meanings and values. Simply put: in internationalism, the temporal projections of outmoded nationalisms are always unsettled by an ample spatiality; and cultural, social, political, and economic forms operate without closure because space disseminates, fractures, and hybridizes them and the related processes through which identities are formed. For Mariátegui, nationalism has as its perhaps impossible task to engage the possibilities of configurations of identities in this excess of space. "Reality," Mariátegui says, "is less finite."[2] Mariátegui has a concrete grasp of this excess of space as a material condition: "Internationalism is not solely an idea or a feeling; it is, above all, a historic fact." It has to do with practices of commerce that are aligned with global capitalism, as well as with diasporic movements, and with the configuration of international economic classes. And all this leads to a different spirit, since the world has a "new nervous system." He writes, "Transmitted through wires, through hertz waves, through the press, etc., every great emotion instantaneously traverses the world." And this proliferation across space flattens out of time, especially progressive, developmental temporal projections that position one locality "before" another.[3]

At first, it seems that Mariátegui is off the mark, since the phenomenon of internationalism, especially as linked to capitalism, seems to bring about the reduction of space and the instantiation of a homogeneous dominant culture. Mariátegui himself states that "Buenos Aires, Quebec, Lima, copy the fashion in Paris. Their tailors and fashion designers imitate Paquin's models. This solidarity, this uniformity are not exclusively western. European civilization attracts, gradually, towards its orbit and customs all peoples and all races. It is a *dominating* civilization that does not tolerate the existence of any concurrent or rival civilization." Mariátegui's point may indicate, however, that the expansion of an Anglo-European bourgeoisie is not yet a moment of internationalism and is the result of the power differential inherent in capital through which this class becomes dominant on a global scale. Mariátegui writes in this respect, "Capitalist interests developed independently from the growth of the nation. The nation, finally, could not contain them within its boundaries. Capital lost its nationality . . . goods did not know about confinement and fought to circulate freely throughout all countries . . . free commerce was a step toward internationalism."[4]

The first step of internationalism takes the form of the dominance of capitalism and it happens together with the emergence of an international perspective that is not anchored in nations. In this way, capitalism, together with the hegemony of Western civilization, is a transition toward a proper internationalism that sets up the conditions for a new sense of nationalism. The socialist revolution is part of this process toward a spatiality that enables a pluricultural and transcultural international space beyond Western hegemony. This is the complex context from which to read the following statement: "For a century . . . one can see in the European civilization the tendency to prepare an international organization of humanity. . . . The free market, as an idea and as a praxis, was a step toward internationalism, in which the proletariat already recognized one of its objectives, one of its ideals."[5]

SPACE, COLONIALISM, AND IMPERIALISM

In Mariátegui's view, capitalism is expansive, growing out of a center, radiating from an axis. Its axis is the United States. He finds there a particular set of values, sensibilities, and modes of experience anchored in individualism that are expressed spatially through what appears to be a dominant sense of unrestricted mobility: "While in Europe the individuals of the working class and the middle class feel themselves ever more trapped within class boundaries, in the United States they believe that fortune and power are still accessible to anybody that has an aptitude to conquer them. And this is the measure of the subsistence, within a capitalist society, of the psychological factors that determine its development." By "a sense of unrestricted mobility" I mean a disposition toward the possible infinite expansion of the domain of the individual. It is grounded in an actual spatial mobility originating in colonizing practices. The projection of space as a virginal land is the concrete manifestation of this: "Upon the virginal land of America, where they erased all indigenous traces, the Anglo-Saxon colonizers laid, since their arrival, the foundations of the capitalist order." This colonial legacy in the North is actualized in the social and economic value of private property tied to a mobile individualism. Mariátegui quotes Charles A. Beard (through Waldo Frank): "The Constitution was essentially an economic act, based on the notion that the fundamental rights of private property are prior to any government and are morally beyond the reach of the popular masses."[6]

In the United States, private property is the sublimation of the violence of colonialism, of the eradication and enslaved labor of indigenous and black populations, and sustains the basic subjective constitution of the individual as mobile. This colonially constituted, expansive capitalist individualism is the substance of US imperialism: "The capitalist growth of the United States had to led to an imperialist conclusion. North American capitalism cannot be developed within the confines of the United States and its colonies anymore. It reveals, for this reason, a great power of expansion and dominance." Ultimately, Mariátegui shows that the formation of the United States as an imperialist power is embedded in an individualism structured by colonialism and defined by the possibility of undeterred spatial expansions. The individuals here are forged by coloniality and supported by racial, gendered, and epistemic colonial structures of power that deem those different from them across the colonial difference to be subhuman, which implies that their lands are always available for occupation.[7]

For this reason, Mariátegui looks for a different spatiality and economic structure delinked from private property, one in which everyone is materially supported and nobody's life is dispensable, and collective spatialities are grounded in the communal use of the resources of the land. He finds this alternative spatiality and economic structure in the convergence between socialism and the legacies of Andean indigenous peoples. He leaves unexplored, however, the relationship between this convergence and the pluricultural and transcultural international space discussed earlier. Yet in this unfinished gesture he begins to engage, and construct, the possibility of an indigenous, socialist revolutionary project.

RECLAIMING THE MEANING OF "NATION"

In Mariátegui's view, colonialism is the interruption of the development of the economy of the Inka empire, an economy that he claims "grew freely from the Peruvian land and people." His analysis begins with a retroactive projection of the idea of "nation" onto the precolonial Andes and with the conception of a specific and actual Peruvian nation that reaches back to at least the Inka era. Peru as nation, a land, and a people seems to indicate a deep social, economic, and political reality that continues despite the conquest.[8]

This presentation of the Peruvian nation is decisive for Mariátegui's economic analysis. He characterizes the Inka people as "laborious, disciplined, pantheist, simple" but, more important, as collectivist and endowed with "humility and religious obedience." All these psychological and social characteristics constitute the conditions for the consolidation of a people for whom collective work becomes the axis of all social, political, and cultural life and for whom the land, rather than being an abstract, empty factor, is the source of their concrete, differentiated lives. In this way, Mariátegui envisions the Inka empire as providing an economic reality that identifies a new sense of nation that is not defined by enlightenment political ideas such as private property, citizenship, representative and participatory government, or even equality and freedom. Thus, his understanding of "nation" is informed by non-Western Andean economic forms and incorporates a spatiality beyond that of the projections of individualism.[9] Rather than imposing a modern concept onto the Andean pre-Columbian past, Mariátegui engages this past to find a different sense of "nation" that complicates and redetermines the modern one. Mariátegui's challenge and deconstruction of the Enlightenment's nation shows the power and implications of his historical reflection. Setting aside the question of historical accuracy, Mariátegui unearths a different genealogy of the concept "nation" in Peru, one that is anchored in the Andean context rather than in Europe, enabling political and economic options to appear in a non-Eurocentered frame and opening up another history. Opening alternative historical lineages is the intent of his historical method.[10]

This historical dimension of his analysis dislodges the concept "nation" from Eurocentrism for the sake of enabling a radical conceptual shift, one that allows him to use "nation" as an indigenous concept in order to critique both colonialism and the social, political, and economic structures of the Peruvian republic. Mariátegui's indigenous socialism cannot be properly understood outside this shift through which the meaning of "nation" is reclaimed. His critical move is similar to the one Dussel finds in Guaman Poma's *The First New Chronicle and Good Government*. These words could be applied to Mariátegui's analysis: "This is a categorical critique of Modernity on the basis of the world that preceded it; on the basis of an ecological utopia of ethical-communitarian justice, where there existed 'good government' and not violence, theft, filth, ugliness, rape, excess, brutality, suffering, cowardice, lies, arrogance, . . . death."[11]

TWO POLITICO-ECONOMIC PARADIGMS

Mariátegui maintains that Spanish colonialism "destroyed the machinery of production" of the Inkas, in such a way that "the nation was dissolved into dispersed communities." The Spanish did not establish a nation as a life-sustaining economic form because they were invested in the exploitation of land and laborers rather than in the lives of the laborers as a force of production: "The Spanish pioneer also lacked the aptitude to create nuclei of labor. Instead of the utilization of the indigenous peoples, they seemed to want their extermination. And the colonizers could not rely on themselves to create a solid and organic economy." The Spanish were concerned with military and ecclesiastic authority rather than with labor as the center of the political and social organization of the colonies. In this sense, Mariátegui's critique of the colonial economy is not strictly historical or even economic in the narrower sense of the term. It, rather, theorizes two politico-economic paradigms (here I am supplying a conceptuality extraneous to Mariátegui's text). The first paradigm is the indigenous nation, defined by a sustainable relationship with the land and the principle that every human being is given the means necessary to maintain her life. This paradigm is socialist in Mariátegui's analysis and reclaims the term "nation" as operative within an indigenous lineage. Mabel Moraña helps me understand this point: "Socialism appears, then, as a restitution, that is, as the instance that returns to the indigenous people their productive and spiritual relationship with the land, a connection that was dismantled by Spanish colonialism, and that when reconstituted would confer to the peasant forms of sociability the communitarian sense lost through the adoption of capitalist modes of production."

The second paradigm is the colonial state, understood as an exploitative economic and political structure in which the land is seen as an infinite resource for the production of wealth, and race operates as the distinction between the human (whites) and the subhuman (nonwhites) (where the latter's lives are dispensable and thus the material base for slave labor and servitude). This paradigm is dominant in both colonialism and the Peruvian republic.[12]

These two paradigms, in my view, constitute hermeneutic lenses that allow Mariátegui to grasp the economic history of Peru and the Andean region, and they are decisive for his vision of a possible Peruvian nation. Perhaps the most interesting aspect of Mariátegui's analysis is condensed in the statement "On top of the ruins and residues of a socialist economy, they [the Spanish] laid out the bases for a feudal economy." This phrase is remarkable not only because of the apparently anachronic evocation of socialism but also because it provides a way to imagine the Peruvian economic reality so that two politico-economic paradigms coexist in it, where one (the colonial state) dominates the other (the indigenous nation) but without extinguishing it, without stopping it from being a continuous referent not only for the economic analysis of Peru but for an indigenous socialist revolutionary praxis.[13]

In this way, just like Bolívar and Martí, among others, Mariátegui comes to posit an identity, that is, an "Indian" identity, linked to a revolutionary project, one in which the indigenous nation helps articulate a redemptive future. Appealing to an indigenous lineage, the nation is reclaimed as a redemptive ideal exceeding its operation as a critical notion.[14] It links an indigenous past to contemporary political movements, setting the stage for the figure of the socialist revolutionary "Indian" on the basis of a fabricated "Indian" identity.[15]

A "SECOND COLONIZATION" AND "INDO-SPANISH AMÉRICA"

A continuous and growing contact between South America and Western civilization was established. The most favored countries by this traffic were, naturally, due to their greater proximity to Europe, the countries located in the Atlantic shore. Argentina and Brazil, above all, attracted European immigrants and capital in large quantities. Strong and homogeneous western barrages accelerated in these countries the transformation of the economy and culture that acquired gradually the function and the structure of the European economy and culture. Bourgeois and liberal democracy was able to take secure root there, while in the rest of South America was stopped from doing so due to the continuation of extensive and tenacious residues of a feudal order.

Mariátegui, *Siete ensayos*

This paragraph captures what Mariátegui thinks of as a second kind of colonization, which in his analysis constitutes another defining critical perspective. The second colonization involves the imposition of a capitalist economy and liberal democracy (the latter being the political form that serves the former) on Latin America. Its success is based on the transplantation of an economy that relies on constant traffic with Europe and, what is perhaps most important, on European immigration and its resulting demographic, social, and cultural expansions. Mariátegui's concept of the spread of capitalism as a second colonization underscores the fact that capitalism is not a transferable ideology or economic form but is tied to people with particular histories, lineages, and cultures. In his view, for example, just as one cannot dissociate capitalism from liberalism, one cannot dissociate capitalism from Protestantism. The spread of capitalism constitutes, then, a cultural imposition whose efficacy depends on coercive processes of assimilation into Western civilization or, more effectively, on European immigration. This means that the spread of global capitalism depends on the continuance of colonial processes. The geographic and spatial conditions that facilitate such continuance constitute definitive factors for the consolidation of the bourgeoisie in the Americas. This critical perspective opens ways of understanding the relation between race and the spread of global capitalism. Aníbal Quijano takes up this discussion showing the heterogeneity of modes of labor in global capitalism and the relationship between this heterogeneity and racial classification. Mariátegui's second colonization, then, can be seen as a precursor to Quijano's "coloniality of power."[16]

The second colonization challenges the unity of America because it fractures a sense of shared destiny for American or Latin American peoples. It thus undermines the integrity of an American identity. Mariátegui writes about Peru, "the general historic process of Peru enters into a stage of differentiation and disentanglement from the historic process of other peoples of South America. Given their geography, ones were destined to develop faster than others. The Independence had joined them in a common enterprise, only in order to separate them later in individual enterprises." The fracturing of America is a guiding intuition in Mariátegui's work. From the critical lens of the second colonization, the identity of America, Bolívar's dream and even Martí's version of it, fail. This complex deconfiguration of América is at stake in Mariátegui's famous yet difficult text "The Unity of Indo-Hispanic America."[17]

Mariátegui, attending to economic factors and to the connection between global capitalism and imperialism, rejects the centrality of a continental American identity as the entrapment of a futile and materially baseless creole imaginary and proceeds with an analysis that does not capitalize on such an identity to secure the efficacy of an indigenous socialism. He is more interested in unearthing, from underneath an American identity, silenced indigenous lineages. Decentering this identity, Mariátegui focuses on complex economic conditions relying on his analysis of an indigenous national economy surviving at least as a politico-economic paradigm. Mariátegui calls for the recovery of alternative economic forms operative beneath coloniality and for the political agency of subjects for whom this alternative economy is evident as a guiding ideal. This, for Mariátegui, does not imply a continental identity but a project sensitive to the heterogeneity of what he sometimes calls "Indo-Spanish America."[18]

Earlier I suggested that reclaiming an indigenous nation brings into play investments in cultural continuities tied to logics of redemption that sustain an Indian identity, an indigenous socialism and its iconic figure, the socialist revolutionary Indian. At the same time, the material, cultural, and political heterogeneity operative in Mariátegui's notion of Indo-Spanish America is grounded on spatial determinations that localize such political projects and expose them to disruptive spatial differentials that limit their field of efficacy. This tension is apparent when Mariátegui writes, "in contemporary Peru coexist elements of three economies. Under the regime of a feudal economy born with the conquest, some living residues of the indigenous communist economy subsist in the sierra. In the coast, on top of a feudal soil, grows a bourgeois economy that, at least in its intellectual development, gives the impression of a delayed economy." It turns out, then, that the two politico-economic paradigms that appear to inform Mariátegui's indigenous socialism, the indigenous nation and the colonial state, are apparent from a particular location: the sierra. In the coast the colonial state coexists with an incipient bourgeois economy. In other words, the coast and the sierra are spatial differentials that complicate the reach of the indigenous nation as part of a socialist project. Moreover, these spatial differentials also disseminate different temporalities. The episodic stages of feudalism, capitalism and socialism, articulated through a Eurocentric linear temporality, are thrown in disarray. In Peru, not only are these stages simultaneous but they also involve different temporal projections. Socialism is both past and futural; colonialism is in the past and the present, and capitalism may appear futurally in the coast, but outside the range of temporal projections in the sierra. Space disseminates time so that political projects become spatialized and temporalized in specific ways and intersect with one another disruptively, beyond linear history and spatial homogeneity. The redemptive dimension of Mariátegui's indigenous socialism will always be unsettled by such disseminations.[19]

THE REDEMPTIVE FRAME OF "THE PROBLEM OF THE INDIAN" IN THE *SEVEN ESSAYS*

What Mariátegui has done is to offer a vision of society in which the Indian population is seen as an essentially creative and dynamic participant in the productive process, on a par with everyone else. In addition, he has tied the cultural identity of the nation to the identity of the redeemed or regenerated Indian, thus reversing and surpassing to the fullest extent the social and economic effects of the Spanish conquest.

Ofelia Schutte, *Cultural Identity and Social Liberation in Latin American Thought*

The essay "The Problem of the Indian," within the *Seven Essays*, constitutes the core of Mariátegui's work. It is famous as an example of Mariátegui's Marxist method since it presents this "problem" as an economic one. If one reads only this text through an unquestioned orthodox Marxist lens, however, many aspects of it may not become apparent, some of which are central to the whole of the *Seven Essays*. I will read this text, rather, on the basis of Mariátegui's interpretation of socialism as a myth in which Marx's main accomplishment, beyond his materialist and economic analyses, is the identification of the proletariat as a revolutionary agent. From this perspective, the economic approach in "The Problem of the Indian" cannot distract us from an analogous identification in Mariátegui's socialism, namely, that of Indians, and those in solidarity with them, as the emerging revolutionary agents in Peru. In this identification, the liberation of the Indian (an identity configured through Mariátegui's work), promised through the overturning of the colonial structures that continue to assail them, becomes also a restoration and a final redemptive affirmation of their humanity.[20]

Mariátegui inherits the problem of the Indian from very different political positions, and his analysis to a large extent is a critique of the ways the problem is posed by both liberals and conservatives. Later in the work (in the sixth essay), he quotes the Spanish conservative academic Eugenio d'Ors as having already posed the problem. It is worth quoting this statement since it appears to be at the background of Mariátegui's approach:

Bolivia, like Peru and like Mexico, has a great local problem—which also signifies a great universal problem—it has the problem of the Indian; of the situation of the Indian in the face of culture. What to do with this race? It is known that there have been, traditionally, two opposed methods. The Saxon method has been to make it regress, to weaken it, to eliminate it slowly. The Spanish method, to the contrary, attempted an approximation, *redemption*, mixture. . . . One must establish . . . the obligation to work with one or the other method. It is morally impossible to be content with a kind of conduct that simply avoids the problem, and that simply tolerates the existence and swarming of the Indians next to the white population, without caring for their situation, except to take advantage of it.

The point of Mariátegui's recalling this statement seems to be, at first, to show that even thinkers who do not share his own political commitments recognize the centrality of the problem of the Indian. Immediately after quoting d'Ors, however, Mariátegui distances himself from his statement. In particular, Mariátegui challenges the supposed humanitarianism of the Spanish in its contrast with the "will to extermination" of the Saxons—an extermination of indigenous peoples that, according to d'Ors, is still a moral option. Mariátegui underscores that both the Saxon and the Spanish methods deem Indians to be subhuman and consider their lives dispensable. In a parenthetical remark, Mariátegui writes, "Probably, for Eugenio d'Ors, the Spanish method is represented by the generous spirit of the priest de Las Casas, and not by the policies of the conquest and the viceroyalty that were completely impregnated with prejudices against not only the Indians but also the mestizos." Mariátegui thus puts into question a Spanish humanitarianism, referring to the colonial structures of racism and exploitation that are covered up in uncritical and aggrandizing interpretations of Spanish colonialism, interpretations that d'Ors exemplifies and that are insidious to approaches to the problem of the Indian.[21]

Eugenio d'Ors's statement articulates the problem of the Indian in specific ways that Mariátegui will return to in his own analysis. For d'Ors, the problem appears in terms of the externality of the Indians with respect to culture (which coincides with Western civilization), their inability to contribute to culture and, thus, to justify their existence. In this assessment, the dichotomy civilization-barbarism defined from a Spanish colonial perspective is still operative as a racist framework. In this sense, the problem is the very existence of indigenous peoples, the fact that they are alive and that their lives are worthless in their own right.

Mariátegui's rethinking of the problem seeks to overturn the racist ways in which this problem has been posed prior to him (by both liberals and conservatives), as if the problem were the mere lives of indigenous peoples, lives that are an obstacle to the smooth unfolding of (Western) civilization. Mariátegui's supposedly economic approach to the problem recognizes that the humanity of indigenous peoples is in question, that their existence has been deemed dispensable. Borrowing a terminology not available to Mariátegui, one could say that the problem of the Indian has to be thought from the colonial difference, from the space of contestation of the difference between the categories human and subhuman.[22]

Eugenio d'Ors is worried about the immorality of not addressing this problem for the sake of furthering (Western) civilization. The moral options are the extermination or the redemption of the Indians (the latter meaning their approximation to Western civilization). His question and framing of the problem, then, can be rephrased as "What to do with this dispensable, subhuman, race?" It goes without saying, since indigenous peoples are outside culture, that those who ask this question, and those who could act and do something about this race, are not the Indians themselves but, rather, those who belong to "civilization." In other words, the racist assessment of the dispensability of indigenous lives has to be connected, for d'Ors, to the moral disposition of having to do something about these lives, since Indians, in their pointless existence, should not be left alone. D'Ors makes explicit this "having to do something about the Indians" as an urgent moral issue. He wants to bring forth a type of moral imperative. The two moral options, then, which characterize the Saxon and the Spanish methods, do not constitute two different valuations of indigenous lives but are informed by a shared sense of their subhumanity. This is probably why Mariátegui does not want to differentiate these two methods as d'Ors does, why he sees them as the same in a fundamental way and why he implies that the Spanish were racially prejudiced against indigenous peoples and mestizos, despite the appearance of working toward the redemption of the Indians.

It seems to me that Mariátegui continues, not without irony, to call the Spanish method as described by d'Ors humanitarian because it involves the decision to act in order to give value to dispensable Indian lives, a decision that presupposes the subhumanity of Indians. What can be more humanitarian than such actions? D'Ors specifies the outcomes of the actions he has in mind: "approximation, *redemption*, mixture." Approximation and mixture imply actions that bring indigenous peoples into civilization, methods of inclusion that could range from political and social integration to miscegenation. By redemption, d'Ors means giving value to Indian lives by including them in Western civilization. Thus, the redemption of Indians is not a method like the other ones but the moral outcome of them. In their inclusion into civilization, through approximation and mixture, their lives are given worth, not having any worth in themselves—a gift that binds them to the superiority and generosity of the Spanish with an infinite debt because it justifies their existence.[23]

D'Ors's position is that during Spanish colonialism the moral, redemptive obligation toward Indian lives is evident. He is concerned that the newly independent republics may lose sight of this important colonial heritage and of the true nature of the problem of the Indian. For that reason, he posits the question "What to do with this race?" In his view, the new republics are obligated to ask the question. The consequence of not doing so would be allowing the continuation of a life without value, one that, he fears, would only be exploited. At this juncture, d'Ors argument becomes complex. He presents himself as a defender of Indians, but how can he both be a champion of indigenous peoples and consider their lives intrinsically worthless?

It seems that d'Ors's position does not necessarily condemn the exploitation of indigenous labor in colonialism nor does it imply a call for stopping it during the republican epoch. Rather, it implies that exploitation can be reevaluated so as to acquire a redemptive meaning through the exposure of indigenous peoples to civilization. Namely, that the exploitation of indigenous labor has to be understood as part of the larger moral project of Indian redemption. Strangely enough, in d'Ors's moral proposal, and within the larger context of redemption, the very practices that take advantage of the Indians are bestowed with redemptive meaning, especially for the creoles. He wants to reveal the moral significance of the exploitation of indigenous peoples and, thus, put the creoles in good moral standing. In this twisted logic, Indians are both exploited and enculturated, and the creoles take on the moral purpose of redeeming them. His concern is with the moral integrity of the creoles rather than with indigenous lives. I call this approach to the problem of the Indian the "colonial logic of redemption." One can speculate that this logic informs the creole identity as an emerging bourgeoisie in the new republics and gives it political and economic meaning and purpose.

MARIÁTEGUI'S ESSAY "THE PROBLEM OF THE INDIAN"

What I call the "colonial logic of redemption" is an implicit allusion to Mariátegui's own analysis of the problem. The stance from which the inclusion of indigenous peoples into civilization appears as a redemptive process continues to define how the problem of the Indian is addressed in Mariátegui's time. The economic approach that is at the core of Mariátegui's discussion acquires a layered sense once it is seen to be a critical response to this colonial logic. Mariátegui explains the originality of his approach to the problem of the Indian as follows: "The socialist critique discovers and clarifies it [the problem of the Indian], because it seeks its causes in the economy of the country and not in its administrative, juridical or ecclesiastic mechanisms, nor in the duality or plurality of races, nor in cultural and moral conditions. The indigenous issue starts in our economy. It is rooted in the regime of land property." It should be noted that Mariátegui does not begin with the supposed subhumanity of the Indian. In fact, his economic approach is, above all, an implicit challenge to racist framings of the problem. I will trace some of the ways in which the quotation puts the reader on a path of systematically dismantling how Mariátegui's contemporaries understand the problem of the Indian. In particular, he undermines them because they put forward a series of noneconomic theses (I will address the administrative, racial, moral, and educational ones).[24]

Administratively, Mariátegui notes that the decrees and laws issued since the independence with the intent to protect indigenous peoples from abuse have been ineffective because under the regime of *gamonales,* the "gamonal has . . . very little to fear from administrative theories. He knows that the practice is different." Gamonalismo, as the continuance of a colonial regime of land property in which indigenous labor is exploited and indigenous lives deemed dispensable, is effectively untouched by administrative policies. Mariátegui also observes that the "individualist character of the legislation of the Republic," in an economic context in which colonialism remains operative, enables the appropriation of indigenous communal land for the benefit of the gamonales. Gamonalismo both creates a sphere in which the law to protect the Indians is suspended and undermines the process through which a feudal economy can develop into a capitalist one. Mariátegui states, "without the dissolution of feudalism liberal rights have not been able to function."[25]

Approaching the problem on the basis of race posits its solution as miscegenation, through "an active mixing of the aboriginal race with white immigrants." Mariátegui challenges this position in two ways. First, he questions the idea of racial inferiority itself, pointing to its function within imperialism: "The concept of inferior races served the white West in its work of expansion and conquest." In other words, racial inferiority is an instrument of colonialism and imperialism and is meaningful only in that context. Second, Mariátegui opposes the notion of racial inferiority by pointing to a practice of active transculturation on the part of the colonized: "The Asian peoples, to whom the Indian people are not in the least inferior, have admirably assimilated western culture, its most dynamic and creative characteristics, without the transfusion of European blood." While the colonial/imperial concept of racial inferiority presupposes a kind of racial stasis in which racialized peoples are unable to develop on their own (this is at the background of d'Ors's position and of the "colonial logic of redemption"), Mariátegui affirms the capacity of indigenous peoples to actively engage in transcultural processes of absorption, negotiation, and assimilation that involve the selection and evaluation of traits of the dominant culture without compromising their integrity as a people. To the biologistic, static, colonial/imperial concept of race, Mariátegui proposes a transcultural, historical, and geopolitical one, seemingly shifting toward a concept of ethnicity rather than race, at least at this juncture. Miscegenation cannot be the solution to the problem of the Indian because it is based on a colonial/imperialist, racist perspective that does not recognize the conditions for the transcultural flourishing of colonized peoples. Mariátegui's economic solution to the problem has to align itself with such conditions.[26]

Mariátegui also disagrees with the position that the solution to the problem of the Indian depends on a moral sense and humanitarianism. He questions the efficacy of the "leagues for the rights of man" and of the "anti-slavery conferences and societies." In his short discussion, Mariátegui engages Manuel González Prada twice. The first time he clearly distances himself from the first option in the following quote: the "indigenous condition can improve in two ways: either the heart of the oppressors is moved to the extreme of recognizing the rights of the oppressed, or the spirit of the oppressed acquires enough virility to chase away the oppressors." Mariátegui dismisses González Prada's hope in the good heart of the oppressors for two reasons. The first, and most explicit one, relies on González Prada's own insight into indigenous oppression during the colonial regime: one cannot expect humanitarianism in a political and economic context where structures for the exploitation of indigenous labor are in place, where the ends that humanitarianism seeks could be achieved only through the overthrowing of the whole colonial regime. Mariátegui seems puzzled about why González Prada would think that the issue would be different after colonialism, that somehow the creoles would act with a "moral sense" when the feudal economic structure of gamonalismo remains in place. Mariátegui notes (in a statement that could also challenge d'Ors) that in the postcolonial era "the humanitarian preaching has not ashamed European imperialism nor has it appeased its methods." In other words, just as the economic structure of gamonalismo suspends the law, it also suspends any humanitarianism.[27]

The second, and implicit, reason why Mariátegui dismisses the moral solution is that it presupposes the passivity of indigenous peoples, something that is obvious in d'Ors's position. That is, it puts the burden of action and decision on the creole elite, turning them into redemptive agents advocating indigenous rights. This solution, in fact, disempowers the indigenous masses and bolsters the disposition toward them as a static, uncivilized people whose well-being depends on an external force bringing them into Western civilization. The humanitarian solution, then, is not far away from the colonial logic of redemption. Mariátegui rejects this kind of indigenous passivity as a racist projection and affirms the political power and agency of the indigenous masses. His rejection is clear in the statement "The struggle against imperialism does not rely on anything but in the solidarity and strength of the movements of emancipation of the colonial masses." In this respect, then, he seems more agreeable to Gonzales Prada's second option: the indigenous masses chasing away the oppressors.[28]

Mariátegui's rejection of the thesis that the problem of the Indian would be solved by educating Indians has two interrelated aspects. The first is his insistence that education happens within social and economic conditions that overdetermine it: "The modern pedagogue knows perfectly that education is not merely an issue of schooling and didactic methods. The economic and social medium inexorably conditions the work of the teacher." The values of individualism and self-development that define the aims and pedagogies of modern education cannot flourish in the context in which indigenous peoples find themselves under gamonalismo. What is the point of a modern education for indigenous peoples while their economic role is servitude? The issue seems to be, again, the mismatch between enlightenment ideals ostensibly held by the creole elite and the economic system of gamonalismo. The second aspect of Mariátegui's critique addresses the specific way gamonalismo seeks to shape the character and the economic and political potential of indigenous peoples through a regime of servitude: "Gamonalismo is fundamentally adverse to the education of the Indian: its subsistence has the same interest in the maintenance of indigenous ignorance as in the fostering of their alcoholism. . . . [T]he mechanics of servitude would completely annul the work of [modern] schools. . . . [S]chools and teachers are unavoidably condemned to be denatured under the pressure of the feudal atmosphere." Mariátegui focuses on servitude as a structure that singles out indigenous peoples and that systematically attempts to diminish their power of political self-affirmation. While the moral and racial theses were based on indigenous passivity as a racial "fact," the educational thesis ignores the structures of the republic that foster passivity.[29]

The foregoing discussion lays out the substance of Mariátegui's essay "The Problem of the Indian." The point of it, then, is not to explain the precise sense in which this "problem" is an economic one. Such an explanation is undertaken in the third essay. It would be accurate to say, rather, that the second essay attempts to reframe the way the problem of the Indian is understood, that it deconstructs the ways it is overdetermined by racist denials of the humanity of indigenous peoples. A superficial reading would understand this analysis as a process in which Mariátegui simply discards attempts to understand the problem through noneconomic approaches in order to leave the economic approach as the only viable one. Such readings have been put forth to reveal the extent of Mariátegui's Marxism, namely, his apparent reduction of social, cultural, and political problems to a strictly economic plane.[30]

A more accurate reading, however, shows the complexity of the second essay beyond such an economic reduction. The first clue comes from Mariátegui himself: "This critique repudiates and disqualifies the diverse theses that consider the issue through *one* of the following *unilateral and exclusive criteria*: administrative, juridical, ethnic, moral, educational, ecclesiastic."[31] In other words, the failure of the noneconomic theses is not that they are irrelevant to addressing the problem of the Indian but, rather, they fail because they address the problem exclusively from a specific purview, without noting how the economic and noneconomic reciprocate one another as a result of their shared colonialist, racist assumptions. In my view, Mariátegui is suggesting that, in order to address the problem correctly, the criteria underlying the noneconomic theses need to be mobilized in conjunction, articulated with one another under a decolonial guiding perspective that clarifies the problem. This guiding perspective defines the economic thesis that Mariátegui proposes.

Mariátegui's challenge to the noneconomic theses reveals what they overlook: the entanglement of the new republic with an economy of gamonalismo sustained by colonial social and political structures. In fact, racism defines the perspective from which the noneconomic solutions to the problem are articulated, and it is a primary, though implicit, target in Mariátegui's rejection of them. His discussion reveals that racism enforces a perspective from which indigenous peoples appear dispensable as a static race, unable to shape for themselves a cultural environment and historical trajectory that could be part of civilization. In particular, this perspective cannot see the transcultural praxis indigenous peoples engage in, one in which their historical development consists of the deliberate integration of other people's economies and social systems and worldviews. In this way, transculturation challenges the construction of Indians as premodern, since modernity can be integrated into the historical development of indigenous peoples through it, even yielding a different sense of modernity. The opening of a new non-Eurocentric modernity, one that is not grounded in racism, may be envisioned, then, from indigenous lineages and, for Mariátegui, from an indigenous socialism informed by what I have called the indigenous nation.

In Mariátegui's analysis, such a transcultural praxis goes hand in hand with the national and world-historical potential of indigenous peoples as agents of their own liberation and as the core of a socialist revolution articulated from a non-Eurocentric modernity. Mariátegui's insight is that the colonial state, which the noneconomic theses implicitly endorse, is the first field for transformation by an indigenous revolutionary praxis guided by the ideal of the indigenous nation (challenging the human-subhuman distinction in its economic structure). Ultimately, Mariátegui's economic thesis reconfigures noneconomic theses away from their racist axis so that ethnic/racial criteria would affirm indigenous transculturation, moral criteria would affirm indigenous autonomy and solidarity, and pedagogic criteria would affirm indigenous lives outside servitude. In this sense, indigenous socialism appears as a redemptive project that configures the identity Indian as the basis of an indigenous revolutionary agency toward the restitution of the "indigenous nation."[32]

THE PROLOGUE TO *TEMPEST IN THE ANDES* AND INDIGENOUS SOCIALISM

A footnote to the essay "The Problem of the Indian" makes an explicit reference to another text that has to be read in conjunction with it: Mariátegui's prologue to Luis E. Valcárcel's *Tempestad en los Andes*. A joint reading of these texts reveals the intention behind the *Seven Essays* as a whole. In his first footnote to "The Problem of the Indian," Mariátegui quotes his prologue extensively. Perhaps the most important statement is the following: "The faith in indigenous resurgence does not come from a process of 'westernizing' the material of the Quechua soil. It is not the civilization, not the alphabet of the whites, that raises the soul of the Indian. It is the myth, the idea of the socialist revolution." The footnote posits the revolutionary and historic role of indigenous agency and its relation to socialism. In this way, Mariátegui configures an Indian identity as anchoring a critical perspective. From it, it becomes evident that gamonalismo stunts the development away from colonialism and its feudal structures and that the creole class cannot consolidate itself as a bourgeoisie. This means that capitalism maintains itself nationally and globally through the interrelation of various modalities of labor (that is, communal, feudal, free labor) rather than by overcoming all forms of labor toward free labor; an insight that departs from orthodox Marxist positions. The implication is that there is no internal mechanism for historical development that assures a linear process through which feudalism is followed by capitalism, and capitalism by communism. Mariátegui's socialist analysis of economic legacies of colonialism, from the perspective of an Indian identity, dissolves this illusion. Freed from conceptualities based on linear progression, he studies particular conditions of labor and production, as well as institutional and ideological structures that limit the formation of the bourgeoisie. The figure of the socialist, revolutionary Indian makes this critique concrete by incarnating its locus of enunciation.[33]

Through socialism, Mariátegui argues, Indians come to realize that their own experiential, social, and political horizons, articulated in terms of the immediate struggle for their subsistence, could bring about a radical, liberatory change for all Peruvians. As he writes: "Socialism has taught us to pose the indigenous problem in new terms. We have stopped considering it abstractly as an ethnic or moral problem in order to recognize it concretely as a social, economic and political problem. And then we have felt it, for the first time, to be clarified and demarcated."[34]

Socialism here is a theoretical and practical perspective that weaves together a critique of the bourgeoisie and gamonalismo, the "indigenous nation" as an economic ideal, and the identification of the Indians as national and world revolutionaries. This latter point makes indigenous socialism a faith or myth that projects toward an open future without the support of a developmental and progressive history. In fact, Mariátegui does not offer a practical path toward the instantiation of an economic and political form of indigenous socialism in Peru, which only reaffirms that for him indigenous socialism is primarily a redemptive hope. This elucidates his investment in configuring an Indian identity sustained by a volitional subjective and intersubjective structure, one that gives liberatory meaning and purpose in the absence of concrete historical paths and developmental temporalities. I call this structure the "indigenista logic of redemption."[35]

THREE CONFLICTING ASPECTS OF MARIÁTEGUI'S INDIGENOUS SOCIALISM

Indigenous socialism is geared toward a political deed that seeks to destroy gamonalismo and the colonial state supported by it. Mariátegui writes,

> The term "gamonalismo" does not only designate a social and economic category: the one of the landowners or large agrarian property owners. It designates a whole phenomenon. Gamonalismo is not represented only by the gamonales themselves. It comprehends a long hierarchy of functionaries, intermediaries, agents, parasites, etc. . . . The central factor of this phenomenon is the hegemony of the large semi-feudal property over politics and state mechanisms. Therefore, in order to attack the root of an evil that some are invested in not contemplating except for its episodic or subsidiary expressions, it is on this factor that one must act.

Mariátegui's point is that dismantling gamonalismo as a system of land property would also dislodge racism and colonialism from other institutional and ideological structures that form the total phenomenon that gamonalismo in fact designates. The revolutionary political deed, then, must target the concrete economic regime of gamonalismo in a concerted effort to destroy the political, ideological, and institutional structures that surround it. Without this broader range of revolutionary praxis, the gamonales would be simply replaced by other colonial, semifeudal systems.[36]

At the same time, an abstract bourgeois rhetoric has to be avoided, otherwise the problem of the Indian would be seen upside down, and the efficacy and priority of the political deed would be missed. Mariátegui states that this abstract perspective opposes "the revolutionary dialectic with confused and absurd critiques, according to which the solution to the indigenous problem cannot begin with a reform or political deed because its immediate effects would miss a complex multitude of customs and vices that can only be transformed through a slow and normal evolution." Thus, Mariátegui critiques the bourgeois position for misunderstanding the nature of radical political praxis that cannot be prejudged and replaced by strictly theoretical and rhetorical approaches.[37]

Indigenous socialism has a critical dimension (the critique of the creole elite as a bourgeoisie and of gamonalismo as a colonial economic structure), an ideal dimension (the shift from the colonial state to the indigenous nation), and a volitional/mythical dimension (the redemptive mobilization of an Indian identity). All these culminate in the concretion of a political deed, one whose results cannot be anticipated in theory or by developmental, progressive temporal projections, a deed that is the interruption of an old order and the opening of a new epoch. In this sense, Mariátegui's indigenous socialism does not engage the telos of political praxis but, instead, prepares the conditions for an unprecedented political event. It is in this context that one should read "Revolutionary thought, and even the reformist one, cannot be liberal anymore but socialist. Socialism appears in our history not randomly, or by imitation or fashion, as superficial spirits assume, but as a historic fatality."[38]

Mariátegui's indigenous socialism also implies the transcultural praxis of indigenous peoples. In his work, this capacity for transculturation appears once again through Valcárcel: "The case of Valcárcel shows the same as my personal experience. He is a man of a different intellectual formation, influenced by traditionalist tastes, oriented by a different kind of suggestions and studies; and Valcárcel resolves his indigenismo in socialism. In this book he tells us, among other things, that the 'indigenous proletariat awaits its Lenin.' A Marxist's language would not be different."[39]

Valcárcel is an indigenista promoting an indigenous revival for the formation of a new Indian nation. He posits the cultural and racial superiority of indigenous peoples and calls for indigenous racial purity (condemning the mestizos as an unviable race). He appears to reject racial and cultural mixing. Mariátegui, however, interprets him differently. He generally disagrees with Valcárcel's biologistic and essentialist racial positions yet finds in him (perhaps despite Valcárcel's own intentions) proof of the operation of a kind of indigenous transculturation. Unless he were to posit ahistorical Indians,

Valcárcel must accept processes through which the indigenous masses preserve their integrity and traditions while adapting, negotiating, reconfiguring their own destiny in the context of other cultures, particularly those to which they are exposed through colonial differences. In this sense—and this seems to be Mariátegui's conclusion—even in the most radical indigenismo, the indigenous embracing of socialism emerges as a transcultural process rather than as a simple revival of old traditions. He writes, "Universal history, today more than ever, tends to be guided by the same quadrant. Why would the Inka peoples, having constructed the most developed and harmonic communist system, be the only ones insensitive to the world spirit?" This rhetorical question implies global and local transcultural processes that dislodge the European axis of socialism.[40]

The redemption of the Indian is another aspect of Mariátegui's indigenous socialism: "The elimination of gamonalismo, or of feudalism, could have been realized in the Republic within liberal and capitalist principles. But, for reasons that I have already laid out, these principles have not fully and effectively directed our historical process. Sabotaged by the very class that was supposed to apply them, these principles have been unable for over a century to *redeem* the indian from a servitude that was a fact in full solidarity with feudalism." Mariátegui weaves together the task of the socialist revolution in Peru to overcome the colonial state with the redemption of Indians from the servitude and subhumanity they have been reduced to since colonialism. In this way, the creole bourgeoisie is dispossessed of the role assigned to them by both capitalism and Eurocentered Marxism. A comparison with d'Ors's "colonial logic of redemption" is helpful here. In his case, the logic of redemption was the ideology that gave worth to indigenous lives by charging the creoles with bringing indigenous peoples to civilization and modernity. Mariátegui's indigenous socialism interrupts this logic. He replaces this logic of redemption with another one, with an indigenista logic of redemption, in which the task of the redemption of the Indians falls on indigenous peoples as socialist revolutionary agents.[41]

Redemption seems to be a word that Mariátegui drops here and there although, in fact, it names an implicit rigorous logic that sustains his thought. The logic depends on coherent and robust configurations of an Indian identity in his work. At this juncture, the difference between the adoption of a critical indigenous perspective and the positing of a transhistorical Indian identity can be dangerously blurred, revealing tensions within Mariátegui's indigenous socialism. The indigenous awakening to which Mariátegui avers suffers from a fracture between the political attempt to invoke essentialized identities and socialist local and global revolutionary projects nourished by proliferating critical loci across geopolitical differentials within an international field.

Moreover, the redemption of the Indian is in conflict with both transculturation and the nature of political deeds. The indigenista logic of redemption draws from the questionable construction of a historically continuous and delimited Indian identity (from precolonial to modern times) as a source of moral and political meaning and purpose for indigenous masses invested in the restitution of their humanity through the dismantling structures of coloniality. Such a logic is at odds with the historical transformations that peoples undergo in processes of transculturation, especially in the radical encounters that define colonial and postcolonial formations. Transculturation preserves the integrity of peoples, but *also* affirms—in a way that may threaten the indigenista logic of redemption—cultural, political, social, and economic shifts and *new* historical trajectories that result from the encounters between peoples, especially within the dynamics of the colonial difference. In fact, indigenous critical perspectives within the colonial difference can be critical of both the oppressor's and the indigenous cultures, thus resisting transhistorical constructions of Indian identities. In this double critique, indigenous subjectivities can come to be both attached and detached from their cultural lineages, eluding the scope of the identity Indian (which has narrow colonial origins in first place), undermining this category as an axis for a redemptive project.[42]

The indigenista logic of redemption can also be at odds with the political deeds it seeks. Political deeds, in Mariátegui's sense, imply the heterogeneity and unpredictability of historical events and a sensibility to them that detaches itself from the values of continuous historical narratives and identities. Furthermore, redemption here is necessarily understood futurally as a defined event, while the nature of political deeds challenge investments in the possibility of such projections of single futural horizons. These conflicts define Mariátegui's *Seven Essays* in ways that he can't fully resolve and that remain mostly implicit in this work.

For example, seriously compromising the transcultural strains of his thought, he makes the following statement: "The blacks were dedicated to domestic service and errands. The white easily mixed with the blacks, producing this mestizaje that is one of the types of coastal populations with characteristics that adhere more to the Spanish and resist more the indigenous." This racial fabrication is one of the most problematic aspects of Mariátegui's commitment to the redemption of the Indian. For the sake of keeping intact the figure of the revolutionary Indian, Mariátegui adopts an antiblack racist position in order to preserve the polarity Indian-white. His redemptive project, thus, becomes a racist mechanism. He portrays black slaves as complicit with their oppressors and projects onto them the racist views that whites project on indigenous peoples. He endorses, for example, constructions of black slaves as passive. He dismisses the agency of oppressed peoples that do not fit within his configuration of an Indian identity and ends up embedding his indigenista redemptive logic in the colonial, racist frame that it was supposed to over-come. In this way, his redemptive logic ceases to contest the distinction human-subhuman, a colonial distinction that grounds the exploitation of indigenous peoples in the first place.[43]

AVATARS OF COLONIALITY

Mariátegui quotes Castro Pozo's list of the various types of surviving indig-enous communities that are organized around specific forms of collective labor. He directs the reader to the correct interpretation of Castro Pozo's variety of forms. Rather than dissolving the original, Inka form of indigenous community, they "show . . . the vitality of the indigenous communism that invariably propels indigenous peoples toward varied forms of collaboration and association." These forms of indigenous community represent, accord-ing to Mariátegui, the only defense against a system that renders indigenous lives dispensable. In my terms, indigenous peoples appear to operate under the paradigm of the indigenous nation as a matter of survival. Mariátegui interprets this from his socialist perspective: "in indigenous towns, where families are gathered among whom the ties of communal property and work have been extinguished, there subsists, robust and tenacious, habits of coop-eration and solidarity that are the empirical expression of a communist spirit. The 'community' corresponds to that spirit. It is its organ." Under the colonial state, indigenous peoples live a split life between the way the racist colonial logic of redemption constructs their Indian identity and their lack of vitality, and their economic and cultural survival, expressed in the variegated per-sistence of their communities. For Mariátegui, this split reveals practices of resistance and is the condition for the emergence of an indigenous socialism. This resistance is evident as a transcultural process: "When expropriation and re-distribution appear to liquidate the community, indigenous social-ism always finds a way to remake it, maintain it or subrogate it." This process involves the preservation of the indigenous nation as a legacy and as an ideal of resistance, and with it, the continuity of an Indian identity.[44]

Transculturation, however, involves not only the preservation of the past but an engagement with cultural, social, and political forms in the present, especially in the context of the colonial difference, where the dominant "other" is adapted to, negotiated, assimilated, reinterpreted, and even adopted as a perspective, all of this being a form of survival and resistance. And transformative transcultural processes determined by alterity rather than by a reclaiming of the past are also operative in the development of new social, political, and economic forms, including ones that are constituted by indigenous peoples but not through commitments to a continuous lineage or identity.

An extensive footnote gives an indication of this other, more complex and fractured, aspect of transculturation. It begins by positing the differences between Inka communism and modern communism: "One and the other communism are expressions of different human experiences. They belong to different historical epochs. They constitute the elaboration of different civilizations. The Inka civilization was agrarian. Marx's and Sorel's is an industrial one. In the former man submitted himself to nature. In the latter nature submits itself sometimes to man." The formation of indigenous socialism implies, then, a process of transculturation of indigenous communal forms that would even appropriate Eurocentered liberal ideals that are constitutive of the structures that marginalize them. The complexity of this process, especially within the power dynamics within of the colonial difference, is left out of Mariátegui's analysis. Yet it reveals a radical process of transculturation adapting to pressing and coercive contemporary constraints, one that does not resonate with the indigenista logic of redemption. In my discussion, this logic seems consistent with only one aspect of transculturation, one in which the values of cultural continuity and of transhistorical Indian identities are at the forefront. Yet transculturation also implies the dissemination of such identities.[45]

This tension disrupts the *Seven Essays*, where sometimes Mariátegui embellishes the Inka past, as if feeling an urgency to force and protect an Indian identity by presenting the integrity of a heritage that is worth restoring and redeeming. For example, Mariátegui feels the need to defend the Inka society against the charge of the suppression of individual freedom: "The man of the Tawantinsuyo did not feel absolutely any necessity for individual freedom," and "The life and the spirit of the Indian were not tormented by the desire for intellectual creation and speculation." These statements are issued to deny that the Inka empire was a tyranny. He reflects that "A tyranny . . . is real to the extent that it oppresses the will of a people, or that it goes against or suffocates its vital impulse. Many times, in antiquity, an absolutist and theocratic regime has embodied and represented, to the contrary, this will and this impulse." With these statements Mariátegui walks on a dangerous path. In order to glorify the Inka past for the sake of preserving an indigenista logic of redemption, he mobilizes constructions of Indian passivity that are part of the racist colonial logic of redemption, revealing that these two logics may not be rigorously differentiated in his analysis.[46]

Furthermore, the tension between Mariátegui's transcultural strain and the redemptive one takes a revealing form in the fifth essay, "The Religious Factor." Mariátegui reflects on the relationship between the Inka state and religion and notes that "The fundamental characteristics of the Inka religion are its collectivist theocracy and its materialism," traits that make the Inka religion more of a "moral code than a metaphysical conception." He emphasizes that the Inka religion does not focus on anything other than earthly life, and so it depended entirely on the state, having "temporal rather than spiritual ends." This absence of metaphysics is connected to a lack of individualism that he embellishes but that eventually causes a crisis in his thought.[47]

The crisis begins to appear if we pay close attention to Mariátegui's statements about the Conquest, which he admires: "After the tragedy in Cajamarca, the missionary continued to dictate zealously its law to the Conquest. The spiritual power inspired and drove the temporal power." In this respect, he makes a distinction between the conquistadors and the colonizers: "The conquistador was from spiritual stock, the colonizer wasn't." Thus, Mariátegui laments the loss of the conquistador's spirituality. He also suggests a similarity between this spirit and the puritan spirit that led the conquest of Anglo America. On this issue, Mariátegui relies on the writings of Waldo Frank in order to establish the spiritual essence of Puritanism: "he discovered a power over himself, over other people, over the tangible world." He adds: "In the mystical impulse of Puritanism, Waldo Frank recognizes correctly, above all, the will to power." Metaphysics appears here as a source of power over the world, a creative, disciplined power that Mariátegui deems necessary for revolutionary praxis. He finds a similar discipline, for example, in the bourgeois revolution: "the Reformation forged the moral weapons of the bourgeois revolution, paving the way to capitalism." He also asserts the essential role this discipline and morality play in the organization of the proletariat toward the socialist revolution. Thus, in terms of discipline, morality, and religiosity, Mariátegui underscores a will to power that links the conquest of the Americas, the bourgeois revolution, and the socialist revolution.[48]

Two important populations are missing from this lineage. First, we have the Spanish colonizers who followed the conquistadors. The establishment of the Catholic Church by them shows, according to Mariátegui, an undisciplined people deprived of will to power: "Catholicity is characterized, historically by the mimetism through which, in the formal aspects, it has molded itself to the environment.... But this faculty to adapt is, at the same time, the strength and weakness of the Roman Church. The religious spirit is not tightened except by combat and struggle." Here Unamuno's *Agony of Christianity* is also a reference, especially his assertion that Christianity was not a doctrine but "life, fight, struggle."[49]

The other missing population, because of its lack of metaphysics, is the Inka one. Mariátegui suggests parallels between colonial Catholicism and the Inka state religion. In fact, he sees in their confluence the coming together of two forms of morality without will to power that adapted to each other. This leads Mariátegui to one of his most remarkable—and troublesome—statements on this issue: "The passivity with which the Indians allowed themselves to be catechized, without comprehending the catechism, spiritually weakened Catholicism in Peru."[50] Without metaphysics, indigenous peoples offered no resistance, and that sapped Catholicism's spirit.

This is one of the most vexed aspects of Mariátegui's indigenista logic of redemption: Indians lack the will to power to carry out the revolution. The myth of socialism, then, needs to be embraced by them as a discipline, which calls for a kind of second conversion to Christianity. It is as if the Indians need to first be redeemed by socialism, and only then can they redeem themselves. This prior conversion is problematic in at least three ways. First, it presents socialism as a foreign, rather than indigenous, project, which contradicts the intention of Mariátegui's own reclaiming of an Indian past. Second, it calls for a different agent to carry out this originary redemption of the Indian (socialist intellectuals, perhaps?). And third, it falls back into the racist perspective of the colonial logic of redemption, positing the passivity of the Indian. At this juncture, the indigenista logic of redemption collapses, and the figure of the revolutionary Indian that brings about the redemption of indigenous peoples shows itself to be an embodiment of the colonial logic of redemption.[51]

NOTES

1. For parallel and influential interpretations of Mariátegui's socialism as myth, see Aricó, *Mariátegui*; Becker, *Mariátegui*; Löwy "Marxismo Romántico"; Melis, *Leyendo Mariátegui*; and Salazar Bondy, *Historia de las ideas*, 285–312. See the related discussion of the relationship between nation and tradition in F. Rivera, "Mariátegui." See also Mariátegui, "Man and Myth," 144.

2. Mariátegui, "Nacionalismo e internacionalismo," 65. Ibid. See also Moraña's discussion, "Mariátegui," 66–67. Henceforth *JCME*.

3. Mariátegui's concern with the spatiality of internationalism anticipates and departs from Castro-Gomez, "No Longer Broad," 35: "the binding force of the of the discourses that set out to posit an organic identity between nation, people, and culture also dries up. In Latin America, these discourses were part of the political arsenal of both the political right and the political left.... Beginning in the 1980s, however, it starts becoming clear that that this crusade for the recovery of values of the people is illusory, since neither the state nor any other instances are capable of controlling that global expansion of information and symbols." The point of disagreement here is that an excess of spatiality in Mariátegui, "Nacionalismo e internacionalismo," 66, an excess that Castro-Gómez tries to capture temporally. Schutte traces this spatialization in Quijano in Schutte, "De la colonialidad." Ibid.

4. Mariátegui, "Nacionalismo e Internacionalismo," 65.

5. Fornet-Betancourt states about this reduction that "humanity does not globalize itself, but rather it is becoming globalized by the totalitarian process of a civilizing model. Thus, globalization is not growth in universalization or universality. On the contrary, it represents a reductive process that, in the name of the deceitful promise of building one world, instead levels differences and homogenizes the planet, at least on the surface" (Fornet-Betancourt, "Alternative to Globalization," 230). Mariátegui, "Nacionalismo e internacionalismo," 66; See also Mariátegui, "Nacionalismo e internacionalismo," 67–68.

6. There is some important secondary literature on space in Mariátegui that informs my discussion here. See Méndez, "De indio a serrano"; Quiroz Rojas, "Otra modernidad"; and Ruiz, "Mariátegui." See Mariátegui, "Destino," 416, 417. Hernando de Soto in *Misterio del capital*, 141–44, has a similar account of the role of space and private property in the development of US imperialism.

7. Mariátegui, "Imperio," 83. This observation opens the issue of the relationship between coloniality, modernity, and space. I won't thematize it, but I have found helpful Coronil, "Beyond Occidentalism."

8. Fanon can be an important interlocutor here, especially in his analysis of the colonized intellectual's relationship to nationalism and the past. In many ways, his analysis can be understood in relation to dynamics of redemption in nationalist projects. See Fanon, *Wretched of the Earth*, 145–69. Mariátegui, *Siete ensayos*, 17.

9. Ibid.

10. Ruiz Zevallos in "Mariátegui," 105, elaborates on Mariátegui's approach to history in its relation to myth: "Mariátegui is more explicit in his reflection on the ways to relate us to the past when he levels lyricism with science, and indicates that science, if it puts itself above myth and legend, 'does not help us' to understand history. ... I consider evident the lyricism of all of the greatest historical reconstructions." Mariátegui, "Heterodoxia," gives us an account of

his approach to history and its entanglement in myth: "The faculty of thinking history and the faculty of making it and creating it, become identified with one another. The revolutionary has perhaps a subjective image of the past, but a lively and alive one, while the *pasadista* is unable to represent the past in its disquiet and fluidity." See also Mariátegui, "Destino," 408. Italics mine. *Pasadista* here means "traditionalist."

11. *AC*, 38. See also 38–39.

12. Mariátegui, *Siete ensayos*, 17, 18. Ibid. See the account of Mariátegui's heterodox understanding of nationalism in Moraña's "Mariátegui," *JCME*, 66–68. *JCME*, 66. This interpretation of Mariátegui resonates well with Quijano's account of the nation-state, which corresponds to what we have called the colonial state, and he finds it to be at the center of the coloniality of power. Our account of the indigenous nation corresponds to Quijano's call: "In a very precise sense, the 'nation' in Latin America would imply . . . a radical redefinition of the category, removing it from its Eurocentric matrix, even if that does not appear as viable" (Quijano, "Raza").

13. Mariátegui, *Siete ensayos*, 18.

14. Moraña, "Mariátegui," 66, captures the redemptive logic operative here: "Socialism is perceived here as a *restitution*, that is, as the instance that gives back to the indigenous person her productive and spiritual relationship with the land, a connection that was dismantled by Spanish colonialism, and that when reconstituted it would confer upon social peasant forms the communitarian sense lost with the adoption of capitalist modes of production."

15. The resonances between this "Indian" and Martí's "natural man" are evident.

16. Quijano, "Colonialidad del poder." See Mariátegui, *Siete ensayos*, 21, 22. Fornet-Betancourt asks, "And is not what is being spread with the resounding name of 'planetary civilization' *only one* version of *one* cultural variant of humanity?" ("Alternative to Globalization," 234).

17. See Mariátegui, "Unity of Indo-Spanish América," 445–49. Mariátegui, *Siete ensayos*, 22. This is the ambivalence in Martí between a transamerican and a Bolivarian approach to America analyzed in chapter 2 in this volume. I am suggesting here that there is an implicit difference in Mariátegui between the unity of América or Hispanic América and the unity of Indo-Hispanic América. Mariátgui recognizes the revolutionary potential of both (as in Bolívar) but does not see the material basis for the former. In this sense, he shifts from Hispanic América to Indo-Hispanic América, the latter being grounded in new material conditions. In my view, the text "Unity of Indo-Hispanic América" would suggest this shift and tension. Ibid.

18. Chavarria, *José Carlos Mariátegui*, states about the approach to the bourgeoisie in the *Seven Essays*: "What Mariátegui meant here was that

essentially feudal attitudes had continued to coexist alongside the selective assimilation of capitalist ones. From then on, to the Europeans the Peruvian bourgeoisie tried to appear as another bourgeoisie, but within their own milieu they preserved the pursuit of aristocratic privileges and avoided any changes running to the contrary to the colonialist status quo" (112).

19. Mariátegui, *Siete ensayos*, 31. This heterogeneity drives Moraña to see in Mariátegui's work a heterogeneous revolutionary subject. She states that Mariátegui "suggests that at least in postcolonial societies, there is not one single revolutionary subject" (Moraña, *Mariátegui*, 54). I think it is important that Mariátegui is making a suggestion, not an explicit point.

20. Llorente, in "Amauta's Ambivalence," 228–48, offers a sound economic interpretation of "The Problem of the Indian" as one of property relations and sets up an interesting argument about the limits of the concept of race in Mariátegui. Our interpretation here disagrees with his basic interpretation of the problem. Augusto Castro states, "Mariátegui concludes that the exceptional merit in Marx consists in having, in this sense, invented the proletariat. The Revolution demands a subject and, in this case, it is the proletariat. . . . Mariátegui himself, in order to construct the Peruvian social myth, would invent—in Marx's style—the Indian that he would call socialist, in charge of the transformation and the social revolution in Peru" (*Filosofía y política*, 111).

21. Mariátegui, *Siete ensayos*, 179. Italics mine. The immoral option would be to do nothing about the Indians (Mariátegui, *Siete ensayos*, 180).

22. The "colonial difference" is discussed in Mignolo, *Local Histories/Global Designs*, 49–90.

23. Mariátegui, *Siete ensayos*, 181. Italics mine.

24. Mariátegui, *Siete ensayos*, 38.

25. Mariátegui, *Siete ensayos*, 39, 40.

26. Ibid. For Mariátegui's interest in Asia from a decolonial angle, see Kim, "José Mariátegui's East-South Decolonial Experiment." I draw this term from Rama's understanding of it. See Rama, *Writing across Cultures*, 21–23. For a succinct comparative account of the concept of race in the Americas, see Mendieta, "Making of New Peoples."

27. Gonzalez Prada is an anarchist who influenced Mariátegui, including his treatment of the problem of the Indian (Gonzalez Prada, *Pájinas libres*). Mariátegui, *Siete ensayos*, 40, 41.

28. Ibid.

29. Mariátegui, *Siete ensayos*, 41, 42.

30. For a thorough study of Mariátegui's Marxism, see Sobrevilla, *Marxismo de Mariátegui*.

31. Mariátegui, *Siete ensayos*, 39. Italics mine.

32. For a related discussion, see the chapter "Critique of the Myth of Modernity" in Dussel, *Invention of the Americas*.

33. See Valcárcel, *Tempestad en los Andes*; Mariátegui, *Siete ensayos*, 42; and Tucker, *Marx-Engels Reader*, 475–83. See also Quijano's critique of this sequence in "Colonialidad del poder."

34. Mariátegui, *Siete ensayos*, 43.

35. Mariátegui, *Siete ensayos*, 43.

36. Mariátegui, *Siete ensayos*, 43.

37. This is expressed in the noneconomic essays. See Mariátegui, *Siete ensayos*, 43.

38. Mariátegui, *Siete ensayos*, 43. There is a Sorelian influence here. For Mariátegui's ambivalent relationship to Sorel, see Paris, "Mariátegui," 155–61; García Salvatecci, *Georg Sorel y Mariátegui*; and Mazotti, "Fuerza del mito," 139–52. The last article in particular is helpful to our study, since Mazotti links myth in Mariátegui to cultural investments in a departure from Sorel. See also Mariátegui, *Siete ensayos*, 44.

39. Mariátegui, *Siete ensayos*, 42.

40. For Mariátegui's problematic relationship with mestizos, see de la Cadena, *Indigenous Mestizos*, 24–27.

41. Mariátegui, *Siete ensayos*, 43. Italics mine.

42. Arguedas's *Deep Rivers* should be read as written from this kind of mestizaje, one that is influenced by Mariátegui.

43. For a discussion of the concept of race and racism in Mariátegui, see Manrique, *Piel*, 59–84, and Forgues, "Mariátegui." See also Mariátegui, *Siete ensayos*, 47.

44. Mariátegui, *Siete ensayos*, 81.

45. Mariátegui, *Siete ensayos*, 82.

46. Mariátegui, *Siete ensayos*, 82, 83.

47. Mariátegui, *Siete ensayos*, 150, 151. Ibid.

48. Ibid. Mariátegui, *Siete ensayos*, 156, 160, 163, 63. See the discussion of discipline in Mariátegui as a morality of producers in Schutte, *Cultural Identity*, 47–57.

49. Mariátegui, *Siete ensayos*, 158. Mariátegui understood revolutionary sensibilities as a form of agony at play in Unamuno, *Agony of Christianity*.

50. Mariátegui, *Siete ensayos*, 159.

51. Along these lines, Sanjinés has written an exceptional article in which he mobilizes some of the themes I have traced in Mariátegui—in particular, spatiality (which connects with my reading of "internationalism," and even "transculturation") and the indeterminacy of revolutionary events (which connects with my reading of "political deeds"). He retains a sense of redemption, however. It differs, though, from the way I have defined it. An interpretation of

this work in relation to my discussion would be productive to open up new ways of encountering Mariátegui especially in the context of decoloniality and border thinking. He states at the beginning of the essay: "These reflections about the work of José Carlos Mariátegui do not seek to explain his thought framing it in the historical context of his epoch, but to exude it and actualize it, with the intent that it continue the work of those, utopian like ourselves, who still fight for the re-encounter between socialism and nation." See San Jinés, "Between Doubt and Hope," in Moraña and Podestá, *José Carlos Mariátegui.*

FOUR

—〰—

LIMINALITIES

Schutte's Transcultural Reading of Mariátegui

THE PREVIOUS CHAPTER shows tensions in Mariátegui's socialism, especially as it is articulated in his *Seven Essays*. One of these tensions occurs between an indigenista logic of redemption (which essentializes the identity Indian) and the transcultural strains of his liberatory project. It attests to the role of culture in decolonial movements of liberation and the difficult relationship between liberatory philosophy and transcultural processes within dynamics of coloniality. This chapter focuses on these issues in order to put forward a transcultural delimitation of philosophy that would complement the contextual one put forward by Martín Alcoff and discussed in chapter 1. For the most part, I will remain within Ofelia Schutte's interpretation of Mariátegui.

OFELIA SCHUTTE'S READING OF MARIÁTEGUI

Schutte's *Cultural Identity and Social Liberation in Latin American Thought* includes an important analysis of Mariátegui in relation to Latin American philosophy. In her text, an interpretation of Mariátegui's general approach and of his main works sets the stage for an engagement with well-studied figures of this philosophical lineage: Ramos, Zea, Roig, and Dussel, among others. Through Schutte's reading of Mariátegui, I will revisit the place of cultural identity in Latin American philosophy. Schutte's describes her text thus: "It is about the construction of a philosophical perspective on the subject of cultural identity based on concerns expressed by a diversity of political and intellectual movements interested in social liberation within the Latin American continent."[1] I take the "philosophical perspective" on "cultural identity" under construction in Schutte's text to be a transcultural delimitation of Latin American liberatory thought. I am interested in uncovering the complexity of its "construction."

In particular, the philosophical perspective that Schutte unpacks can guide an articulation of the relationship between cultural identity and social liberation in Mariátegui's work. In this sense, Schutte uncovers what I call a Nietzschean matrix, provocatively showing that not only Mariátegui's indigenous socialism but also an important strain of Latin American philosophy are informed by Nietzsche.[2]

FROM NATIONAL TO SOCIAL LIBERATION

The focus of my analysis is on the notion of social liberation, understood broadly to include cultural, political, and economic aspects. Social liberation refers to the need to liberate individuals from structures of social oppression, particularly those that create or reproduce inequities due to economic class, sex, race, or national origin.

Schutte, *Cultural Identity and Social Liberation in Latin American Thought*

Starting an analysis of Mariátegui in this way provides a particular interpretive angle: his works will not be approached as leading toward national liberation. National liberation has as its purpose, according to Schutte, namely "displacing from political power certain national governments characterized by the liberation groups as governments . . . controlled by U.S. economic and/or military interests." In other words, the liberation movement expressed in Mariátegui's works is not understood here as having the liberation of a nation as its principal aim in its anticolonial and anti-imperialist commitments. Rather, the liberation at issue is the liberation of peoples oppressed on the basis of their social identities, and its target are the structural and everyday social marginalizations that undermine their survival. Decentering liberation from being merely a national issue, Schutte states, in a way that arguably reflects accurately Mariátegui's stance, "I take social and personal liberation as the fundamental goals of liberation, rejecting the argument that only a victory at the level of a national liberation movement can guarantee the former."[3]

Schutte acknowledges possible complementary interests between social liberation and national liberation, but the reorienting of the aim of liberation toward social, and specifically cultural, identities in her work is definitive. This reorienting sheds light on a difficult aspect of Mariátegui's thought, which often appears to be aligned with nationalism as a revolutionary movement.

Also, in this reorienting, Schutte conceives of the possibilities and character of liberation from social and political conditions for the articulation of identities and interprets Mariátegui indigenous socialism from this perspective.[4]

Focusing on the Latin American identity as a defining factor in the formation of anti-imperialist and decolonial liberatory movements, opposing social as well as economic and political structures of oppression, Schutte turns to cultural identities. She finds in them the basis for struggles of self-determination that can be part of processes of liberation. In particular, she values the way in which cultural identities can provide a sense of continuity and, thus, purpose, by connecting peoples to a shared past and future. There is an implicit ethical and agential dimension here. Cultural identity "creates rational links between the stated origin of the group's values and the goals and actions of its members." Such links can motivate liberatory actions in people whose values and traditions are systematically marginalized or excluded. As she states, "to speak of a Latin American cultural identity could also refer to a process aimed at rectifying the imbalance of power between the United States and Latin American countries, which to a significant extent puts at risk the cultural production of the latter."

Schutte identifies Martí, in his "Latin America for Latin Americans," and Mariátegui, in his "affirmation of the values of the continent's indigenous pre-Columbian heritage," as examples of thinkers for whom the defense of a Latin American cultural identity is connected to liberatory struggles. Schutte thus opens a singular and productive interpretive approach to them. Her approach is part of a general delimitation of Latin American philosophy that is at the core of Schutte's book, one in which "The philosophical values attached to notions of cultural identity are very often linked to political movements for self-determination and to indigenismo or other expressions of native cultural ties in the arts and literature."[5]

Schutte presents Latin American liberatory thought as a philosophical perspective on the relationship between cultural identities, expressions, and values and political movements of social liberation. This insight and its complex exposition is perhaps the greatest contribution in her work. But also, here is the place where possible critiques begin to unfold, especially in connection to her reading of Mariátegui.[6]

CULTURAL IDENTITY AND POLITICS OF LIBERATION

In terms of the relationship between the cultural and the political, the latter understood here as the possibility of social liberation, it seems that Schutte finds a somewhat continuous transition from one to the other. That is, the affirmation of cultural identity leads to self-determination, which leads to political liberatory movements. It is important to underscore the continuity, but one might wonder about whether it reduces the liberatory/political to the cultural. Some indications in the text point to such a reduction. For example, according to Schutte, the imbalanced relationship between the United States and Latin American states is one in which "There is no corresponding penetration of U.S. culture by Latin American-oriented values and products."[7] Even more explicitly, "For liberation theory dealing with the North-South tension there arises the problem of how to assess the weight of European or North American *culture* vis-à-vis *cultures* of particular Latin American nations."[8] Schutte is not necessarily denying the difference between the cultural and the political here. In fact, she calls attention to their relationship because her argument is meant to challenge positions that value the articulation of liberatory projects at the expense of cultural identities and demands. Yet, after having benefitted from Schutte's work, it may be of interest to begin to revisit the difference as it bears on Martí's and Mariátegui's thought, since she engages these two figures as part of her argument.[9]

One could ask the following questions: What is the relationship, in Martí's "Our America," for example, between the cultural identity implied in a "Latin America for Latin Americans" and the assumption of an oppositional stance to US imperialism? Is the latter an outgrowth of the former, or is it the reverse? Or is this a political situation that includes factors that cannot be simply absorbed into the defense of a "Latin American" cultural identity? Or does it need a larger frame of reference that attests to imposed transnational political and economic realities?[10]

Furthermore, is Mariátegui's problem of the Indian, the exploitation under the land property system of gamonales, one that can be countered solely through processes of indigenous cultural affirmation? Or is there need to supplement such processes with liberatory practices and political programs that attest to imposed local and global structures of power whose comprehension does not emerge organically from indigenous cultural referents? This is the problem of the relationship between socialism and indigenous culture in Mariátegui, whether the former can be an extension of the latter, or whether socialism arises within a global economic and political structure with inherent characteristics that cannot be simply inscribed within a critical Andean cultural frame. In other words, is Mariátegui's socialist program of "Indo-Spanish America" a movement that arises from Andean indigenous practices of cultural self-determination?

These questions are about the relationship between the coconstitutive economic and political configuration of imperialism and coloniality as a global exploitative structure and the imaginaries of cultural groups submitted to it; about the expectation that those groups, many of which are non-Western, will engage in a reflection on their origins, historical continuity, and values in a way that would articulate or endorse a political program that tackles global capitalism; and, in Mariátegui's case, about the complex configuration of a revolutionary Indian who, on the basis of continuous ancestral knowledges and wisdom, supposedly holds the key to solve global economic, political, and environmental crises. The issue is not whether Schutte believes in a redemptive Indian, or whether she identifies the cultural with the political. Rather, I focus on whether she sufficiently explores this redemptive figure and the distinction between the cultural and political in Mariátegui's texts, especially when she writes: "What Mariátegui has done is to offer a vision of society in which the Indian population is seen as an essentially creative and dynamic participant in the productive process, on a par with everyone else. *In addition, he has tied the cultural identity of the nation to the identity of the redeemed or regenerated Indian, thus reversing and surpassing to the fullest extent the social and economic effects of the Spanish conquest.*"[11]

CULTURAL IDENTITY AND THE COLONIAL DIFFERENCE

I don't deny that cultural identity is fundamental to liberatory projects, and I endorse Schutte's shift from national to social liberation. But, taking this shift as a basis, it may be useful to see whether an explicit differentiation between the cultural and the political is productive in the context of liberation. One may recall Fanon's position in *Black Skin, White Masks*, in the chapter "The Lived Experience of the Black Man" in particular. Fanon's text shows the excruciating failure of the black man's efforts to find cultural referents that would allow him to resist and revert the social and political structures that oppress him. It reveals the ways in which global imperialism and coloniality undermine such an attempt by fabricating, emptying out, resignifying, and reevaluating the meaning of the cultural identity of the oppressed, establishing an alienating distance between the oppressed and her cultural identity, one that is racialized and embodied. In these processes, the oppressed can come to reject her cultural identity, encountering it as an obstacle to her development and well-being and as elusive to any attempt to positively and affirmatively appropriate it in order to open up liberatory political options. In this plight, Fanon has to find the articulation of a political program that would undermine structural racial oppression in sources that include and exceed cultural self-reflection, sources that seem to arise within the colonial difference, that is, in between, and thus irreducible to, cultural identities and the structures of coloniality and imperialism. Perhaps one could read Mariátegui retroactively from Fanon and find in his works a similar plight.[12]

Bringing into play the colonial difference here is helpful, especially in the following elucidation of it by Mignolo, who states that it is "the space where local histories inventing and implementing global designs meet local histories, the space in which global designs have to be adapted, adopted, rejected, integrated or ignored." The dynamics within this space between subaltern local histories and global designs may demand practices and epistemologies that exceed the kind of cultural reflections about origins, values, and historical continuities that Schutte envisions. In Mignolo's terms, we need to be attentive to the emergence of "border thinking." As Mignolo also states, in this space there is no cohesive cultural perspective defining the oppressed: "The colonial difference creates the conditions for dialogic situations in which a fractured enunciation is enacted from the subaltern perspective as a response to the hegemonic discourse and perspective."[13] In this "fractured enunciation," inscribing the liberatory-political into decolonial resistances may be needed and in a way that is not reducible to the expression of defined cultural identities. Quijano seems to suggest this much in his assertion that modernity (understood non-Eurocentrically and decolonially) was the advent of something new, unprecedented: "a universe of social relations, both in its material and intersubjective dimensions, whose central question and, consequently, whose central field of conflict is human social liberation as a historical interest of society."[14]

The resonances with Schutte are evident, but I am tracing a slight variation in meaning here that becomes apparent when one views Quijano's words in light of the colonial difference, recognizing the fractures of cultural identities and preserving a project of social liberation that does not seek to resolve them in order to anchor itself in them. Something analogous to this is operative in Boaventura de Sousa Santos's works. He finds within the colonial difference a new liberatory political opening: "My analysis highlights some of the emancipatory potential of a new insurgent cosmopolitan politics, culture, and law based not on the ideas of European universalism but rather on the social and political culture of social groups whose everyday lives are energized by the need to transform survival strategies into sources of innovation, creativity, transgression, and subversion." I suggest that these survival strategies exceed the ways in which one's culture is devalued and turned against oneself, affirming both attachments to and detachments from one's own culture, even investments in options where the value of cultural continuities is suspended, allowing for critical perspectives to arise from fractured liminal positionalities. De Sousa

Santos thinks of these processes as "anthropophagy" and "transculturation." He finds the resultant excesses and liminalities to be the conditions for utopianism as a liberatory political phenomenon: "By utopia I mean the imagination's exploration of new modes of human possibility and styles of will and the confrontation by imagination of the necessity of whatever exists—just because it exists—on behalf of something radically better that is worth fighting for and to which humanity is entitled." De Sousa Santos not only bases his analysis of a counter-hegemonic globalization along these lines on Martí's work "Our America" but also names Mariátegui as one of the inheritors and key figures of this subaltern political lineage.[15]

To return to Schutte's text, she does emphasize the fluidity of cultural forms. She even qualifies further her earlier statements on the continuity of cultural legacies and their relationship to liberation movements:

> In short, the standpoint of identity adopted here refers ultimately to a differential reality, not to a centrally regulated force. The "identity" of which I speak here is not derived from a fixed origin, but is a result of multiple configurations always in the process of reorganizing and redefining themselves. In terms of liberation theory, such identities-in-the-making result from a process of endangered or forgotten differences and bringing them to public attention. This involves breaking through the silence imposed on some forms of thought and only subsequently trying to "position" such differences within the general purview of the culture for the enrichment and benefit of all.[16]

Schutte's nonessentialist position on identity recognizes the transformative power of cultural practices and reflections, and, following Roig, she finds in this power the enactment of a cultural legacy that includes a creative social praxis that unsettles oppressive social and political forms. This praxis is tied to a project of memory and cultural recovery. Thus, she warns against US imperialism because it undermines the "cultural vitality of a people" and its "cultural development."[17]

Schutte retains values of cultural integrity and coherence and finds liberatory potencies in the defense of cultures that are in danger of extinction: "Just as environmentalists speak of endangered species, so we could speak of endangered cultures." She does not appear to focus, however, on the liberatory force of processes of detachment from one's own culture, processes that do not negate the relationship between cultural identity and social liberation but that are also part of the conditions within which political liberatory projects emerge. They are conditions that fracture identities, where being between cultures exceeds their framings, enabling transcultural critiques from multifocal positions where the valence of one culture does not necessarily overdetermine others. In my view, my critical departures from Schutte are subtle.[18]

In fact, Schutte's commitment to cultural identity is ambivalent. She emphasizes continuities and legacies, as well as multiplicity, alterity, fluidity, and transformation. The ambivalence may be ultimately productive as informing a philosophical approach to cultural formations within oppressive contexts and in view of liberation. It can be mobilized to shed light on coloniality and globalization, on the complexities of the colonial difference and of the fracture of loci of enunciation that Mignolo points to, on Fanon's understanding of the limits of cultural legacies for enabling the dismantling of colonial systems, on Quijano's opening of a new global, economic, and political horizons for projects of social liberation irreducible to the cultural horizons of marginalized cultures, and on de Sousa Santos's transcultural conditions for the emergence of utopias. It is important to note that all these figures agree with Schutte: cultural identities in their fluidity and transformations are relevant factors in the articulation of anti-imperialist and decolonial movements. The point here is, then, not to dismiss the liberatory potential of cultural identity formations but to understand them as irreducibly intersecting with epistemologies, practices, and commitments, even survival strategies, that may exceed them or even fracture them, intersections that arise from unprecedented situations and transcultural contexts, especially under the pressure of a modern colonial global and economic order. Liberatory political options come to pass in these intersections without single horizons and structures of meaning.

A TRANSCULTURAL DELIMITATION OF LATIN AMERICAN PHILOSOPHY

I have noted that the shift in focus from national liberation to social liberation leads Schutte to turn to cultural identities, and that this shift determines her approach to Martí (whom she mentions briefly) and Mariátegui (whom she studies extensively). I have built critically on this approach, mainly by applying to Schutte's discussion insights from the decolonial constellation Martí-Mariátegui-Quijano-Mignolo-de Sousa Santos. In doing so, I have suggested fracturing the referents for social liberation, including cultural identity, in the context of the colonial difference. In this way, I have tentatively and broadly inscribed within this context the political that is in excess of the cultural, specifically as regards liberation. Thus far I have, then, studied and problematized the relationship between two elements of Latin American liberatory thought: cultural identity and social liberation. Now I turn to Schutte's philosophical perspective on this relationship.[19]

This issue is part of the larger problematic of a delimitation of Latin American philosophy. As Schutte states, "Advocates of a universal view of reason in history generally hold that the most rational civilization prevails in the end. When their attention turns toward Latin America, they tend to be drawn to the 'universal' values found in Latin American philosophy rather than to the philosophical importance of cultural-specific values found in Latin American thought. Their respect for a particular cultural formation is only a consequence of the respect for the universality of human reason, with the latter usually understood in exclusively Western terms."

Bringing Schutte into a dialogue with Quijano, Mignolo, Vallega, Martín Alcoff, and others, "a universal view of reason," which is a trait of modern Western philosophy, sets the standard both for the legitimacy of non-Western philosophies and for the humanity of non-Western peoples. This double effect happens through a complex process in which a particular instantiation of philosophy is codetermined by practices of colonization. In the modern West, universality is not recognized as an ethnocentric Western value enforced by the dominant positionalities of white Europeans that suppress others, and is, rather, understood as an inherently philosophical trait. Thus, as a result of coloniality, philosophy comes to be anchored in universality (which actually is the forceful exclusion of non-European cultures) and seems to be beyond cultural determinations. This peculiar philosophical delimitation makes Western philosophy not only ethnocentric but also Eurocentric. In this way, Western philosophy appears as the standard of all philosophical thinking. Eurocentrism is not a derivative characteristic of modern Western philosophy; it, rather, comes to define how Western philosophy articulates the systems of knowledge and truth that characterize it.[20]

This delimitation of modern Western philosophy intersects with race as an instrument of coloniality. Philosophy becomes a factor in the determination of the difference between human and nonhuman through which colonized peoples are exploited and eradicated. This is because human rationality as such is seen as the adoption a universal standpoint, and as thinking through universals. Eurocentrism then, is also the process through which a self-defined universal view of reason, worked out in modern Western philosophy, becomes naturalized as human. The entanglement between modern Western philosophy and the structure of human rationality furthers coloniality and supports a progressive, linear view of history in which the "most rational civilization prevails in the end."[21]

This framing of Schutte's statement sheds light on the delimitation and possibility of Latin American philosophy as emerging within the colonial difference, where the difference between the human and the nonhuman is at stake. Not only is the Eurocentric philosophical stance interested in Latin American philosophy to the extent that it yields universal values, as Schutte states. But also it recognizes as legitimate only those forms of Latin American philosophy that happen within the element of the universal. Furthermore, the legitimacy of Latin American philosophy implies a decision about the humanity of Latin Americans. These latter points are suggested in Schutte's statement "Their respect for a particular cultural formation is only a consequence of the respect for the universality of human reason."

Latin American philosophy can contest Eurocentric/colonial philosophical framings. Through it the humanity of Latin Americans can be affirmed beyond Eurocentrism by means of the critique of a universal view of reason and the positing of alternative rationalities. Latin American philosophy can be, in de Sousa Santos's phrase, a transformation of "survival strategies into sources of innovation, creativity, transgression, and subversion." That is, Schutte's approach to Latin American philosophy is a way to inhabit the colonial difference as a field of contestation, where a hermeneutic, situated philosophical perspective can become operative within the Latin American context as the undoing of a universal view of reason and consequently of the distinction between the human and the subhuman that it enforces. In this way, Schutte retains a contextual approach to Latin American philosophy such as Martín Alcoff's. Moreover, from universalism she turns toward the "philosophical importance of cultural-specific values found in Latin American thought." By "philosophical importance" she does not mean the universalization of cultural values but the recognition, beyond Eurocentrism, that such cultural values have to be interpreted within, and as contributing to, a transcultural, horizontal philosophical dialogue. Schutte makes an epistemological choice for a hermeneutic model of reasoning over against a universalist view of reasoning and delimits Latin American philosophy as a hermeneutics that sustains a transcultural dialogic space.[22]

In this sense, Latin American philosophy is aligned with cultural pluralism: "advocates of a cultural pluralism would be more willing to accept the peaceful coexistence of various culturally identified groups without prior appeal to a universal norm that would grant each group its particular legitimacy." For Schutte, such a hermeneutic transcultural philosophical perspective is rooted in processes of reflection so that "each group would have access to its own cultural legacy in a relationship of parity and mutual respect toward other groups." In this view, philosophy's role is to allow a specific cultural reflection that is based on the articulation of communal memories and legacies to enter into a transcultural dialogue. Thus, philosophy becomes an interpretive practice that facilitates such a dialogue by giving cultural values and histories a level of translatable intelligibility without anchoring the possibility of this translation in a universal and dominant universal perspective. It is not defined by a universalist view of reason because through this hermeneutic function it underscores differences rather than universal norms and attempts translations and communication across cultural alterities. Schutte recognizes that this specific philosophical function arises within a political situation defined by the colonial difference: out of the need for the social liberation of marginalized cultural identities in between colonial power differentials.[23]

How is this transcultural delimitation of Latin American philosophy connected to social liberation? For Schutte, it is a particular way of taking up the issue of cultural identity so as to act "as a buffer between models of 'liberation' based on the notion of full assimilation of minorities and marginal sectors into the already constituted framework of values of the society at large, and a defense of the particular interests of disadvantaged groups." Opening a horizontal space of transcultural dialogue means that the demands of marginalized groups can be heard without their legitimacy depending on their ability to assimilate, that is, without compromising the integrity of their own cultural positionalities and without questioning their humanity. Yet this transcultural dialogue also opens cultural identities to alterities in ways that recognize their fractures within the colonial difference and in relation to other cultural positions. Latin American philosophy can assist them in this respect through a two-tiered process: "This involves breaking through the silence imposed on some forms of thought and only subsequently trying to 'position' such differences within the general purview of the culture for the enrichment and benefit of all." It is easy to see that the second step, the positioning of differences within a transcultural dialogue for the benefit of all, is at stake in the hermeneutic transcultural philosophical delimitation I described earlier. Attending to the relationship between cultural identity and social liberation within the colonial difference, it seems that the transcultural delimitation of Latin American philosophy is invested in values of cultural continuity and of the integrity of cultural positionalities even if recognizing them as fluid and transformative. Yet opening these positionalities to a transcultural dialogical space may precisely decenter the force of such values.[24]

A subtle distinction and a connection are also to be made between philosophy as opening cultural positionalities to transcultural dialogues through a hermeneutic operation and philosophy itself being destabilized by a proliferation of fractured loci of enunciation, including ones that inform hermeneutic perspectives. Localizing pluricultural, hermeneutic philosophical perspectives shows that they are always already tangled up in irreducible power differentials that condition their enunciation within the colonial difference, that they can never fully open transcultural dialogues that are in fact horizontal. In this respect, perhaps a hermeneutic, transcultural, and communicative philosophical delimitation can overstate its emancipatory potential, and even mask a universalizing—even if dialogical—disposition. A transcultural delimitation of Latin American philosophy must include, then, a social and political critique of the conditions of its own enunciation.[25]

This level of critique is connected to the possibility of: "breaking through the silence imposed on some forms of thought." For Schutte, this possibility is a necessary condition for entering into a pluricultural dialogue. It is hard to see how a strictly hermeneutic philosophy could bring about such an interruption, since the silencing happens because a distinction between the human and the nonhuman operates within the colonial difference, a distinction that pervades all knowledge production by tying constructions of rationality to racial configurations. There is nothing to assure that even a pluricultural hermeneutic philosophy will operate outside the intimate relation between racism and rationality in postcolonial settings in its multiple possible instantiations. What would be needed here is to, again, expose the appearance of emancipatory power that philosophy can take on and generate constant critiques of insidious racial-rational formations by continuously dismantling the frames that come to define the "rational" within the colonial difference, with attention to power structures and decisions about the humanity of knowing subjects. It seems to me that the transcultural delimitation of Latin American philosophy that in my view Schutte makes manifest necessarily implies a self-critical practice of philosophy in which it submits itself to constant scrutiny in order to keep in check its tendency to further racism. In this sense, Schutte's positing of a hermeneutic, pluralist philosophy has to be critically developed in view of seeking an interruption of the particular hold coloniality has on subaltern philosophical thought. And in this critical dimension, it seems to me, Latin American philosophy may be more than expressing the "philosophical importance of cultural-specific values found in Latin American thought."[26]

The self-critical philosophical practice of dismantling philosophy's emancipatory, and even redemptive, appearance can be sustained by submitting philosophy to the larger interests of liberatory movements and by embedding it in the immediacy of praxis, which is a characteristic of Mariátegui's thought.

Once liberatory praxis is allowed to guide philosophical thought, the latter enables silenced forms of thought to emerge as critical perspectives (indigenous ones, for example) within liberatory projects that are attentive to insidious power structures even within transcultural dialogical settings. Furthermore, commitments to liberation can set the stage for philosophical reflection to become a critique of the ways in which liberatory projects themselves can fall prey to dominant interests and reconfigure hierarchies implicitly or explicitly connected to the designation of who is human and the related determination of whose rationality and knowledge production ought to be validated. This turn needs to belong to a transcultural delimitation of philosophy. I take this to be a kind of Fanonian call to action as the ground of theory. In this sense, philosophy has to remain in the present as a liberatory juncture and articulate border positions attached and detached from cultural positionalities that allow for intercultural and transcultural critiques on multiple fronts, fronts that correspond to subversive liminalities between Eurocentered and marginalized sites of knowledge production.

Gloria Anzaldúa refers to this kind of liberatory philosophy as "mestizo theorizing":

> Theorists of color are in the process of trying to formulate 'marginal' theories that are partially outside and partially inside the western frame of reference (if that is possible), theories that overlap many 'worlds.' We are articulating new positions in these 'in-between,' Borderland worlds of ethnic communities and academies, feminist and job worlds. In our literature, social issues such as race, class, and sexual difference are intertwined with the narrative and poetic elements of a text, elements in which theory is embedded. In our *mestizaje* theories we create new categories for those of us left out or pushed out of existing ones. We recover and examine non-western aesthetics while critiquing western aesthetics; recover and examine non-rational modes and 'blanked-out' realities while critiquing rational, consensual reality; recover and examine indigenous languages while critiquing the 'languages' of the dominant culture. And we simultaneously combat the tokenization and appropriation of our literatures and our writers/artists.

This statement lays out the characteristics of a transcultural delimitation of Latin American philosophy that I have begun to articulate through an interpretation of Schutte's text *Cultural Identity and Social Liberation in Latin American Thought*. Anzaldúa centers on multifaceted critical border positions in between cultures and other categories of difference and power. She affirms the interruption of the silencing of colonized voices through the creation of new

epistemic categories. Yet she critiques the constitution of pluricultural dialogical spaces as sites where tokenization and misappropriation of cultures can
happen and where expectations of rational consensus exclude subaltern epistemologies and knowledge production. And she sees this marginal theorizing
happening precariously and indeterminately in the border between Western
and non-Western frames. Anzaldúa shows a way of articulating the transcultural delimitation of Latin American philosophy I find in Schutte, an articulation that can also be traced within Schutte's reading of Mariátegui's texts.[27]

SCHUTTE'S INTERPRETATION OF MARIÁTEGUI

In my view, an implicit delimitation of Latin American liberatory philosophy as transcultural, hermeneutic, and dialogical defines Schutte's approach
to Mariátegui, and she finds in him a similar philosophical perspective. The
section "Mariátegui's Interpretation of Peruvian Economic Reality" in her
book is particularly relevant in this respect. It contains Schutte's rendition
of Mariátegui's socialism as rooted in an indigenous cultural identity and in
the possibility of the liberation of Andean indigenous peasants: "Mariátegui's
appreciation of the Peruvian indigenous heritage led him to place an accent on
the respect for the cultural diversity of the region and on political organizing
based on grass-roots coalitions rather than on centrally controlled, foreign-
dominated political parties."

Schutte, as I noted above, provocatively aligns Mariátegui's socialism with
a project of social, rather than national, liberation, the liberation of indigenous
peoples in particular. This social liberation appears to be fundamental for solving the political and economic problems of Peru. She stresses that Mariátegui
does not impose socialism on Andean peasants but rather finds socialism as a
faithful manifestation of their demands on the basis of their traditions. In other
words, she attributes to Mariátegui a socialism that arises from indigenous
contexts and in relation to indigenous cultural identities.[28]

There are two important implications here. First, Schutte argues that
Mariátegui is interested in the correspondence between socialism and traditional indigenous economic and political forms. She supports this by quoting him: "*Aside from reasons of doctrine* [emphasis added], I consider that our
agrarian problem has a special character due to an indisputable and concrete
factor: the survival of the Indian 'community' and of elements of practical
socialism in indigenous agriculture and life." Leaving open the factual issue of
whether socialism can indeed evoke an Andean indigenous communal tradition, Schutte's point is that Mariátegui posits it as a political form that can be

retrieved through indigenous cultural memory and as a testament to indigenous legacies. In fact, socialism in this context would be an accurate example
of a practice of cultural memory that brings to light marginalized aspects of
cultural heritages, motivating grass-roots movements of liberation from below.
Furthermore, Mariátegui's socialism, as a practice of cultural memory, would
enable a transcultural dialogical space by translating indigenous legacies into
contemporary political options. In this sense, Mariátegui's socialism would be
a good example of Latin American philosophy as transcultural.[29]

Second, Schutte interprets Mariátegui's essay "The Problem of the Indian"
as addressing not only an economic problem but also a social one that is tangled up with it. She finds it to be the problem of the self-determination of an
indigenous cultural identity. But Schutte's insight can be extended. Mariátegui
recognizes not only that indigenous peoples are marginalized in terms of culture but also that they are treated as subhuman through forced labor and by
not being under the law (for the indigenous Andean peasant the law is effectively suspended). Thus, one needs to approach this "problem" by extending
Schutte's analysis. Beyond cultural impositions and penetrations (something
that Mariátegui is explicit about), one has to analyze the field of contestation
of the delimitation of the human and trace the aspects of Mariátegui's thought
that engage this field, the space of the colonial difference, explicitly. Schutte
reveals, however, a number of dimensions in Mariátegui's indigenous socialism
that address the contestation.[30]

First, by assigning a historical role to the indigenous masses, Mariátegui
expands and unsettles a Eurocentric construction of history and identification
of historical agents. The difference between history and nonhistory, or between
historical agency and historical nonagency or passivity, is grounded in the
distinction between human and subhuman. So, the inclusion of indigenous
peoples that appears in Schutte's interpretation as a cultural aspect of socialism
that decenters its European determination further implies the circumscription
of a political, epistemic, and subversive positionality within the field where
the determination of the human is negotiated. Schutte writes, "Thus his
understanding of socialism was quite different from the normative one in
which a Western paradigm of scientific progress is superimposed on a given
reality in the name of a higher truth. With its unquestioned concept of 'science'
derived from a linear interpretation of history, such an approach would merely
supplant capitalist with socialist economic policies, without regard for grass-
root level knowledge gained from centuries of experience."[31] The inclusion of
indigenous peoples, then, implies the inclusion of knowledges and experiences
from below that are silenced by a teleological concept of history bound up with

the supposed superiority of scientific reasoning. Since European socialism included these Eurocentric commitments, the reference to indigenous experience and knowledge as the basis for articulating socialism is a clear departure from it.

Schutte emphasizes the practical and political implications of this reference but not the epistemic ones, which include critiques of the configuration of human rationality. This is a fundamental issue since, if the difference between human and subhuman is operative here, much more than a practical inclusion of indigenous peoples has to be at stake. A radical epistemic shift that would dismantle the connection between scientific reasoning, teleological history, and racist framings of human reason is needed. That is, the positing of scientific, universal reasoning as the end of a linear historical trajectory toward Europe (in both its Kantian and Hegelian determinations, for example) has to be interrupted by an emerging temporalizing of thinking that liberates non-Western epistemologies. Such an interpretation is also connected to an aesthetic challenge to the construction of modern Western rationality.[32]

Second, Schutte gives a provocative take on the meaning of class as a critical concept in Mariátegui. Class, in her view, is not simply an economic category. It allows one to see the operation of race as a sociopolitical structure of coloniality. She writes, "Mariátegui argued that the Peruvian bourgeoisie identified primarily with 'white' values and did not feel it shared a common culture and history with the rest of the Peruvian people, whose ancestors were indian." This racial factor, as it intersects with class determinations, complicates the sheer economic front through which Eurocentric socialism understands itself. A dismantling of racial structures as part of the material conditions of life has to complement the praxis of liberation in geopolitical sites like Peru. In this particular juncture, and in relation to cultural identities, Schutte explains that "Thus Mariátegui realized that the cultural values tilted in the direction of capitalism were loaded with racial values that underestimated the civilizing potential of indigenous cultures."[33]

The affirmation of indigenous culture, then, has to challenge racist structures as well. It is unclear, however, as I noted earlier, particularly in relation to Fanon, whether a cultural affirmation can undo racism. DuBois, a critical thinker who in many ways is close to Mariátegui, also discusses a specific operation of race that reveals the limits of an emancipatory appeal to culture. Double consciousness shows not only that the racialized has no alternative to understanding herself other than through the views of her racist oppressor. It also shows that the racialized internalizes the values that dismiss her own cultural milieu as a source of experience and knowledge, an internalization that problematizes the possibility of cultural affirmation that Schutte finds necessary in processes of social liberation such as Mariátegui's. This is where Anzaldúa's border positionalities can be helpful in their attachments and detachments from culture because they attest to sites for critical thinking that are not exhausted by the dominant gaze in the ways that Fanon's and DuBois's accounts make explicit. These border positionalities, however, while arising from cultural ones even in their articulation of political demands, do not draw validation from values of cultural integrity, coherence, and continuity. They rely, rather, on a spectrum of cultural determinations among proliferations of power differentials that fracture them, constituting a heterogeneous field from which liberatory options arise.[34]

A NIETZSCHEAN MATRIX IN MARIÁTEGUI'S WORKS

Schutte's delimitation of Latin American philosophy as transcultural, hermeneutic, and dialogical allows her to posit an implicit interpretive matrix of Mariátegui's texts that is informed by this delimitation and that arguably elucidates his comprehension of the relationship between cultural identity and liberation. In my view, this is perhaps Schutte's most provocative contribution to the study of Mariátegui.

Even when she acknowledges the mobilization of European sources in Mariátegui's socialism, she sees it as part of a commitment to the retrieval of indigenous cultural identities: "socialism could not appreciate the contribution of an indigenous heritage of the sort valued by Mariátegui without assimilating a large dose of antipositivist Western thought, often labeled 'irrationalist' by traditional Marxists." Schutte's interpretive genius is evident when she constructs what I call Mariátegui's "Nietzschean matrix" on the basis of antipositivist Western thought. Schutte brings Nietzsche, Bergson, and William James in particular to the center of Mariátegui's thinking, but Nietzsche remains the main figure. Thus, she attributes to Mariátegui a "life-oriented concept of socialism." From this perspective, first, cultural identity is understood as a "result of a life-oriented process of activity, rather than as a fixed origin or point of departure that must be duplicated indefinitely in order for identity to hold," which moves away from essentialist views of cultural identities. Second, through the matrix of antipositivist thought, Mariátegui's critique of Western reason becomes explicit, one that rejects the strictures of a goal-oriented rationality, and enables the validation of colonized epistemologies. With Nietzsche as a referent, then, these two facets place Mariátegui's indigenous socialism within a broader delimitation of Latin American philosophy in a way that puts into question stable cultural identities and Western constructions of rationality.[35]

But one dimension of this Nietzschean matrix curbs the liberatory potential here. It has to do with the role that life-affirming forces, creativity, and spontaneity take on. In Schutte's account, these three are at play in processes that synthesize revolutionary praxis and Mariátegui's own thinking, spontaneous processes for the creation of new realities that are inherently life-affirming. Theory and praxis emerge bound together as an expression of the same life force. Schutte develops this interpretation in a provocative way. In her view, Mariátegui finds pre-Conquest indigenous economies and political forms to arise spontaneously from an attachment to the land. She quotes him in this respect: "Until the conquest, an economy developed in Peru that sprang spontaneously and freely from the Peruvian soil and people." In this way, Schutte constructs a scenario in which there is an organic affinity between the integrity of the earth, of indigenous cultures, of revolutionary praxis, and of Mariátegui's own revolutionary thought. It is as if all of them were part of the same life-affirming, creative process. She states, "The connectedness of the Indians to the land and of the writer to his lived experience are two figural themes found at the outset of Mariátegui's study. The indigenous economy before the conquest—an economy 'that sprang spontaneously and freely from the Peruvian soil and people'—is analogous to the author's thoughts that gather themselves spontaneously into a book, following a model highly reminiscent of Nietzsche's notion of free spiritedness."[36]

A possible essentialization of identities suggests itself here, which becomes apparent when Schutte characterizes colonization as a "cut," that marks a "before and after," where "before" designates a more authentic life-affirming process embodied in pre-Columbian societies, life forms that were interrupted by colonization. In this construction, however, one can see the possibility of an overdetermination of indigenous forms, of substantialist projections upon them, that reinscribes into this Nietzschean matrix values that affirm the integrity and continuity of indigenous cultural identities and that can counter Schutte's attentiveness to cultural alterity and fluidity.[37]

According to Schutte, Mariátegui's socialism espouses a critical perspective that positions itself in an indigenous world before the "cut." This leads her to the following intriguing, and defining, statement: "If such a position 'before the cut' is to be taken as a starting point of a cultural critique, one would assume that the notion of connectedness, continuity or proximity would have a very strong place in the critic's perspective." Perhaps my subtle departure from Schutte's reading of Mariátegui is best expressed through these dispositions toward connectedness, continuity, and proximity. Would they be still at play if one were to engage Mariátegui operating from fractured loci and border positionalities within the colonial difference? Wouldn't this kind of thinking also be disposed to disconnection, interruptions, and distance, especially in relation to cultural identities?[38]

By mobilizing a Nietzschean matrix in order to understand Mariátegui's stance on the relationship between cultural identity and social liberation, Schutte is able not only to cast Mariátegui's thought as contributing to a hermeneutic and transcultural view of philosophy but also to resolve some of the tensions of his indigenous socialism. The Indian, the critic, and the revolutionary become intertwined; socialism and indigenous Andean culture have an originary resonance, and Mariátegui's critical positionality is anchored in a pre-Conquest socialist perspective that generates a trans-European political and cultural narrative that forms a new revolutionary consciousness. One could even say that this last point puts Mariátegui in the lineage of Guaman Poma, bringing to light a deep and long genealogy of Latin American philosophy.[39]

I recognize the value of such a reading, but I read Mariátegui's works as having a slightly different emphasis. She positions Mariátegui before the cut of colonialism and characterizes his thought as a cultural critique rooted in indigenous culture. For me, the cut of colonialism, rather, opens the space of the colonial difference that can be circumscribed neither by a pre-Conquest cultural heritage and projection nor by the global reach of Europe through colonialism. The cut even undermines the clear temporal distinction between a "before and after" of colonialism, opening a field of differences that articulate political, economic, and cultural dynamics of power that are irreducible to totalizing logics and structures, including temporal and historical ones, and I see Mariátegui positioned within such a field. So, in my view, Mariátegui's *indigenismo* and claims to an indigenous heritage have to be scrutinized and contextualized from fractured loci of enunciation and border positionalities. This, however, does not mean that I simply dismiss Schutte's interpretation of Mariátegui and the transcultural delimitation of Latin American philosophy that I find in it. In fact, I am deeply indebted to them.

A THREEFOLD APPROACH TO MARIÁTEGUI'S MARXISM: OPENING INTERPRETIVE OPTIONS

The last section of the first chapter of Schutte's book, "Mariátegui's Reconciliation between Artistic Free-Spiritedness and Marxist Commitment" sketches further interpretations of Mariátegui. She writes, "In Mariátegui's use of Marxism one may see a combination of three factors: his conception of Marxism as a science, as a faith, and as an aesthetic impulse stimulating the artistic, creative side of what is otherwise considered a political process. It is not easy to discern these three interactive levels of Mariátegui's Marxism, since he himself never outlined them—their union was probably 'spontaneous' for him."[40]

Extending Schutte's analysis, I approach these three aspects of Mariátegui's Marxism from the perspective of the Nietzschean matrix I just posited. For Schutte, Mariátegui understands Marxism as science insofar as it is a method: "Marxism should not be seen as a philosophy of history without qualification, but only as a 'method of historical interpretation' most relevant for the period in which capitalism is the dominant economic system. It is, in other words, an interpretive method that allows us to understand the root causes of certain major (structural) social problems and to envision the dawn of a transition to a more just social system." The view of Marxism as a method works well within Schutte's perspective, and a Nietzschean matrix. This method has no conceptual rigidity, and no metaphysical structures of stable meanings that underpin a historical progression—not even the projection of a linear history. It is transient, adaptable, and prone to self-overcoming. Marxism is, thus, stripped of idealizations and values. It is, a Nietzschean hammer that tears down rigid structures of values and of social and political power.[41]

The aesthetic aspect of Mariátegui's Marxism also fits well within Schutte's Nietzschean approach, since it "relates the art of creating a revolution to the revolutionary power of art. For him [Mariátegui], creativity itself contained a revolutionary potential." This relationship is central to Mariátegui and calls for an analysis not only of Mariátegui's indebtedness to Nietzsche but also, perhaps even more fittingly, to surrealism. In fact, one could argue that in Mariátegui's interpretation of surrealism one finds his most revealing statements about the nature of the revolutionary impulse.[42]

Marxism as myth or faith, however, does not quite fit in this Nietzschean configuration: "Indeed his own spirit was moved by the belief in the transformation of Peruvian society and the 'redemption' of the Indians through a social revolution. This brings us to the second important aspect of Mariátegui's Marxism—his conception of Marxism as faith." She senses in this revolutionary faith a tendency in Mariátegui toward dogmatism, a lack of conceptual and historical sophistication, a problematic assertion of values, and a limited awareness of their contingency. Schutte herself does not focus on how this tendency is applicable to Mariátegui's indigenista commitments, but her writing "redemption" in quotations suggests suspicion on her part. She writes, "When this perspective has the ascendance in his thinking, his writing becomes excessively rhetorical." One could approach this departure from Mariátegui as the revelation of an inner tension in his thinking that is expressed through the contradiction between the methodological and aesthetic aspects of his Marxism, on the one hand, and his revolutionary faith, on the other. In my view, by exposing this tension Schutte allows for revisiting Mariátegui and engaging him beyond redemption.[43]

NOTES

1. Schutte, *Cultural Identity*, 1.

2. A complementary text here is Schutte, "Nietzsche." Another text that informs my analysis here is O. Rivera, "From Revolving Time." For transculturality in Schutte, see also Schutte, *Cross Cultural Communication*.

3. Schutte, *Cultural Identity*, 10, 11. Ibid.

4. The connection between cultural identity and social liberation in Schutte should be read here in relation to Martín Alcoff's delimitation of Latin American philosophy I discussed in chapter 1 in this volume.

5. Schutte, *Cultural Identity*, 13.

6. I will not cover this problematic in Schutte's reading of the many other Latin American thinkers that she covers; my project here is oriented to a precise understanding of Mariátegui's thought in relation to Latin American philosophy.

7. Schutte, *Cultural Identity*, 13.

8. Schutte, *Cultural Identity*, 14. Italics mine.

9. The issue is part of a larger discussion of the notion of culture as it fits within a decolonial theory and its critique of Eurocentrism. See the recent Castro-Gómez, "Qué hacer."

10. A seminal essay on the relationship between Latin American philosophy and power is Salazar Bondy, "Existe una filosofía de nuestra América?"

11. Schutte, *Cultural Identity*, 66. Italics mine.

12. Fanon, *Black Skin, White Masks*. It is important to note that Schutte is attentive to these issues in later essays. See, for example, Schutte, "Negotiating Latina Identities," and Schutte, "Cultural Alterity."

13. Mignolo, *Local Histories/Global Designs*, ix.

14. Quijano, "Coloniality of Power," 193.

15. De Sousa Santos, *Epistemologies*, 51, 52, 56.

16. Schutte, *Cultural Identity*, 15.

17. Schutte, *Cultural Identity*, 14.

18. Schutte, *Cultural Identity*, 14.

19. For a discussion parallel to this one, see Dussel, *Transmodernity*. A natural extension of this discussion would be a critical engagement with intercultural philosophy. Especially see Fornet-Betancourt, "Alternative to Globalization."

20. Schutte, *Cultural Identity*, 14.

21. I am here drawing from Robert Bernasconi's work on race. See, for example, "Who Invented the Concept of Race?" 11–36. I am also working from my essay, "Reading Alejandro Vallega," and from Wynter, "Ceremony."

22. Any attempt to assimilate to the universality of Western philosophy constitutes the restriction of thought to a specific manifestation of it. De Sousa Santos, *Epistemologies*, 51.

23. Schutte, *Cultural Identity*, 14. Ibid.

24. Schutte, *Cultural Identity*, 15.

25. Mignolo's movement from hermeneutics to "pluri-topic hermeneutics" could be a helpful corrective here, as well as his notion of border thinking. See the development of a decolonial epistemology in Mignolo, from a pluritopic hermeneutics to border thinking. The important texts are Mignolo, *Darker Side of the Renaissance*, and Mignolo, *Local Histories/Global Designs*, 49–90. See also a defense of hermeneutics in response to Mignolo in Martín Alcoff, "Mignolo's Epistemology."

26. See Lugones's discussion of infrapolitics in "Toward a Decolonial Feminism." See also Schutte, *Cultural Identity*, 14.

27. Anzaldúa, *Gloria Anzaldúa Reader*, 137.

28. Schutte, *Cultural Identity*, 21.

29. Schutte, *Cultural Identity*, 22.

30. There is an intersection here with Giorgio Agamben in Mariátegui's understanding of the relationship between Indians and the law (Agamben, *Homo Sacer*). See, for example, the relationship between race and colonialism in Mariátegui essay "El Problema de las Razas en América Latina," in *Siete ensayos*, 370–77.

31. Schutte, *Cultural Identity*, 22.

32. For an example of a decolonial opening of alternative rationalities in relation to temporal sensibilities, see Mignolo, *Darker Side of Western Modernity*, 149–80.

33. Schutte, *Cultural Identity*, 23. See Mills, "Materializing Race."

34. See "Of Our Spiritual Strivings," in DuBois *Reader*.

35. Schutte, *Cultural Identity*, 24–27.

36. Schutte, *Cultural Identity*, 29.

37. Schutte, *Cultural Identity*, 28.

38. Schutte, *Cultural Identity*. Ibid., 29.

39. As in the lineage traced out in Dussel, "Anti-Cartesian Meditations," 36–51.

40. Schutte, *Cultural Identity*, 29.

41. Schutte, *Cultural Identity*, 31. For a discussion of Mariátegui and Surrealism, see Fernanda Beigel *El Itinerario*.

42. Schutte, *Cultural Identity*, 33.

43. Schutte, *Cultural Identity*, 33.

REPRESENTATION

Mariátegui's and Lugones's Invisibilities

Literature's intense representativity . . . lies at the core of this [Mariátegui's] and other Andean traditions of indigenismo in modernity.

Jorge Coronado, *The Andes Imagined*

OFELIA SCHUTTE'S work allows for an articulation of a transcultural delimitation of Latin American philosophy. Yet she also signals an aesthetic dimension to Mariátegui's socialism, which is the main theme of the rest of this book, culminating in an aesthetic delimitation of Latin American philosophy. In this chapter in particular, resources in Mariátegui's writings on aesthetics are mobilized to dislodge the representativity implied by the indigenista logic of redemption, opening up aesthetic liberatory options that I will explore in the next chapter and the conclusion. The indigenista logic of redemption configures an Indian identity in order to bolster a socialist project of indigenous redemption. My concern is whether Mariátegui is committed to a rigid representation of this identity that essentializes it abstracted from indigenous peoples themselves. Such essentialization would mean that Mariátegui's indigenous socialism is an ideological imposition of a lettered class upon indigenous peoples. This concern is perhaps best articulated by Jorge Coronado's and Luis Alberto Sanchez's critiques of Mariátegui's indigenismo as a representational aesthetics, which are the focus of the beginning of this chapter. In response to them, and through an interpretation of Mariátegui's approach to Enrique López Albújar's indigenista literature, a transrepresentative facet of Mariátegui's indigenismo comes forth. At the end of the chapter, Mariátegui's transrepresentative aesthetics appears in relation to Lugones's understanding of the invisibilities of the oppressed and is connected to the possibility of liberatory praxis beyond redemption.[1]

CORONADO'S CRITIQUE AND TRANSREPRESENTATION

In the chapter "The Revolutionary Indio" of *The Andes Imagined*, Coronado gives a devastating critique of Mariátegui's indigenismo as an ideological use of an artificial representation of the indio for the sake of a lettered and imposed socialist revolution in Peru. His argument has shortcomings, particularly in the way it is framed. Focusing on the core of this frame, I will recover Mariátegui's aesthetics beyond the representativity implied in the indigenista logic of redemption.[2]

In the process of deconstructing Coronado's critique, a transrepresentative dimension in Mariátegui's approach to indigenismo can become apparent. This point hinges on what this transrepresentative approach means. It does not suggest that Mariátegui denies that representations of indigenous peoples are part of indigenismo's aesthetics. Rather, it implies that Mariátegui finds an unsettling of such representations already operative within indigenista aesthetics. From his perspective, as it relates to the work of López Albújar in particular, indigenismo represents indigenous peoples and simultaneously calls for undermining such representations, in a movement of self-overcoming that manifests itself within indigenista works. This complex aesthetic phenomenon is the culminating thematic of Mariátegui's transrepresentative aesthetics, and it reveals indigenismo to be, beyond its representation of indigenous peoples, an aesthetics of invisibilities.[3]

In this respect, Mariátegui's approach includes a critique of indigenista representations in the very process of laying out the indigenista aesthetics that informs his socialism, which suggests that Coronado, Sánchez, and Mariátegui are not so far apart, at least in their recognition of the need for such a critique. This point will come back at the end of the chapter in order to gauge the extent of their disagreement. In the meantime, in the first part of this chapter, I analyze Coronado's critique, and Sánchez's as a version of it, in their aesthetic and political implications and trace Mariátegui's transrepresentative approach to López Albújar's literary work, revealing three representative layers in it, the last one being an aesthetics of invisibilities.

THE DOUBLE FRAME OF CORONADO'S
CRITIQUE OF MARIÁTEGUI

Coronado's analysis is framed in two interrelated ways. First, it denies that Mariátegui could position himself critically in relation to indigenista representations, mainly because he was not exposed to indigenous peoples. For this reason, he maintains that Mariátegui's "representation of the indio, in the end, cannot be taken to be identical with the indigenous peoples themselves." This first frame assumes in a problematic way that critiques of indigenista representations can come only from genuine knowledge of indigenous peoples (being, thus, critiques of the inaccuracy of indigenismo's representations). As a result, Coronado claims that Mariátegui is part of a movement whose intent is to produce an ideological representation of Peruvian indigenous populations and cultures. He states, "Mariátegui subsumes the indio into his own revolutionary discourse. . . . The socially acceptable and valued practice of literature is thus made to speak the figure of the indigenous while at the same time silencing the indio's own voice." In this respect, he sees Mariátegui passively accepting the lettered representations of indigenous peoples, endorsing his contemporary lettered class (who were also mostly nonindigenous) as the vanguard of indigenous populations while these populations were in fact silenced by it.[4]

Second, Coronado's critique is framed by taking Mariátegui to be invested in a representation of indigenous populations that allows him to set up a dialectic opposition that leads to a socialist revolution. This dialectic, in Coronado's view, is the core of Mariátegui's ideological and strategic manipulation of the representation of the "revolutionary indio" he adopts from indigenismo. The dialectic opposition works like this: (1) Mariátegui's opposes indigenous peoples to Peruvian Western/colonial socioeconomic forms. Or, more precisely, Mariátegui opposes a representation of indigenous ways of living as "communism" to Peruvian postcolonial capitalism. (2) This opposition would resolve itself dialectically, through an indigenous revolution, into a socialist state as a new synthesis in which Peru would be indigenous and modern at the same time. Coronado warns the reader that this manipulation is the true intention behind Mariátegui's indigenismo, which would explain and undermine the naive interpretations of Mariátegui either as a genuine channel for the self-representation of indigenous populations or as a liminally situated "border thinker" invested in a critical encounter between indigenous and Western epistemologies and political practices. This framing, however, erroneously assumes, in light of Mariátegui's engagement with López Albújar's writings, that Mariátegui is interested only in representations of indigenous peoples that present them as potential socialist revolutionaries, representations that he could manipulate.[5]

This chapter tackles the center of Coronado's critique: the claim that Mariátegui is interested in indigenismo as a representative aesthetics that he could manipulate. Coronado's claim supports a view of indigenismo's representations that positions Mariátegui as a passive recipient of them and that allows

Mariátegui to set up the dialectic explained above. Challenging Coronado's critique in this way, one can recover Mariátegui as a critic of indigenismo's representational function, as well as a transrepresentational aspect that expands indigenista aesthetics beyond Coronado's analysis.[6]

SÁNCHEZ'S CRITIQUE AS AN EARLIER VERSION OF CORONADO'S AND THE CASE OF LÓPEZ ALBÚJAR'S INDIGENISMO

Coronado is correct in pointing to Mariátegui's connection to indigenismo as central to his indigenous socialist program. The *Seven Essays* in particular shows the essential role that the relationship between the indigenous populations of Peru and socialism plays in Mariátegui's thought. There Mariátegui tackles this relationship through the study of indigenismo as both a literary and a political movement. Luis Alberto Sánchez, a contemporary of Mariátegui's and a member of the anti-imperialist APRA, understood the depth of Mariátegui's investment in indigenismo and made it a focus of his critique of him.[7]

Against Coronado's views, a close reading of Mariátegui shows that he is well aware of the representational restrictions of indigenismo and that he positions himself explicitly as a critic of it. This is apparent in his controversy with Sánchez in 1927. Sánchez, like Coronado, puts into question the lettered representation of the indigenous populations in indigenismo, challenging it as a fabrication of *costeños* who do not share the ethnicity and race of the indigenous populations, belonging ethnically and racially, rather, to their oppressors. Sánchez, then, anticipates Coronado's critique of the legitimacy of the representation of the indio in indigenismo and is also suspicious of the political programs that could come from the strategic manipulation of it. Sánchez underscores an important aspect of Coronado's later critique, namely, that the colonial difference between creoles and indigenous populations defines indigenista aesthetics as a representation of the oppressed by their oppressors. In this sense, this aesthetics could set up the stage for political programs that ostensibly advocate for indigenous peoples while, in fact, continuing to enforce social structures that oppress them.[8]

Mariátegui's response to Sánchez's critique is illuminating. He does not challenge the main points of it: that indigenismo is not the self-representation of indigenous populations, that it is enunciated by costeños, and, thus, that it could be a distorting representational aesthetics with dangerous political implications. This view is consistent with the *Seven Essays*. The difference from Sánchez position (and, one could extrapolate, from Coronado's) lies in

Mariátegui's engagement with this representational failure as a facet of indigenismo that can reveal decolonial aesthetic and political dimensions of indigenismo beyond its strictly representational content.[9]

There is a further aspect in Sánchez critique that Coronado does not share. For Sánchez, indigenismo, as a movement, claims coherence by expounding a series of formulated and definitive positions that include representative claims about indigenous populations. On this basis, Sánchez proceeds to find contradictions within these representations, which leads him to question the coherence of the movement as a whole. From this perspective, attention to the representative function of indigenismo reveals both the inadequacies of its representational claims (inadequacies linked to the fact that it was costeños who represent the Indians) and the untenability of its political aspirations.

Sánchez's critical position differs from Coronado's in other respects. First, beyond questioning the accuracy of indigenista representations, Sánchez challenges the coherence of these representations, showing the possibility of critiquing indigenismo without having the burden (which Coronado tacitly assumes) of pointing to what authentic representations of indigenous peoples would be like. For Sánchez, it is enough to issue a critique of these representations by noting both the colonial difference that determines them and the lack of coherence in them. He does not believe that one needs to have access to or posit a genuine indigenous representativity in order to see the problems with indigenista representations. In this respect, Sánchez and Mariátegui are, in fact, strange allies. Second, Sánchez sees in indigenismo a broken movement, and so, for him, Mariátegui's use of it is an intentional and original ideological revitalization of it. For Sánchez, Coronado's view of Mariátegui as passively adopting the indigenista movement would make no sense. Nevertheless, Sánchez and Coronado agree in a fundamental way: they see Mariátegui manipulating indigenista representations, the representation of the revolutionary indio in particular, for the sake of his socialist ideology.

Mariátegui responds to Sánchez as follows. He sees the indigenista movement in a process of development rather than claiming coherence and finality; namely, as "barely a debate, within which diverse voices and ideas take place that recognize themselves to be animated by the same spirit of renovation. . . . The tendencies or groups seeking renovation do not yet have a clearly formulated nor uniformly accepted program." He understands contradictory positions in indigenista representations in view of their still possible complementarity. This understanding implies uncovering the political sense of the movement through and beyond the representational incongruencies that Sánchez points to, finding complementarity in its "spirit of renovation" rather than in the movement's representational output. Mariátegui is not manipulating indigenista representations for the sake of a laid-out political program. He is, rather, looking to uncover the political originality of indigenismo before asking the question of its possible relation to socialism. For that reason, as a critic of a movement in formation, he states, "my effort does not intend to impose a criterion it rather seeks to contribute to the formation of one."[10] To the extent that Sánchez and Coronado miss this element of Mariátegui's indigenismo, they bury the ultimate sense of Mariátegui's practical and heterogeneous revolutionary indigenous socialism, one that I am trying to recover here in an aesthetic register.

Sánchez's particular understanding of indigenismo can, nevertheless, help structure an analysis of Mariátegui's approach to it. Sánchez sees a contradiction in the indigenista movement because it attempts to hold, simultaneously, the representational work of two indigenistas: Luis E. Valcárcel and Enrique López Albújar. Sánchez contrasts Valcárcel's exaltation of Andean indigenous peoples—one could say, using Coronado's phrase—as potential revolutionary indios, with López Albújar's negative portrayal of them. From López Albújar's writings, according to Sanchez, "emerges the necessity to go to the indigenous race, but to exterminate it." The works of Valcárcel and López Albújar also constitute for Mariátegui two aspects of indigenismo. If Mariátegui were interested only in the manipulation of the representation of the revolutionary indio, he would dismiss López Albújar's indigenismo and embrace Valcárcel's. (As discussed in chapter 3, Valcárcel is a referent for an "indigenista logic of redemption.") Instead, Mariátegui is interested in the complementarity between them beyond their representative contradictions as moments of the same movement in formation.[11]

THREE REPRESENTATIVE LAYERS IN LÓPEZ ALBÚJAR'S INDIGENISMO

Mariátegui's transrepresentative approach remains implicit. It displays López Albújar's indigenismo as an aesthetic field in which differences emerge within representations of Andean indigenous peoples, representations explicitly determined by the context of coloniality and, especially, by different perspectives defined by the colonial difference (indigenous peoples on one side and the *Mistis*, landowners and the lettered class, on the other). Three layers of representations of the psychology and agency of indigenous peoples emerge here, namely, as (1) barbaric and primitive (as the Mistis and landowners perceive them), as (2) rooted and situated in a colonial context (as López Albújar sees them from the position of an indigenista writer), and as (3) potentially self-determining beyond the purview of the Mistis, landowners, and indigenistas. The third layer constitutes lapses in representation more than representations, lapses that indicate the limits of the perspective of the landowners, Mistis, and indigenistas. In it, an aesthetics of invisibilities begins to be manifest in López Albújar's works (whose explicit representational work fits in the second layer).

Mariátegui's approach is suggested by his retort to Sánchez, specifically by his appeal to López Albújar's "warning to the reader" (which he quotes extensively) and by his brief response to it. Before looking into these passages in detail, it is important to note the temporal sensibility at work in López Albújar's warning. This is a sensibility that implies the determination of time as a linear progression, as sequential (a new epoch leaves the previous one behind) and as absolute (space being overcome as a differential factor). In such a temporal sensibility, the future is the dominant temporality and it retroactively justifies and compensates for the past. In this way, peoples attain self-understanding, purpose, and cultural validation from the future. López Albújar writes from this sensibility without making it explicit. The manner in which this futural temporality excludes space and the past as sources for meaning and purpose is at the core of López Albújar's indigenista representations.

The First Representative Layer:
"Nostalgia" and "without Care for the Future"

López Albújar's warning to his readers begins thus: "The Indian is a sphinx with two faces: with one it looks toward the past and with the other to the present, without care for what is to come. The first serves him to live among his own; the second to deal with strangers." A sensibility defined by a linear, futural time sheds light on López Albújar's warning. In his view, Indians look toward their past to find their proper space: their *ayllus*, their communities, are in the past, even though they are in some way contemporaneous with them. From the perspective of this spatiotemporal sensibility, their past is static, left behind, outside progressive, futural, meaningful time; their space, their ayllu, where they live among each other, excludes them from the thrust of history. Their present belongs to a future that is not theirs. López Albújar suggests that, seeing their ayllus in the past allows indigenous peoples to inhabit their proper place and manifest themselves to one another, but this inhabitation and dynamic of recognition is useless, senseless, historically ineffective.[12]

The representation of this spatiotemporal entrapment of indigenous existence is a constant in López Albújar's stories, which render the pathological patterns of the psychology of the "indio huanuqueño" specifically as nostalgic and without care for the future. Such representations are intensified in relation to their ayllu. The communal space of the ayllu emerges in this first representative layer as a definitive spatiotemporal referent that confines Indians within an irresolvable nostalgia. Nostalgic, reckless without foresight, impossibly and desperately attached to their ayllu—all these representations constitute the perspective of the racist landowners and gamonales, their view of Indians as backward, primitive, uncivilized, even as needing to be exterminated, in Sánchez's words. This point is crucial: these characteristics are ascribed to them not because of their customs or beliefs, but because they are seen as being pathologically attached to them, entrapped in the past. Indians refuse to progress, to jump into the movement of history.[13]

It is easy to note that there is a slippage here: a *perception* of indigenous peoples from the point of view of the landowners and Mistis, one that is determined by coloniality and by the sensibility of futural time, is naturalized as an indigenous trait. Thus, indigenous peoples come to be nostalgic and futurally reckless. This slippage is accomplished in the first representative layer of López Albújar's indigenismo. Within it, Coronado's and Sánchez's concerns are warranted: if this perception influences Mariátegui, then his idealization of the Indian community and past is an ideological manipulation of indigenista images.

The Second Representative Layer: Contextualizing López Albújar and Indigenous Existential Duality

López Albújar's warning to his readers continues: "To the former [those like him], the Indian manifests himself as he is; to the latter [strangers], as he would not like to be." This part of the warning shows that the representations of indigenous peoples as nostalgic and without care for the future are, in fact, projections onto them. This second representative layer is critically aware of the one-sidedness of the first. Furthermore, it reveals that indigenous peoples manifest themselves doubly, since they are also manifest to those like themselves. This double manifestation is not made explicit in the first layer as a representative issue. López Albújar, self-reflectively as an indigenista writer, focuses on this double manifestation and states, "One thing, then, is the Indian in his ayllu, in his community, in his intimate life, and another is the Indian in the Misti's city in his relations with him, as his servant or as a free man."[14]

López Albújar, in these reflections, differentiates his position from that of the Mistis, claiming greater insight into indigenous existence—even a kind of neutrality that enables his indigenista literature. One could say that the indigenista's neutrality (as opposed to the first layer) attends to the appearance of indigenous peoples as contingent on coloniality and on the perspectival differences implied by colonial differences. From this privileged position, an indigenous duality is apparent, and the fact that indigenous peoples themselves are aware of their own duality is also apparent. They seem aware of wavering between appearing as what they are and as "they would not like to be." The representation of this self-awareness is absent in the first representative layer.[15]

This last point has an interesting implication. Indigenous peoples, from López Albújar's perspective, reject the way they appear to the Mistis. More specifically: they are aware of and reject the characterization of them as nostalgic and without care for the future. At the same time, from López Albújar's perspective, the only other context for their manifestation as "what they are" is their ayllu. It is precisely the attachment to their ayllu, however, that enforces the representation of their nostalgia and futural recklessness. Within the indigenista horizons in López Albújar's works, indigenous peoples' rejection of how they appear to the Mistis can bring them to also detach from their ayllu as the site for their authentic manifestation among themselves. They can be existentially suspended in an aporetic duality. In this duality, Indians reject their appearance in front of the Mistis but are irremediably trapped in it, without an alternative self-image and self-understanding beyond the viewpoint of the Mistis. They are existentially trapped in nostalgia and a carelessness about the future, disposed to these unavoidable appearances through self-hatred. Their self-awareness cannot overcome and define itself beyond the representations projected upon them.

Lopez Albújar writes about this duality and entrapment in relation to his representative work "This duality . . . is the one that determines his life [the indio's], the one that exhibits him underneath this double personality, which sometimes is disorienting and leads to errors, and other times makes one renounce one's observation deeming the Indian impenetrable." In this second representative layer, nostalgia and carelessness about the future as natural indigenous traits are put into question: their character as projections and as rooted in the context of coloniality has become evident. Now, instead, existential duality and self-hatred become objects of representation, representations of Indians trapped with self-awareness of the Mistis' projections of them. They are represented not as nostalgic, for example, but as trapped in the appearance of nostalgia. In López Albújar's view, this second order of representation constitutes the foremost challenge to his writing, one that he cannot overcome fully. It is the limit of his representative work. He cannot envision and represent the aporetic duality of indigenous existence. He has, effectively, two options: to either produce erroneous representations or, in a stunning turn within representation, to recognize this limit and project it onto indigenous peoples as their own characteristic. In this latter option, the limit of the indigenista writer's perspective becomes naturalized and represented as indigenous impenetrability. "Impenetrability" is a third basic representation of indigenous peoples in indigenista literature and operates in a second layer of representation. To the slippage in the first representative layer, one has to juxtapose a second slippage, namely, one in which the limit of indigenista representative power is itself represented as an aporia belonging to indigenous existence.[16]

The Third Representative Layer:
From Double Consciousness to Invisibility

The second representative layer engages a problematic similar to DuBois's double consciousness. DuBois states: "It is a peculiar sensation, this double-consciousness, this sense of always looking at one's self through the eyes of others, of measuring one's soul by the tape of a world that looks on in amused contempt and pity."[17] For DuBois, double consciousness is a defining experience for those who are oppressed on the basis of race. The predicament lies, in this context, in the fact that those who are racialized see the distorted, negative view of them held by those who racialize them, recognize that this view does not correspond to who they are and aspire to be, and despite this recognition, cannot construct a self-image that is not mediated by these negative projections of them because there is no alternative referential option that allows them to cultivate their self-understanding. This corresponds to the experience of Indians that López Albújar finds at the limits of his representative work.

DuBois captures this intersubjective dynamic through the image of a veil: "Then it dawned upon me with a certain suddenness that I was different from the others; or like, mayhap, in heart and life and longing, but shut out from the world by a vast veil." The veil signifies that racialized oppressed peoples are concealed from those who racialize them underneath their projections. The veil indicates concealment, but a concealment that is apparent only to those who are concealed. Despite this recognition and awareness of double consciousness, however, there is no way out of this concealment since there is no opportunity for a self-determined manifestation that would break through the veil. Being trapped in concealment is being trapped under the racialized projections that others impose on oneself.[18]

DuBois's double consciousness is at issue in my interpretation of the second representative layer of López Albújar's work but in a modified way. In my discussion above, the colonized are not the only ones aware of their entrapment in double consciousness. Indigenista writers, such as López Albújar, can also become aware of it even though they do not inhabit the same positionality as Indians. For López Albújar the most difficult task is to represent double consciousness as it is manifest in and for indigenous experience. This is a limit in indigenista representations that becomes, through a slippage, represented as an indigenous trait: "impenetrability." In this slippage, the aporia that indigenistas can face becomes represented as an aporia that constitutes the entrapment of "Indians" in their existential duality. In this sense, their existence is taken as not only aporetic when viewed from the outside, but as essentially aporetic. López Albújar, then, adds to DuBois's account a third perspective (that of the indigenista writer). The veil thickens.

Situated in the Andes under the complex system of gamonales and ayllus as differential spaces, the aporetic nature of indigenous double consciousness as it is treated in López Albújar's work is based on a futural sensibility, one that determines the representation of Indians from the other side of the colonial difference. It is due to this sensibility that life in the ayllu (located in the "past") appears to not be an option for the cultivation of self-understanding beyond the Mistis' gaze. That is, a temporality of pastness determines the entrapment in double consciousness. In this particular indigenista aesthetics, double consciousness is aporetic, impenetrable, and tangled up in futural, linear time, which sets the parameters of the Mistis' and even of López Albújar's own perspective. The neutrality of the indigenista writer's now shows itself to be an illusion.[19]

In this sense, indigenous peoples themselves would understand their double consciousness as aporetic if they shared this futural sensibility and understood their existence as somehow stuck in the past, as not having meaning and purpose in their present. Can one affirm this, or are there indications that indigenous peoples may be operating from a different temporal (and maybe even spatial) sensibility than that of the Mistis? This question will be addressed later. Now Mariátegui's comments on López Albújar's warning and the third representative layer of this indigenista's work are at issue.[20]

Mariátegui states, "The majority of the observations of López Albújar correspond to the attitude of the Indian in front of the whites, in front of the Misti. They represent the face that López Albújar, from his position, could bring into focus more." López Albújar situates himself in a privileged, neutral position as a writer: one from which an Indian double consciousness becomes apparent as an existential fact. Diverging from this indigenista's self-positioning, Mariátegui contextualizes this privileged position itself, questioning its neutrality and making apparent the limits of its scope. Mariátegui, more alert to ideological structures of coloniality, begins an interpretation of López Albújar's indigenista representations in terms of the shared positionality between the writer and the Mistis.[21]

This critical move defines the third representative layer (and implicitly assumes that the sensibility of futural temporality cannot be simply applied to indigenous peoples). The Indian duality or double consciousness appears to López Albújar as impenetrable because of his positionality and temporal sensibility. In this third representative layer, the limits of the indigenista's purview are not transferred to indigenous existence as manifesting its impenetrability, they simply remain as limits, blind spots of a representative function anchored in a dominant perspective.

At this juncture, there is a transition from an aesthetics of indigenous impenetrability to one of indigenous invisibilities. In this aesthetics, the representations, paradoxically, capture not what indigenous peoples are (nostalgic, without care for the future, or impenetrable), but the way they elude representations. In this sense, accessible through a transrepresentative approach, the representative limits of indigenismo become apparent as limits in the same movement in which indigenous peoples withdraw from the perspective of the indigenista writer and from representations of Indians. Invisible, but manifest in their invisibility, is not the same as being concealed or impenetrable. In this aesthetics of invisibility, the dominance of the indigenista perspective is undermined in a movement of self-overcoming in and of this aesthetic form.[22]

MARIÁTEGUI'S AND CORONADO'S DISAGREEMENT AND A MODIFICATION OF DUBOIS'S DOUBLE CONSCIOUSNESS

This discussion sheds light on the extent of Coronado's and Mariátegui's disagreement introduced at the beginning this chapter. The issue can be articulated as follows: Coronado and Mariátegui agree in that indigenista representations need to be critiqued insofar as they are a projection from the Mistis and lettered class onto indigenous peoples. Does this mean that their disagreement amounts to Coronado seeing such a critique as external to indigenismo while Mariátegui finds it suggested within it?

If the only difference between Coronado's and Mariátegui's position is about the externality or internality of the critique of indigenista representations, then Mariátegui's position does not open up significant options beyond Coronado's critique. This is, however, not the case. Coronado's critique of indigenista representations leads him to posit the possibility of an authentic aesthetics of representation by indigenous peoples themselves as an alternative (one that

Mariátegui also entertains in the *Seven Essays*). In other words, Coronado's critique of indigenista representations is not a critique of it in view of different modalities (or layers) of representation. Mariátegui's transrepresentative approach, as developed here, offers such a critique. It takes indigenismo to the limits of its representative power and, at this limit, attests to the withdrawal of indigenous peoples from its representative grasp in a movement of self-overcoming leading to an aesthetics of invisibilities.

There are two implications of this transrepresentative approach that go beyond Coronado's critique. First, this approach shows indigenismo as able to support a movement of deconstruction of the colonial sensibilities that condition its representativity. Second, the aesthetics of invisibilities reveals the possibility of an indigenous praxis that is not wholly determined and accessible within the horizons (especially temporal ones) of the Mistis' and lettered class's perspective. This would be a praxis that exceeds the sense of the economically, socially, and politically dominant structures that oppress indigenous peoples. A space of indigenous praxis emerges, then, as a possibility suggested by the invisibilities in this aesthetic movement. Specifically, the ayllu, the space that is represented through nostalgia and impenetrability as temporalized in the past, comes to be released to possibilities (including temporalizations) at the borders of the representations that belong to indigenismo's perspective. And in this release, options for indigenous praxis could arise even from the positionality of indigenous peoples themselves without being submitted to essentialized representations of Indian identities.

Going back to DuBois's double consciousness may shed light on this last point. The pathology of double consciousness lies in the fact that the racialized subject is veiled and only seen (even by herself) through the projections of the racist gaze. One way out of this predicament, and the one that DuBois pursued, is to enable the racialized subject to cultivate representations of herself beyond the purview of the racist gaze. In this way, the racialized subject would develop a sense of self-identity that would allow her to counter the racist gaze and demand entrance into an equalized dynamic of recognition with it. This option is also one that aligns with Coronado's call for an authentically indigenous aesthetics of representation.

Another way out of the constraints of double consciousness is that, instead of engaging in acts of self-representation seeking a direct recognition, the colonized could turn their invisibility into a site for praxis in which they give themselves space for self-cultivation and resistance. Certainly, this space may allow for options for self-representation (Mariátegui is open to these) but, and this is the crucial difference, the gaze of the oppressor would be destabilized not only through these acts of self-representation but also through the way the colonized play with their own invisibility with indifference to the need for recognition. In this gesture, indigenismo partakes in a movement of self-overcoming and belongs within a long lineage of resistance and aesthetics of invisibilities that can be traced back to the beginning of colonialism in the Andes.[23]

MARÍA LUGONES'S INVISIBILITIES

Lugones begins her chapter "Structure/Anti-structure and Agency under Oppression" in *Pilgrimages/Peregrinajes* with a concern that puts her in dialogue with Mariátegui. She focuses on the problem of how an oppressed subject can carry out her own liberation in light of theories that configure oppression as an inescapable situation. She writes, "I claim that the account of oppression itself leaves the subject trapped inescapably in the oppressive system. The logic of the particular form of oppression leads me to understand it as inescapable." Her interpretation of Marx is especially insightful: "He gives great importance to class struggle and the production of class consciousness. But given his account of the logic of capitalism, I do not see how that is subjectively possible. I need to understand the subjective mechanisms of its possibility. If class consciousness is to be produced through necessities of particular unstable structures rather than through the subjects' exercises of their agency, such production is uninformative from the point of view advanced here." Unearthing possibilities of liberating agencies in addition to the identification of structural instabilities is the same issue that leads Mariátegui to be interested in indigenous socialism as a political myth and faith. His study of gamonalismo shows that the identification of structural instabilities on their own cannot reveal the subjective conditions for liberation. Even though Mariátegui does not explicitly posit the oppressed indigenous peoples as inescapably trapped in the system, his analysis of the assumed subhumanity of indigenous peoples under gamonalismo, including how gamonalismo undermines indigenous agency and autonomy, can be seen as precisely the kind of theory of inescapability that Lugones refers to.

At the same time, Mariátegui's socialist faith contains an indigenista logic of redemption that is a condition for liberatory agencies that appeals to a continuous history of Andean peoples, to a substantial Indian transhistorical identity, and to investments in possibilities of restoration of indigenous economies beyond legacies of colonialism. Yet this redemptive logic is at odds with Mariátegui's understanding of revolutionary political deeds (since they disseminate temporal trajectories and definitive futural projections) and of transculturation (since it undermines notions of continuous, cohesive, transhistorical identities, and monolithic configurations of cultural legacies, positing instead multifocal positionalities and subjectivities). By putting Mariátegui in dialogue with Lugones, one can delve deeper into these tensions.

The key to Lugones's account of subjective possibilities of liberation is the relationship between ontological pluralism and the practical syllogism (a reasoning that ends in action) as a volitional structure. She understands oppression as stunting the articulation of effective practical syllogisms by the oppressed. The case of the arrogantly perceived woman is helpful here: "The act of arrogating someone's substance ends the possibility of the subject's giving a practical syllogism that she can put into action and is not severely affected by the practical syllogism of the arrogant perceiver." That is, the male oppressor interferes with the syllogism of the oppressed by not allowing her to actualize her syllogism. The male oppressor can also impose his own practical syllogism on the oppressed so that "she chooses the alternative the arrogant perceiver wants her to choose." The power of the oppressor, then, is the elimination of choices for the oppressed that are not in his interest. The disruption of the practical syllogism of the oppressed by the oppressor can happen in three interrelated levels: the oppressor can undermine the processes through which the oppressed form intentions, the oppressor can block the passage from intention to action in the syllogism of the oppressed, and the oppressor can impose his will so that the oppressed generates syllogisms that serve him.[24]

One could argue that the indigenista logic of redemption is not at odds with an unarrogated practical syllogism of the oppressed. A continuous Indian identity and an appeal to redemption from coloniality can operate as an ideal that would direct indigenous praxis. The economic form of an indigenous nation in particular could guide an attempt to dismantle gamonalismo, allowing for the kind of deliberative, syllogistic reasoning that leads to the specificity of concrete action, even if this deliberative process is not fully explored by Mariátegui. But the identity Indian is a colonial projection onto indigenous peoples, and one could argue that the indigenous nation is as well. Moreover, in Mariátegui's own text, especially when the supposed passivity of Indian surfaces, socialism begins to appear as an imposition on indigenous peoples. That is, a redemptive logic could distort the formation of liberatory intentions by the colonized, it could block syllogisms that they articulate on the basis of their geopolitical positionalities, and it could itself be a syllogistic structure that submits their will, furthering their subservience. If this is the case, then, the redemptive dimension of Mariátegui's indigenous socialism could reinforce the dependency of indigenous peoples operative under coloniality.

Ontological pluralism allows Lugones to undermine the hold of arrogated practical syllogisms, especially when she writes from the experience of "bicultural people who are also victims of ethnocentric racism in a society that has one of those cultures as subordinate and the other as dominant"; that is, people within the colonial difference embodying different cultural loci across power differentials. Their multiple selves enable them to form unarrogated practical syllogisms, even if they are structurally oppressed. Lugones writes that such bicultural people "are very familiar with experiencing themselves as more than one: having desires, character, and personality traits that are different in one reality than in the other, and acting, enacting, animating their bodies, having thoughts, feeling the emotions, in ways that are different in one reality than in the other."[25]

This is an experience of at least two positionalities, without a substantial self that brings a larger, synthetic perspective that encompasses its multiplicity. The proliferation of sites of experience means that such multiple selves tend to form practical syllogisms within different realities that hold "such different possibilities for them." Lugones's point is that the oppressed, not being fully subsumed under one social and cultural referent, are in fact, always already articulating practical syllogisms in different realities, and that part of their oppression in this regard comes from understanding these syllogisms from the dominant perspective that arrogates their existence, that is, within the possibilities of the reality in which they are deemed to be subhuman. In this case, recalling practical syllogisms formed in other realities may not preserve their integrity and efficacy: "If one can remember the intentions of the person one is in the other world and tries to enact them in the other, one can see that many times one cannot do so because the action does not have any meaning or has a very different sort of meaning than the one it has in the other reality." Peruvian indigenismo, in the works of López Albújar in particular, is full of examples of this dynamic. Practices that for an indigenous person have meaning and purpose in their ayllu, are emptied out of significance in the dominant reality of the Misti and in the cities. One can imagine that a practical syllogism operating within a subaltern collectivist environment would be nonsensical within an individualist one, for example.[26]

Nevertheless, Lugones finds in the multiple selves of the oppressed a possibility to resist the arrogation of practical syllogisms and even produce liberatory ones. The key statement is "One can see that the very same person may remember herself in another reality and thus be able to form practical syllogisms that have *intentions* that the person she is in another reality would have."[27] Lugones does not pause in the implications of this statement, but it can be unpacked in the context of subjective conditions for liberation. This suggests that an indigenous person, for example, in a gamonal or in the city, could remember herself in her ayllu articulating practical syllogisms for the continuance of her personal and cultural survival that are sustained by, and meaningful in, her environment. She could, then, preserve that memory in order to articulate the intentions driving those syllogisms to form other syllogisms more viable in the gamonal or the city. This would allow her to exist in oppressive contexts with the intentions she has cultivated in her community. If the possibility to do so is blocked, she could find ways to undo those blocks, engaging in resistances articulated with liberatory sense and enacted through practical syllogisms effective in oppressive contexts.

At this juncture, one can see the depth of this statement: "But, of course, her actions would not be visible or heard or understood in the reality in which she performs them in that case. That is the meaning of invisibility." The oppressed, in so far as she remembers herself in the way just discussed, is invisible to the dominant perspective that also dictates the limits of the realm of the visible: her intentions, that is, the meaning and purpose of her actions, do not appear in this realm. This means that invisibility is an ambiguous state. It can be debilitating because visibility validates and gives recognition to one's actions and intentions. But it can also be the condition for the possibility of liberatory praxis, in so far as it allows the oppressed to articulate practical syllogisms that are not mandated by the oppressors even if operative invisibly in their domains.[28]

This is where Lugones's argument and Mariátegui's transrepresentative approach to indigenismo come together. One could understand invisibility in Mariátegui's thought as the moment when the oppressor's perspective recognizes its limits. Exposed to those limits as invisibilities, and open to the possibility of indigenous praxis to operate beyond those limits, as invisible practices, may be the beginning for dominant social and political structures' hold over the oppressor (even if this realm is articulated from the oppressor's locus) to loosen up. This would be an exposure of the oppressor to liminal spaces across power differentials and cultural loci that sustain practices and intentions that do not conform to the totalizing senses of dominant worlds. This would come to pass without the requirement of visibility; without having to fully see the oppressed. In this regard, it is as if Lugones and Mariátegui are thinking from the opposite sides of the invisibility of the oppressed.

Lugones summarizes her argument thus: "So, the connection between the practical syllogism, ontological plurality, and liberatory oppression theory lies in the fact that the oppressed know themselves in realities in which they are able to form intentions that are not among the alternatives that are possible in the world in which they are brutalized and oppressed." Putting this in relation to Mariátegui's indigenismo, and if we turn to our example of the indigenous sub-ject above, it is clear that she inhabits a liminal state that allows for the critique of the reality of the oppressor. Her ability to remember herself in her commun-ity when she is in the city, and to retain the intention of syllogisms formed in the former to form others in the latter, means that she understands both realities at the same time. Lugones writes, "One understands oneself in every world in which one remembers oneself to the extent that one understands that world." This simultaneity and multiple foci means that she is somewhat detached not only from the reality that oppresses her but also from her community and is engaged in at least a double critique, including that of her own community. She is in a liminal state, in "an interstice from where one can mostly stand criti-cally toward different structures." Lugones emphasizes that liminality is a state that is not reducible to one of the realities that the oppressed subject inhabits. This is why: "In the liminal phase, there are no structural descriptions, so the liminal subject does not stand with respect to others in the limen as in a hier-archy. . . . The experience of victims of ethnocentric racism of moving across realities, of being different in each, and of reasoning practically differently in each, can be understood as liminal." The colonized, in this case, may draw from her community in order to articulate practical syllogisms that imply resistance and liberation in the reality of the oppressor, but she is not simply positioned within it. Liminally, attached and detached from her community, engaged in double critique, the cultural horizon of her community does not contain her. This liminal positionality eludes the coherent cultural loci of enunciation, and cultural rigidity, implied in the redemptive logic of Mariátegui's indigenous socialism and the stability of the identity "Indian" in ways that are, rather, closer to Mariátegui's transcultural strain.[29]

Moreover, Lugones's account of the crossing of worlds disrupts the tempo-rality of redemption and of indigenous impenetrability. The indigenous subject, in this sense, does not relate to the reality of her community as in the past, or as something to be redeemed in a futural projection. She, thus, eludes the hold of redemptive, liberatory projects thrust upon her. Otherwise the temporal projections of her community would be reduced to those viable within the domain of the oppressor. Her community is a reality in the present for her, one in which she can form practical syllogisms that turn liberatory in oppressive contexts and is, thus, outside nostalgic entrapments and redemptive logics. It would be more accurate to say that her sense of liberatory agency is sustained by spatial possibilities rather than linear temporal ones. In this regard, the indigenous subject, for example, moves from one reality to the other, and her liminality carries with it spatial rather than temporal senses. In this respect, this disruption of time by space neutralizes liberatory investments in progressive temporalities. Exposing Mariátegui to Lugones's thought in this way, taking invisibility as a notion where these two thinkers could come together, allows for dislodging Mariátegui's thought from the representational strictures of indigenismo and engaging with his aesthetics as a dimension of his liberatory theory that could inform an account of the possibility of revolutionary praxis beyond redemption.[30] Taking this aesthetic opening as a cue, in the next chapter I will revisit Mariátegui's aesthetics in view of his notion of myth.

In a similar vein, Alejandro Vallega focuses on the possibility of a struggle for liberation at the level of sensibility, one through which the affective hold coloniality has on the oppressed could be undone. In particular, Vallega focuses on a linear and sequential temporal sensibility in which the colonized is always placed behind European civilization as underdeveloped and barbaric and on the coloniality of images where the oppressors exhaust the field of representation, including the representativity of oppressed groups, as a way to further structures of coloniality. Vallega is interested in a decolonial aesthetics that can undo these two aspects of coloniality at the level of sensibility. Mariátegui's transrepresentative approach to indigenismo fits within this determination of a decolonial aesthetics, it exposes the linear temporality that determines the projection of both the Mistis and indigenista writers onto indigenous peoples, and, through an aesthetic of invisibilities, unsettles the totalizing reach of the coloniality of images. A thorough encounter between Vallega and Mariátegui would be productive here.[31]

With regard to an aesthetics of invisibilities as a decolonial aesthetics, Vallega studies the work of Alfredo Jaar, the *Rwanda Project* in particular. In it Vallega finds a particular play with images in which Jaar "has created not an image but a space that cannot be made into an image to serve the economy of the coloniality of power, knowledge and thought and its pernicious temporality." In my terms, Jaar is engaged with invisibilities. One of the effects of this, according to Vallega, is that "One's gaze has found a mirror—a most damning image, the gaze of the damned that no longer stands outside of one's 'objective' viewing and comprehension, outside of one's claim to objective (untouchable) rationality and humanity."[32]

NOTES

1. For a complementary essay to this chapter, see O. Rivera, "Hermenéutica, representatividad y espacio." This chapter is intended as a response to Fanon,

Black Skin, White Masks. For a thorough analysis of Mariátegui's relationship to indigenismo, see Beigel, "Mariátegui." In regard to the representativity of the Indian in the *Seven Essays*, see O. Rivera, "Image of the Indio."

2. Coronado complements this argument in a later essay, stating that Mariátegui's work in the journal *Labor* did not conform to his indigenista representation of the Indian. This does not change the tenor of my response here. See Coronado, "Periódico *Labor*," 353–78.

3. For a parallel interpretation of Mariátegui's reading of López Albújar, see Escajadillo, *Mariátegui*, 127–233.

4. Coronado, *Andes Imagined*, 50. See also O. Rivera, "Image of the Indio," 142–45.

5. This representation appears in the *Seven Essays* as the image of the indio. Cornejo Polar has a different reading of Mariátegui in terms of modernity and Andean culture, where he finds productive options for this relationship. See Cornejo Polar, *Writing in the Air*, 131–36. Cornejo Polar may be alluding to Quijano's early reading of Mariátegui here.

6. Coronado understands the importance of this point for his argument and repeatedly points out that Mariátegui did not have a "pure" contact with indigenous populations.

7. This convergence of aesthetics and politics is also the focus of Mariátegui's interest in surrealism. See chapter 6 in this volume. For Sánchez's own engagement with indigenismo, see Sánchez, *Indianismo y indigenismo*.

8. This is evident in Mariátegui's account of the different kinds of indigenismo in the last essay of the *Seven Essays*. For a parallel discussion of the debate between Mariátegui and Sánchez, see Podestá, "Indigenismo," 312–15.

9. By "decolonial" here, I mean a critical engagement that deconstructs ideological, economic, and political structures that continue colonial dynamics of oppression. The implicit question that I pose in this chapter and the next is whether Mariátegui can be read as effecting a decolonial turn. A helpful text in this respect is Grosfoguel, "Epistemic Decolonial Turn." In the *Seven Essays*, Mariátegui understands the limits of indigenismo; he is explicit in maintaining that indigenismo is not an aesthetics of self-representation of indigenous peoples.

10. Mariátegui, "Indigenismo y socialismo," 508–9.

11. Mariátegui, "Indigenismo y socialismo," 508–9. See chapter 3 in this volume for the connection between Valcárcel and the indigenista logic of redemption.

12. This section on nostalgia, especially in its temporal dimension, could be extended into issues of memory and trauma in the context of coloniality. I am thinking here of Oyarzún, "Memory." My interest in approaching decolonial aesthetics on this basis brings my work into dialogue with Acosta López, "Gramáticas." See also Mariátegui, "Indigenismo y socialismo," 510.

13. López Albújar's stories in particular focus on indigenous nostalgia. Mariátegui finds this representation in the whole of the movement and even in Vallejo's poetry, as is clear from the *Seven Essays*. Another important interlocutor here, for its representation of the Indian, is Vargas Llosa, *Utopía arcaíca*.

14. Mariátegui, "Indigenismo y socialismo," 510. Ibid.

15. Mariátegui, "Indigenismo y socialismo," 510.

16. Mariátegui, "Indigenismo y socialismo," 510. "Impenetrability" appears in addition to "nostalgia" and being "without care for the future."

17. DuBois *Reader*.

18. DuBois *Reader*, 28.

19. This discussion is connected to the problematic of the temporality of the perception of race. See Fanon, *Black Skin, White Masks*, 89–94; Alia Al-Saji, "Too Late"; Al-Saji, "Phenomenology of Hesitation"; and Ngo, *Habits of Racism*.

20. Sanjinés could be another productive interlocutor here, especially because of his attentiveness to indigenous exteriority and temporal and spatial sensibilities. He writes,

> the paradox we face is that we have opted for the epistemological outside of Western time, and have accepted the ideologies of our colonizers du jour, while always paying tribute to the time of progress, which, though we have not learned to administer it well, nevertheless molds the supposed essence of our people, so that we forget to check it against that other time, the time of our own original peoples that I marked by a profoundly different ethics of being.... Indigenous experience has a different locus of enunciation. It is an exterior locus, one that uses its exterior positioning to break with the rationality of the discourse of power. This locus differs from the outside of mestizo-creole elite discourse which observes the world around it by adjusting the world to supposedly undeniable and universal Western values.... opposition is always destined for reconciliation, provided the correct logical process can be instigated. Indigenous exteriority is, instead, fundamentally spatial, alien to Western and European perspectives." (Sanjinés, *Mestizaje*, 8–10)

21. Mariátegui, "Indigenismo y socialismo," 510.

22. Cornejo Polar has already suggested the impact of Mariátegui's aesthetics. His aesthetics of invisibilities could amount to a further contribution between Rama's transculturation and Cornejo Polar's heterogeneity. See Cornejo Polar, "*Indigenismo*," and Cornejo Polar, "*Mestizaje*." See also Rama, *Transculturación*, 32–39.

23. At first, invisibility and lack of recognition appear to be merely aspects of oppression. What I am proposing here, following Lugones, is to understand invisibility as a dimension of resistance, as it appears in *Pilgrimages*. Practices of invisibility, then, may ultimately be ambivalent. For an account of indigenous practices of invisibilities in the colonial era, see Dean, *Inka Bodies*.

24. For theorists of ontological pluralism, Lugones cites Bartky, "Toward a Phenomenology." See also Frye, *Politics of Reality*, and Harstock, "Feminist Standpoint," among others. See further Lugones, *Pilgrimages/Peregrinajes*, 56–57.

25. Ibid.

26. Ibid. See the movement from the community to the city in Ushanan Hampi, for example. There López Albújar writes about the exile of indigenous peoples from their communities: "El *jitarishum* es la muerte civil del condenado, una muerte de la que jamás se vuelve a la rehabilitación; que condena al indio al ostracismo perpetuo y parece marcarle con un signo que le cierra para siempre las puertas de la comunidad. Se le deja solamente la vida para que vague con ella a cuestas por quebradas, cerros, punas y bosques, o para que baje a vivir en las ciudades bajo la ferula del *misti*; lo que para un indio altivo y amante de las Alturas es un suplicio y una vergüenza" López Albújar, *Cuentos andinos*.

27. Lugones, *Pilgrimages/Peregrinajes*, 58. Italics mine.

28. Lugones, *Pilgrimages/Peregrinajes*, 58.

29. Lugones, *Pilgrimages/Peregrinajes*, 59, 61.

30. This account of invisibilities in Lugones seems to appear later as a methodology that shows awareness of the limits of a Eurocentered feminism to articulate critical perspectives from an indigenous positionality. See Lugones, "Toward a Decolonial Feminism," and Lugones, "Heterosexualism."

31. See Vallega, *Latin American Philosophy*, 196–208.

32. Vallega, *Latin American Philosophy*, 215, 216.

SIX

—ₘₙ—

AESTHETIC DISCIPLINE

Mariátegui through Quijano and Flores Galindo

THE LAST CHAPTER revealed an aesthetic opening to liberatory praxis, an opening at the level of sensibility and imagination that can constitute a disposition that is not attached to a view of the liberatory praxis of the oppressed that fits the sense of one dominant world with defined social and political structures. This suggests an untethered liberatory praxis released from the hold of stable identities and from the draw of futural, progressive, and redemptive temporalities. This chapter continues to pursue the relationship between aesthetics and liberation in Mariátegui's socialism and revisits his notion of myth. This pursuit leads to the articulation of a mode of aesthetic discipline that sustains a form of liberatory praxis that does not have redemptive investments. The analysis in this chapter is informed by a comparative reading of Aníbal Quijano's and Alberto Flores Galindo's interpretations of Mariátegui.[1]

THEORY AND PRAXIS

Aporetic conditions for theorizing direct my reading of Mariátegui's *Seven Essays* and allows me to explore Aníbal Quijano's and Alberto Flores Galindo's conflicting interpretations of him. Mariátegui writes: "I think that it is impossible to apprehend in one theory the entire panorama of the contemporary world. That it is impossible, above all, to fix its movement in one theory. We have to explore it, episode by episode, facet by facet. Our judgment and imagination will always feel to be lagging behind the totality of the phenomenon."[2]

One can find in theorizing the intention to grasp the totality of the contemporary world, an intention that fails because of this phenomenon's movement.

In view of the problem, Mariátegui does not seem to prescribe a proliferation of theories that would, by complementing each other, apprehend such a totality. Among other difficulties, it seems that he would find in such proliferation a dissemination of theoretical positions that is not conducive to an effective and consistent practical revolutionary intervention. Thus, he retains the practical exigency of facing the contemporary world through a defined theoretical perspective (Marxism in his case), yet he theorizes without a totalizing disposition. His ambivalence prioritizes praxis, which determines the meaning of terms such as *truth, interpretation,* and *method* in his lexicon and politicizes all his theoretical endeavors. Both Quijano and Flores Galindo are attentive to the emphasis on praxis, especially the latter in his concern with Mariátegui's thoughts on utopias. There is no conflict between theory and praxis here, insofar as theorizing is understood within the immediacy, restricted horizons, volatility, and objectives of praxis.[3]

QUIJANO'S EARLY INTRODUCTION TO MARIÁTEGUI AND FLORES GALINDO'S INTERPRETATION

Quijano's early engagement with Mariátegui resonates with this theoretical approach. He attempts to show that Mariátegui retains a strict theoretical Marxism, even if grounded in praxis. He maintains that Mariátegui's Marxism is ultimately not infused and distorted by religiosity and the mythical, voluntarist characteristics of an open Marxism, as some argue. Quijano's account recognizes, then, the subjectivity operative in embedding theory in praxis and its disavowal of systematicity, but he also conceives of a strictly Marxist methodology that is not undermined by the emphasis on praxis. As to the quote above, Mariátegui's Marxism appears to Quijano as the best theoretical approach to trace the movement of the contemporary world "episode by episode, facet by facet" and thus to disclose revolutionary political options that are contextually and temporally effective.[4]

Flores Galindo's approach to Mariátegui may well fall into what Quijano dismissively characterizes as an open Marxism. He focuses on Mariátegui's religiosity as a connecting thread throughout his works that predates his Marxism, determining his Marxism in unorthodox ways. He also identifies an agonic religious sensibility that grounds his practical and theoretical endeavors, as well as key moments in his writings and positions such as his controversies with Haya de la Torre and the Third International. Flores Galindo is sensitive to the way theoretical framings, including Marxism, will always lag behind the totality of the phenomenon. He is concerned that this lag will fail to elicit and direct praxis unless infused by a faith and commitment to a myth that moves multitudes in political struggle. He argues that Mariátegui's notion of myth, as it relates to utopia, can address this problem. In this respect, Flores Galindo sees Mariátegui's Marxism as determined by heterogeneous religious sensibilities, even those of surviving Andean indigenous communities, submitting Marxism to traditions and lineages foreign to it. Thus, Flores Galindo maintains that, for Mariátegui, socialism not only implies Marxist theory, but, more important, is also a faith that is a form of agonic sensibility that can arise from various geopolitical and historical loci.[5]

QUIJANO'S *REENCUENTRO Y DEBATE: UNA INTRODUCCIÓN A MARIÁTEGUI* (1979)

Quijano recognizes that one finds in Mariátegui's writings a religious sensibility that informs his Marxism. He therefore notes the "agonistic tension between a metaphysical conception of existence, the nourishment of a heroic will for action, and the necessary implications of the adherence to Marxism."[6] A central part of his interpretation consists of arguing that Mariátegui's metaphysical proclivities can be excised from the core of his thought, leaving intact a "proper" Marxist theoretical position.[7]

The issue, of course, is what Quijano means by this "Marxist position," since Mariátegui's piecemeal engagement with Marx, for example, left out essential parts of Marx's political economy. Quijano draws from Antonio Melis's influential interpretation that sees Mariátegui as able to "situate the specific traits of an economic-social form within a general model of historical development, which is the only thing that gives an authentically scientific value to Marxism." Quijano underscores Mariátegui's focus on economic-social forms as the basis for understanding political realities and his attention to the geohistorical specificities of these forms, situating them in their appropriate historical processes. Following Melis, for Quijano these two aspects position Mariátegui squarely within Marxism and allow him to elaborate "fundamental ideas about the character and the modalities of the Peruvian revolution." Quijano points out a third aspect that Melis seems to miss: Melis's account does not address the "political implications of such an effort to the character of the Peruvian revolutionary process." In other words, and this is not fully fleshed out in Quijano's analysis, the missing aspect is that Mariátegui disavows a distanced theoretical disposition and inhabits the very historical processes that he reveals, theorizing from a commitment to political praxis in order to clarify his own situation in the midst of and for the sake of revolutionary change. The third aspect of Mariátegui's

Marxism, then, is the practical political disposition that grounds his theorizing and that places him within a lineage of Latin American philosophy as situated critical thinking within a revolutionary political horizon.[8]

Quijano, probably inspired by the eleventh thesis on Feuerbach and its resonance with Mariátegui's work, extends Melis's "authentically scientific value" of Marxism to include a revolutionary-situated thinking and characterizes it as "the quality of a frame and starting point to investigate, know, explain, interpret and *change a concrete historical reality, from within itself.*" He contrasts this quality with the tendency to "stick to the 'application' of the conceptual Marxist apparatus as a classificatory and nominative template, marinated in ideological rhetoric, upon a determinate social reality."[9] Quijano's move here to stay true to the Marxism in Mariátegui's work is subtle and complex. It leads him to posit an authentic Marxism that rejects Marxism as a universal and totalizing theory to be applied indiscriminately, even finding in it the possibility of going beyond Eurocentrism. In this sense, then, Mariátegui's statement on the limits of theorizing would be enunciated from within the strict bounds of an authentic Marxism.[10]

Before I turn to Quijano's interpretation of the *Seven Essays* through this approach, I will look at his excision of the religious and metaphysical proclivities in Mariátegui, which is a fundamental step in his analysis. In this regard, Quijano takes on the responsibility of laying out Mariátegui's Marxism to an extent beyond where Mariátegui himself went.

The Metaphysical "Problem" in Mariátegui

Quijano identifies two problem areas in the way Mariátegui "assumes Marxism." The first problem area is "The unsolved tension between a conception of Marxism as a theory of society and history, and as a method of interpretation and revolutionary action, on the one hand, and a philosophy of history, open to receive the waters of other philosophical currents that, according to Mariátegui, could contribute to the permanence of the will to revolutionary action, on the other." The first side of this tension reflects Mariátegui's authentic Marxism, and the second, the need for a philosophy of history that would sustain the revolutionary will, is the one that has to be excised. The first question that Quijano's analysis brings up is, Why does Mariátegui feel the need to include a philosophy of history? The easy answer would be that Mariátegui is concerned with generating such a permanent revolutionary will. Quijano argues, however, that Mariátegui is not concerned with this at all because Mariátegui's experience is one of a long history of revolutionary action, especially among indigenous movements, which would make his interest in a mobilizing philosophy of history come across as redundant. So why does Mariátegui seem to complement his Marxism in this way?[11]

Quijano begins by presenting evidence that Mariátegui in fact evokes a philosophy of history in *Defensa del Marxismo*, the only text where Mariátegui engages Marxism in a sustained way. In this text Quijano finds that "Mariátegui appears to be fundamentally concerned with problems of an ethical-philosophical character . . . in particular with the problem of determinism and will, or of materialism and the production of spiritual values." In fact, Marxism in this text seems secondary, simply a method guided by a revolutionary will that directs history and is invested in spiritual and even religious sources of meaning. Quijano does not dispute the methodological character of Mariátegui's Marxism and bolsters a version of Mariátegui as a religious thinker that instrumentalizes Marxism by quoting him: "All attempts to . . . catalogue Marxist criticism as a simple scientific theory are in vain, while it operates in history as a gospel and method of a mass movement." Quijano continues by underscoring the sources of Mariátegui's philosophy of history: Croce, Sorel, Bergson, James, and Pareto. He concludes thus: "In this way, a curious amalgam of philosophical tendencies, all of them not only foreign but opposed to Marxism, enter to compose a sort of philosophy of history that, in Mariátegui's view, not only doesn't contradict, but even complements and enriches . . . Marxism."[12]

How Can Quijano, Then, Interpret Mariátegui as a Strict Marxist?

Quijano's solution to this first problem area has two aspects, an explicit and an implicit one. The explicit one is straightforward. Those who attribute a spiritualized Marxism to Mariátegui do not understand his materialism in the correct way. They need to note statements such as the following that dismiss the "false position . . . of supposing that a materialist conception of the universe is not able to produce great spiritual values."[13] That is, Mariátegui does not oppose materialism to spiritual values. He affirms the spiritual aspect of revolutionary praxis without positing metaphysical structures that precede such praxis. Mariátegui believes that spiritual values emerge out of a concrete existence embedded and determined by material structural conditions. These spiritual values can even enact political change.

Once Mariátegui's materialism is framed in this way, his supposed spiritual-metaphysical proclivity boils down to recognizing "the fundamental place of praxis in the determination of history, and the essential relation between the action of objective conditions (that are extraneous to consciousness) and conscious action, *as both participating in the same laws of the movement of society,* as reciprocally active moments in the constitution of the global praxis within society."[14]

In other words, in Quijano's account, materialism for Mariátegui is the interaction between material objective conditions and the human life embedded in them, an interaction that provokes conscious action in response to its objective historical conditions and that constantly yields new social and political environments. In this sense, actions begin at the level of basic human emotive and life-enhancing sensibilities that are unmediated by, and prior to, metaphysical structures of meaning. The position that critiques or characterizes Mariátegui's materialism as spiritualized restricts the meaning of materialism to the immediate efficacy of objective material conditions, something that for Mariátegui was ontologically untenable. The explicit solution to the first problem area, which Quijano labels as ethical-metaphysical, then, amounts to the ontological clarification of Mariátegui's materialism as not positing metaphysical or theological structures as the ground of praxis, while affirming a materially mediated spiritual, agonic praxis.

The implicit solution to this first problem area is at the core of Quijano's analysis. It concerns Marxism as a method. Quijano acknowledges that Mariátegui sees Marxism in this way, the issue is to explain what he intends by doing so. Quijano is critical of taking method to mean here simply a tool, that is, implying an instrumentalization of Marxism, stripping it of any claims to truth. Quijano seems to think that for Mariátegui to be a genuine Marxist, Marxism must provide him with a sense of truth. But what can this sense be? That is the question that Quijano leaves unanswered and is one of the limits of his account. This question is especially pressing since he is aware of Mariátegui's rejection of a theoretical totalizing and universal disposition. It is, then, up to the reader to fill this gap while remaining oriented by Quijano's analysis.

At first the answer is straightforward: if Mariátegui rejects a theoretical truth, he may well be engaging Marxism in terms of practical truth. In this respect, there is a long philosophical tradition, including the truth involved in Aristotelian prudence and in Heidegger's appropriation and elaboration of it into hermeneutics and fundamental ontology in the 1920s (that is, contemporaneously with Mariátegui). In this sense of practical truth, a particular kind of interpretive reasoning yields a contextualized truth linked to deliberation (rather than universal reasoning) and choice. Such reasoning seems to apply to Mariátegui's understanding of Marxism as method: it is an interpretive account that clarifies a specific economic, social, and political juncture and elicits political action as a moment of choice. The important point here is that Marxism is not a method as a tool wielded by a subject or a collective that has grasped a truth beforehand. It, rather, is a hermeneutic method that through its explanatory power carries and brings the subject and collective to a practical, situated truth.[15]

The Permanence of Revolutionary Will

This takes me to Quijano's second problem area in Mariátegui's socialism: "the insistence in the centrality of individual will, as a foundation for historic praxis [acción histórica] and, for the sake of this praxis, the insistence on a nourishing faith and a metaphysical foundation for the restoration of a human morality cleansed of the ballast of bourgeois conscience." This statement needs to be contextualized in terms of my previous discussion of Mariátegui's materialism, specifically with regard to Mariátegui's rejection of metaphysical structures that is related to his reading of Nietzsche and Marx. He affirms, however, another sense of metaphysics, namely, one that is a faith that sustains and conducts revolutionary praxis. Furthermore, *morality* ["moral"] here does not mean a dogmatic sense of right and wrong but a disciplined comportment that gives permanence to a revolutionary will guided by faith. The metaphysical operation that supports such discipline is that of myths, in Mariátegui's view. Socialism as myth, as an aspect of his materialism, has to be brought to the fore and understood, Quijano argues, because it secures revolutionary action and conditions the possibility of such action in a bourgeois environment that constantly undermines the discipline and permanence of the revolutionary will. The question of discipline and myth goes beyond the issue of practical truth to the conditions for the permanent commitment to revolutionary praxis in the context of capitalism.[16]

The socialist myth responds, according to Mariátegui, to a human need that has to be recognized and affirmed, especially in his particular historical moment. Quijano quotes Mariátegui: "only myth possesses the precious virtue of fulfilling human's deep self." This affirmation happens in the context of bourgeois affective orders defined, instead, by nihilism and positivism. These two involve sensibilities that are for Mariátegui affective orders that undermine the possibility of revolutionary action. The bourgeoisie is, thus, not only a social, economic, and political structure but also an affective structure that has to be overcome. Mariátegui engages the bourgeoisie at an affective level as part of revolutionary activity and understands affect as a field of struggles for liberation. Or, more succinctly, and this is the most important insight here, in order to secure the conditions for revolutionary praxis, Mariátegui affirms a discipline and faith based on a combative and creative sensibility over against bourgeois nihilism and positivism (the latter two are for Mariátegui two sides of the same coin). For this reason, Mariátegui turns to sensibilities that inform the will and that come to be operative in collective faith and action.[17]

Quijano recognizes this theme in Mariátegui's writings, particularly in regard to relative truth of myths. He quotes Mariátegui: "Contemporary philosophy has done away with the mediocre positivist edifice. It has clarified and demarcated the modest confines of reason. And it has reformulated the current theories of Myth and Action. It is pointless, according to these theories, to look for an absolute truth. Today's truth will not be tomorrow's truth. One truth is valid only for an epoch. Let's be content with a relative truth." This account of relative truth does not lead to an abstract skeptical position but to a notion of truth as practical, that is, contingent within space and time, a truth of action. Such is the truth that corresponds to the hermeneutic, methodological Marxism I discussed earlier. This truth reveals a contextualized political juncture in its revolutionary potential. Now, by focusing on myth, I am unearthing the affective component of this relative truth in view of sustaining a commitment to revolutionary praxis over against bourgeois sensibilities.[18]

In this regard, Quijano explains the importance of myth for the proletariat: "And in the contemporary struggle, this [relative truth] is the advantage of the proletariat over the bourgeoisie: the former has an affirmative posture; against skepticism and nihilism, it has a faith and a myth. Against positivism it is, in addition, relativist. The bourgeoisie, instead, is prisoner to skeptic negation or a flat positivism. For him, then, upon this basis the will for revolutionary action acquires a secure foundation: myth." The second problem area of Mariátegui's assumption of Marxism, then, is the affirmation of a permanent revolutionary will that has to be understood in terms of a practical, hermeneutic truth and in the context of bourgeois nihilistic sensibilities that undermine the affective conditions for the configuration of liberatory agencies. Quijano, thus, appropriately stresses Mariátegui's indebtedness to Nietzsche.[19]

Quijano's analysis leaves some important questions open. In particular, one could ask, What are the affective sources of the permanence of the revolutionary will, in ethical and aesthetic terms, for example? And, what are the historical conditions for the nihilism and positivism of the bourgeois order? These questions are relevant when this order poses a threat to the affective conditions out of which a revolutionary discipline arises, a threat that Quijano does not focus on. For Mariátegui, beyond Quijano's analysis, there is an affective struggle that needs to be engaged at the level of sensibility and understood in some ways prior to the actualization of revolutionary praxis. He is engaged with what Alejandro Vallega has recently called an aesthetics of liberation.[20] In his early interpretation of Mariátegui, Quijano does not see this issue of sensibility fully.

Quijano's Correction of Mariátegui

After Quijano addresses the two problem areas, he closes any foray into an analysis of the affective field of struggle that his own interpretation opens up. He does so in a central section of his introductory text that defines the remainder of his analysis, "The Sources of Mariátegui's Marxism and Philosophy of History," which lays out the correct path of interpretation of Mariátegui away from his unorthodox spiritual and religious proclivities, especially as they are informed by his reliance on Croce, Sorel, Gobetti, and Bergson. I will look carefully at this point of inflection in Quijano's text.[21]

Quijano attributes Mariátegui's lack of engagement with political economy to his Marxist education within the Italian philosophical and political environment in the early 1920s, where emphasis was put on political philosophy and theory, and on spiritual problems. According to Quijano, this exposure constitutes both the strength of Mariátegui's Marxism and its limitation. In this setting, for example, he learned from Croce a philosophy of history that informed his Marxist historical methodology. At the same time, however, he was swayed by Sorel in particular in ways that Quijano finds unjustified. In fact, Quijano seems bewildered by Mariátegui's open admiration for Sorel, and much of his effort at this juncture goes to show that pursuing this admiration leads to unproductive engagements with Mariátegui.[22]

Quijano recognizes three ways in which Mariátegui uses Sorel as a source: first, Sorel's positing of a social myth as necessary for revolutionary praxis; second, that this myth is an antidote for intellectual skepticism; and third, that it provides an essentially metaphysical conception of existence. Quijano's concern is that Mariátegui's excessive focus on these Sorelian motifs distracts him from his historical-materialist method, which for Quijano is the core of Mariátegui's philosophical and political contribution. Quijano's concern, then, seems to be with the way in which Mariátegui's emphasis on Sorel undermines the valuable, and philosophically sound, dimension of his thinking.[23]

For this reason, Quijano attempts to explain Mariátegui's attachment to Sorel. First, he mentions, again, the particular intellectual and political environment in Italy. Second, he underscores the limits of Mariátegui's education as an autodidact. Quijano suggests that Mariátegui did not have the intellectual sophistication to identify the fact that a true understanding of Marxism would reveal the derivative character of this set of spiritual concerns. Third, he points to Mariátegui's own youthful religious inclinations that continued to have a hold over him. Fourth, he maintains that Sorel could be used to counter the specific socialist reformist and conformist atmosphere that Mariátegui found in Peru. And fifth, he claims Sorel's myth helps articulate a strategic revolutionary program that would apply to the indigenous masses that "were not in conditions to agree to a more sophisticated level of understanding of revolutionary theory."[24]

Quijano's treatment of the last reason is particularly revealing. In his view, Mariátegui had the insight that Sorel's myth had to be understood strategically and not as an essential part of the idea of a socialist revolution. Here, he disagrees with Robert Paris, who thinks that Mariátegui understood socialism to be a myth within the Peruvian reality and one that arose from it. In this disagreement, Quijano makes a definitive move: he separates the idea of the revolution from the myth of the revolution. The latter is an ideological strategy put in place to mobilize ignorant indigenous masses. The former is a historical methodology that yields truths. Quijano seeks to orient the reader toward the idea of the socialist revolution as the core of Mariátegui's contribution. Its corresponding myth would, then, be secondary, contingent, and strategic. This move defines the path that Quijano will follow in the remainder of his early introduction to Mariátegui.

Quijano's Reading of the Seven Essays: The Idea of Marxism in Mariátegui

Two aspects of the idea of the socialist revolution as it is connected to Mariátegui's "strict Marxism" stand out in Quijano's analysis. First, Quijano, echoing Melis, points to the heterogeneity of the historical process of Latin America, Peru in particular, as it is studied in the Seven Essays. The core insight here is that in Peru there are three distinct economies that are articulated with one another. Under the needs and direction of a capitalist economy, both a feudal economy and an indigenous communal one coexist. Mariátegui's original Marxist interpretation is that these three economies need to be understood in their reciprocal articulation, one that comes to be expressed sometimes in his writings as the semifeudal character of the Peruvian economy. Quijano writes, "Mariátegui is able to make manifest how, despite their profound differences, the three economies in force converge in the configuration of a self-same and unified socio-economic structure on the basis of a reciprocal articulation under the hegemonic logic of capital." One of the fundamental characteristics of this threefold economy is the dependent character of the Peruvian bourgeoisie, caught between the interests of gamonales and of global capitalism, unable to take on its responsibilities as the leading class in a capitalist national economy. This issue is one of the disagreements between Mariátegui and Haya de la Torre, the leader of APRA. A second disagreement is, perhaps, as important. Haya de la Torre understood the coexistence of these economies as defined by the opposition between capitalist and feudal forces. In this way, he adhered to a straightforward dialectical understanding of revolutionary processes. Mariátegui, on the other hand, understood the heterogeneity and reciprocal articulation of these economies, which called for an interpretation of them that traced their entanglement in order to understand specific economic and political junctures. Quijano explains: "The unity of contradictory elements, in a determinate and concrete historical situation, where unequal levels of development are combined, constantly interpenetrating and conditioning each other, and where one of its elements cannot be destroyed without affecting the ensemble and inversely, is the categorically Marxist and dialectic vision that Mariátegui gives to us as a specific formulation and as an epistemological and methodological attitude."[25]

Quijano claims that this "epistemological and methodological attitude" is to be found in Mariátegui but not yet consolidated. In fact, this attitude is the one that Quijano himself will pursue, allowing him to articulate his main contributions to decolonial theory. Perhaps the most important insight in this respect, one that enacts the turn away from Eurocentrism that defines the decolonial option, is Mariátegui's rejection of a temporal historical sequence that would provide a logic on which to base his economic and political analysis. Such a basis would fail to address the heterogeneity implied in Mariátegui's position. Quijano notes that the sequence feudalism-capitalism-socialism is the articulation of a specifically European historical experience that cannot be transposed to the Latin American context, where these three economic forms are heterogeneously articulated.[26]

The second aspect of the socialist revolutionary idea that Quijano extracts from Mariátegui's work is connected to the first and focuses on the constitution of a collective revolutionary subject. The heterogeneity of the Peruvian reality means that the overcoming of both feudal and capitalist economies needs to be done simultaneously. Furthermore, the anticapitalist struggle needs to give overriding direction to the revolutionary praxis, since capitalism is the dominant economy. In other words, the dissolution of the feudal structure of gamonalismo has to be taken on at the same time that capitalist modes of production are overturned. The defining implication of this view is that the collective revolutionary agent is heterogeneous and operates simultaneously on different social, political, economic, and cultural fronts. In particular, this het-erogeneous agent has to respond to the needs of both indigenous campesinos and industrial workers, complicating the homogeneity implied in a proletariat class articulated from Europe.[27]

This focus on heterogeneous revolutionary subjects and agencies has at least two implications. First, the collective revolutionary subject does not have a sin-gle horizon through which to articulate its praxis. Rather, it finds itself engaged with differentiated and even contradictory needs, demands, and power struc-tures, even if its praxis is oriented to the dissolution of the capitalist dominant system. Such a complex articulation of revolutionary praxis is the only way to understand how the demands of indigenous campesinos can be addressed in their specificity and not compromised by the demands of industrial workers, for example. So, instead of a single horizon that would suggest a defined moment of praxis that would be the accomplishment of a revolution, Quijano's reading of Mariátegui suggests a heterogenous revolutionary activity that transpires in specific, yet linked, actions acting on different fronts without being resolved into one definitive, even redemptive, act.

Second, the surviving economy of indigenous communities acquires for the revolutionary collective subject a different valence than feudalism and capital-ism. While the latter two are economic forms to dismantle, the first gives an orienting direction since it suggests the possibility of a future socialist eco-nomic form. The indigenous community can operate, then, as a guiding ideal for the revolution in Peru insofar as it may allow for the reciprocal articulation of heterogeneous demands coming from indigenous campesinos and industrial workers. For this reason, Quijano states that, despite the limits of Mariátegui's understanding of the economic form of indigenous communities, the destiny of these communities in his revolutionary vision is "one of the most valuable and original contributions of the Amauta [Mariátegui]."[28]

Points of Inflection in Quijano's Early Reading of Mariátegui

The latter two points concerning the revolutionary collective subject are insights that Quijano does not develop fully in his early *Reencuntro* and end up being undermined there. This becomes evident in Quijano's view that the socialist revolution is a transitional process. In particular, the way he explains how this process affects the identity of the revolutionary class is telling. The process of the socialist revolution, he suggests, "purges itself in its class content, it 'becomes' proletariat as the process matures. . . . [T]he proletariat direction of the revolution is the touchstone. And this can be ensured by a party whose direction is proletariat. But in the concrete conditions of Peru . . . this does not suppose a workers movement, but one with a wider basis and, in the Peruvian case, a basis fundamentally constituted by workers and campesinos."

The difficult issue here is the significance of the process as a "purging." This suggests, it seems, that the heterogeneity both of the specific conditions of Peru and of the collective revolutionary agent are transitional, proceeding toward homogenization. In terms of the configuration of the revolutionary collective, the purging means the gradual adoption of a single horizon for its praxis, as well as the consolidation of a unified identity as the proletariat. The purging also has implications for the indigenous economy as a guiding notion: eventually it becomes purged of its indigenous lineages in order to articulate explicitly proletariat ideals. As a result, then, indigenous agencies and lineages are progressively erased.[29]

I have identified two points of inflection in Quijano's *Introducción*, moments in which his analysis closes paths that it itself opens and turns toward a different trajectory. The first is connected to the affective dimensions of the revolutionary subject and her affective struggle of liberation as the ground for the permanence of a revolutionary will. The second is Quijano's notion of heterogeneity, specifically as it determines the collective revolutionary subject. Is there a way of reading Mariátegui that begins from these points of inflection pursuing the issues of sensibility (or aesthetics more generally), heterogeneity, and myth differently?

INTERMEZZO: FERNANDA BEIGEL'S INTERPRETATION OF MARIÁTEGUI'S AVANT-GARDE

Beigel's book *El itinerario y la brújula* is an indispensable text for those trying to understand the relationship between Mariátegui's politics and his aesthetics, focusing on avant-garde movements such as surrealism from a historical and sociological perspective. As Beigel describes it, her text arose from the realization that "an 'avant-garde' Mariátegui, who revealed himself since the first edition of the publication [Amauta], had not been at the center of the scene of Mariateguian studies in this century. Even though almost half of his work is devoted to cultural issues, in the last 50 years it has been the least studied part of his work."

Beigel, then, offers an important recentering of Mariátegui studies, not only by focusing on his aesthetics but also by considering the social, historical, and political conditions in which his work took shape. These two facets come to the fore in Beigel's analysis by her close attention to Mariátegui's prolific activity as a journal editor (of publications such as *Amauta* and *Labor*) that threw him into the midst of philosophical and political debates. So positioned, Mariátegui was sensitive to the role art and artists played in his milieu. This explains his fascination with aesthetic-political movements such as indigenismo and surrealism, which situated themselves in the whirlwind of political struggle. As Beigel notes, for Mariátegui the editorialist, the connection between politics and aesthetics was a given, even though it may be difficult to discern when one secludes oneself within academic confines.[30]

In particular, Mariátegui appears to be keenly aware of the convergence between political and artistic avant-garde practices since artistic movements such as surrealism were attempts to know and change reality. Beigel shows that Mariátegui understands avant-garde aesthetics, beyond its challenge to conventional and institutionalized art forms, as a dismantling of the opposition reality-fiction that sought to "challenge the very conception of reality." According to Beigel, Mariátegui saw that this challenge necessarily had political consequences and took avant-garde aesthetic practices and sensibilities to be part of a movement to bring about social and political change, especially since, from a Marxist perspective, reality is the expression of social and political conditions. In this way, Mariátegui sensed the deep affinity between the revolutionary praxis suggested by the *Theses on Feuerbach*, for example, and the avant-garde aesthetic spirit.[31]

Beigel's analysis points to an essential issue, even if she does not fully work it out philosophically: avant-garde aesthetics joins a socialist political myth as a guiding force but cannot by itself provide myths. As she suggests, avant-garde aesthetics operates as part of a spiritual movement. Yet she leaves open the precise articulation of the way in which this operation informs a revolutionary will, as a form of discipline, for example. Thus she signals a path to inquire about the volitional, affective dimensions of avant-garde aesthetics that support the collective myth of the socialist revolution. Beigel makes a good start on this path by engaging the avant-garde aesthetic movement as a mode of knowledge that is attentive to the multiplicity and heterogeneity of the real and that informs revolutionary praxis.[32]

Beigel shows that Mariátegui rejected any essentialist engagement with artworks that assign them a meaning detached from sociopolitical realities and that he focused, rather, on the figure of the artist as embedded in a particular context while producing works with certain creative freedom. This freedom has to be conceptualized beyond the dichotomy of subjective-objective interpretations of art, because it engages a function of the artist and her creation distinct from both the artist's subjective intentions and the artwork's objective meaning. In fact, through these observations, Mariátegui opens a productive aesthetic field within which avant-garde art operates. This aesthetic field reveals that the artist can make manifest through art the sensibility of an epoch; specifically, artworks can come to express the tension between decadent and revolutionary spirits, one that parallels the tension I noted earlier between a revolutionary spirit on the one hand and nihilism and positivism on the other.

Thus, Beigel finds in Mariátegui's aesthetics a way of "contributing to the critique or the clarification of the spirit [estado de animo] of humanity." In this kind of engagement with art, art appears as a liberating creative praxis insofar as it reveals and unleashes the revolutionary potencies latent in sociopolitical contexts. It offers, then, a kind of diagnosis of revolutionary sensibilities informing political praxis and a counterforce to the nihilism and skepticism that characterizes the bourgeoisie. Surrealism in particular, both as an aesthetic mode and as a political movement, enacts a transformative engagement with reality at the level of sensibility that informs the revolutionary spirit and allows for this diagnosis.[33]

Beigel correctly points to the difficulty of correlating a spiritual revolution showcased in avant-garde art and a proletarian revolution, a difficulty evidenced in surrealism as an aesthetic-political movement. One of the burning questions for Mariátegui was to find the correct relationship between these two revolutions, their intrinsic collaboration. The specific, conceptual articulation of this relationship is one of the limits of Beigel's incisive analysis. She takes some steps toward this issue in suggesting that avant-garde art reveals the utopian and creative aspect of the revolutionary process, insofar as it expresses and makes manifest a new, revolutionary, sensibility. In this respect, Beigel argues that avant-garde art, as Mariátegui understood it, deconstructs bourgeois art's detachment as art for art's sake through an anarchic and dissolving effect and creates an aesthetic event that expresses a new sensibility that informs revolutionary praxis. The second of these operations in particular points to the structure of this sensibility that commits to the socialist revolution. Through Beigel, then, one can put the issue of the sensibility of a revolutionary discipline, and of the affective struggle for liberation it implies, at the center of Mariátegui's interpretation of the avant-garde. In terms of the previous discussion, aesthetics may be at the center of the possibility of the permanence of the revolutionary will as the field in which the affective grounds of liberation are at stake.[34]

ALBERTO FLORES GALINDO'S UTOPIAN THINKING

Beigel underscores a deep connection between Mariátegui's emphasis on myth and faith and a revolutionary aesthetic sensibility expressed through disciplined praxis. Such a discipline can be informed by aesthetic movements like surrealism and undoes the distinction between reality and fiction in order to be able to imagine, and work toward, a different reality, one that is not limited by hegemonic political and economic orders. The suggestion here is that, for Mariátegui, a surrealist discipline informs a sensibility that can sustain the revolutionary will of the masses in the face of bourgeois nihilism. This kind of discipline has two aspects. First, it has a creative side that corresponds to the capacity to imagine alternative realities, especially from the perspective of oppressed groups. In this sense, the undoing of the distinction between reality and fiction corresponds to a liberatory disposition in which the basic structures of reality are permanently engaged in their overcoming. Second, it is an ethos, that is, a practice that needs to be cultivated in order to shelter, carry out, and motivate the commitment of revolutionary agencies. This latter aspect relates to Mariátegui's concern with the permanence of the revolutionary will, with myth as a faith and with the religious factor. It is also the one that Quijano carefully excises in his early interpretation of Mariátegui. In my reading of Flores Galindo's texts on Mariátegui, I am going to keep in mind these two aspects, both of which address a particular sensibility that has a connection with aesthetics, and I will pay particular attention to a revolutionary ethos and discipline.[35]

In many ways, Flores Galindo seems to draw his understanding of utopia from Mariátegui's conception of myth. Yet, he has some reservations about it. A utopia can garner collective commitment to the actualization of an alternative reality, so that "salvation does not depend that much on human beings and on the exercise of their freedom, but on a revealed truth: in the name of which one could endure any sacrifice and justify any atrocities." Utopia both depends on expectations of salvation or, in my terms, redemption and can elicit actions not on the basis of their likelihood determined through deliberation, but on the promise of a revealed truth. The revealed truth may be operative simultaneously with a practical truth, but ultimately it overrides this truth and exceeds the scope of practicality in mobilizing masses. Flores Galindo's account, then, emphasizes the dangers of utopian commitments but also recognizes that revolutionary collective wills are motivated by them. One of the dangers with utopia is the emergence of authoritarianism within revolutionary movements or, in Flores Galindo's terms, messianism. Yet utopias ground liberatory agencies beyond practical deliberative reasoning, enabling them to affirm radical alternative realities unbounded by the intelligibility and structural restrictions of current ones. Should one affirm utopias and faith as necessary dimensions of liberatory theory despite their clear dangers? Or should one join Quijano and distance oneself from them by separating myth from the idea of socialism?[36]

Flores Galindo gives us some encouragement to pursue the former route. First, like Mariátegui, he believes that we are touching here on a fundamental liberatory issue, especially in the context of bourgeois nihilism and rationalism. So, the task is not to avoid it, but to analyze the possibility of faith and myth as not inherently dangerous. Second, there are positive features of utopia and myth. He puts forward at least two of them: (1) in the face of the disempowerment of the masses within capitalist, bourgeois orders, utopia, as connected to discipline, faith, and myth, comprises the formation of collective agents of change and affirms their power beyond the constraints of capitalistic individualism, opening a different field of political action from below; and (2) this affirmation of the power of the masses changes the scope of what is possible, opening alternative realities as viable, focusing on larger or total changes of oppressive structures, rather than on reformist changes within these structures. Flores Galindo speaks about this while reflecting on his contemporary political milieu:

> May be, in our reflections, there is a lack of a sort of utopic dimension . . . that is, not thinking about problems in order to describe them, in order to see what is happening, in order to see the inevitable tendency we need to adapt to; but, rather, in order to think the problems from a valuative optic. . . . I think that, instead, the best approach to these things . . . is to introduce valuative criteria, introducing a sort of utopic dimension and asking ourselves about alternative solutions that would be radically different.

The affirmation of the power of the masses as configured agents of liberation through myth and utopias enables one to seriously engage in a comprehensive critique that allows for the rejection of the fundamental structures and values of the system of power in place. In particular, Flores Galindo wants to preserve an ethical option to vote against the republican oligarchy by affirming an alternative order, and discipline and faith sustain such a preservation.[37]

The Andean Utopia

Flores Galindo carefully studies the political and social repercussions of the Andean utopia in Peruvian history. It is a utopia that gathers the collective revolutionary will of indigenous and mestizo peoples as a challenge to the colonial and republican order and the systems of coloniality and capitalism they belong to. He states, "By definition, utopia is what does not have a place neither in space or time. But in the Andes, the collective imagination ended up finding the ideal society—the paradigm of any possible society and the alternative for the future—, in the historical stage that preceded the arrival of Europeans."

The temporal characteristic of the Andean utopia is that the positing of an alternative reality from the perspective of the oppressed implies a projection to the past as part of envisioning the future. This utopia, then, has an alternative liberatory vision that could not avoid the idealization of the Inka past. This particular utopic vision arises from coloniality, specifically, from peoples seeking liberation in a context in which a radical break from their own histories has restricted their possibilities for futural projections, a context that continues to deemphasize contemporaneous, historically complex, and heterogeneous indigenous lineages, especially in their transcultural formations. Flores Galindo writes, "These Andean peoples needed to create some instruments in order to understand the terrible cataclysm that was the conquest and for this the Andean mythical thought was insufficient, and they had to create or imagine another way to think about things; and this other way is what could be called a kind of Andean utopia." Flores Galindo's reading of Mariátegui approaches his socialism as working on the basis of the Andean utopia. He describes it thus: "Socialism was an aim that allowed for the galvanizing of peoples, giving them an identity to construct a multitude *and to give a path for which it was worth living*. It was a moral. It was, above all else, a practice."[38] This statement expresses Mariátegui's socialism in its capacity to configure an identity in a revolutionary context and to elicit the commitment of the peoples with the promise of an affirmation of their humanity, the promise of a political praxis and reality "for which it was worth living." It also captures socialism as a myth that is also an ethos or discipline, that is, a practice on what appears to me to be a redemptive path.[39]

According to Flores Galindo, Mariátegui found such an ethos already operative within indigenous peoples in the Andes fueled by the Andean utopia, and, thus, had to anchor his socialism in it in order to construct an effective revolutionary myth. Flores Galindo connects this to the role the indigenous communities, or ayllus, play in Mariátegui's socialism: they are a reference that builds on the Andean utopia as the projection of an idealized Inka past. This idealization, however, as suggested above, is at the core of the dangers of a redemptive logic. In it, redemption, as based on a return to an idealized Inka past, forces an essentialist view of a constructed Indian identity that ends up excluding indigenous peoples from liberatory options. This effect is not disconnected from Flores Galindo's assessment of the dangers of utopianism: the expectation of a revealed truth that, in the Andean context, actually limits the revolutionary possibilities for indigenous peoples, even warranting violence against their cultures, social and economic forms, and lives.

One of the dangerous aspects of this logic of redemption, one that even drove Mariátegui to racist views, is the emphasis on an absolute and exhaustive dichotomy between the Spanish and the Indians for the sake of articulating liberatory projects from this opposition. Flores Galindo addresses this same problem in view of Mariátegui's immersion in the Andean utopia. In Flores Galindo's reading, Mariátegui ends up articulating a revolutionary vision that became detached from reality, a reality in which "Still many runas [indigenous peoples] kept their loyalty to the mistis [their oppressors], and they were even willing to risk their lives for them. . . . 'Indians' fighting against 'Indians.'" Apparently, Mariátegui did not adequately understand the complexity of Indian identities, particularly in terms of how the oppressed can assume the perspective of the oppressors and commit to their interests. Flores Galindo also points out that capitalism differentiates indigenous communities in ways that complicate the polarity Spanish-Indian, submitting the two identities to fractures and differentials that block coherent and single political horizons. This aspect of Mariátegui's socialism (conceived either through the Andean utopia or through a logic of redemption) is particularly dangerous in view of the kind of commitment that socialism as myth can elicit, even promoting, through the very configuration of an Indian identity tied to a liberatory project, conflicts between indigenous peoples that coloniality benefits from.[40]

Should myths and utopias, then, be discarded? Did Quijano's purging Mariátegui's thought of mythical faith open up the most productive engagement with him, even beyond logics of redemption? Or is there a way to preserve the ethos and discipline Mariátegui is invested in and curb its dangerous redemptive aspects? Problems seem to arise when utopianism operates with a restrictive and exclusionary sense of a revealed truth for the sake of which agents of liberation act, and when the discipline of these agents closes them off from peoples within complex cultural, ethnic, and social formations. These two aspects are tied to the single futural horizon of redemption that can delimit liberatory projects and to the exclusion of oppressed peoples through the essentialization of identities in the configuration of liberatory collective agents. Can there be an ethos that is not defined by these dangers and that can be operative as the discipline of revolutionary agents? These may, after all, be irresolvable issues in Mariátegui's thinking, but Flores Galindo does suggest ways to think through them in productive directions.

Multitudes in Festivals

Flores Galindo expresses the beginning of Mariátegui's thought, both chronologically and theoretically, thus: "The power of ideas and of traditions when they are incarnated in the multitudes is . . . the central footing (we could almost say, *a criterion of truth*) for Mariátegui." Mariátegui is fundamentally oriented to the incarnation of ideas, to their life in practices when multitudes commune, sharing embodied intimacies. In Flores Galindo's view, his ultimate "criterion of truth," rather than residing in a practical truth or in the promise of a revealed truth (even if such projections may be operative in his indigenous socialism), belongs to the possibility of liberatory projects to be articulated through present exposures and vulnerabilities of peoples within multitudes. This is an aspect of community making that could offer a budding sense for the configuration of liberatory collectives without investments in futural, definitive, and redemptive projections. Flores Galindo argues that Mariátegui is attuned to events given to the affirmation of the life of the other as one who could always come to, and could always arrive at, such a multitude; as the other coming down the street, for example: "This is how . . . [Mariátegui] discovers the mobilizing power of myths, beliefs, traditions, religion, when, transcending individual fervor . . . they are mixed up with the multitudes and the streets of a city."[41]

It is not only the other that comes, but beliefs, myths, and traditions come as well, with and through others; but in the festive multitudes, peoples mix, thrown into a larger yet concrete event that sustains their communing with one another. That is, there are no determinate, revealed truths or redemptive promises that control the meaning and purpose of the event or the multitude. The multitude in its eventuation is larger than revolutionary myths and utopias, yet they become incarnated. People arrive and myths are embodied in the multitudes rather than the multitudes being homogenized by myths. There is a religious factor that informs Mariátegui's reflection on the configuration of liberatory collectives, one found in events of community making that are fluid and unpredictable yet vital and transgressive of oppressive structures. This may be a dimension of liberatory praxis that exceeds the restrictive and exclusionary aspects of myths and their truths, one that is not subjected to redemptive structures—and one that is instantiated in events communities can always return to in order to renew themselves through nondefinitive encounters with others. Flores Galindo states, "the concern for the religious event leads Mariátegui to discover the multitudes, and religion began to be important to him, *not so much because of the answers to metaphysical problems* but, rather, for its capacity to bring multitudes together and mobilize them toward a common project."[42]

Flores Galindo, opening an engagement with the religious factor that exceeds Quijano's critiques, finds the origins of Mariátegui's thought in religious festivals like that of El Señor de los Milagros, during which the streets of the center of Lima are flooded by multitudes. In his account, Mariátegui appears fascinated by the discipline that drives those who carry the figure of Christ in particular: "this is not a matter of . . . resignation, but, on the contrary, of the enthusiasm that enables, year after year, in the month of October, the effort to carry the platform." Discipline, then, is sustained by a particular ethos, a habit and practice that drives people to arrive at the multitude, to be exposed to, and to affirm and be affirmed by, the alterity of others in bodily communion; to engage the way revolutionary myths get mixed up in these multitudes, open to dissemination in the larger context of vulnerable and exposed bodies in which communities are made with indifference to definitive futural projections. This is the discipline to come, arrive, and return, to these collective destabilizing, deindividualizing events that exceed the power of truths to be revealed; the discipline to remain within the multitude rather than the discipline to pursue a redemptive goal. Flores Galindo also finds such festive events in the lineages of the Andean utopia, where one could see even this utopia as energized by the multitudes in ways that are not restrictive but creative of indigenous senses of being that elude substantialist—and dangerous—constructions of Indian identities. This festive community making gives an aesthetic footing to Mariátegui's socialism that may enable one to engage it beyond redemption.[43]

This religious factor allows one to conceive of a configuration of collective agents of liberation based on heterogeneous and open senses of identity that do not curb exposure to the alterity of others, recognizing critical positionalities in them as well, and cultivating discipline and commitment to liberation as a form of communing with others and of making community in the present.

Surrealist Discipline

Flores Galindo notes that Mariátegui's festive ethos is based on a mode of sensibility, one that Mariátegui finds in psychoanalysis and surrealism: "The relationship with Psychoanalysis . . . must be understood from the enthusiasm the Mariátegui felt for Surrealism: Freud's method, breaking the repressions and the barriers of the unconscious, allowed for the flow and discovery of an intense interior life that, when transposed to literature, amounted to a predilection for imaginations and creativity."[44]

Both surrealism and psychoanalysis challenge stable delimitations of comprehensive or even practical truths in order to open a field of indeterminate life and senses of purpose that can arise beyond conscious awareness in concrete events and that can be externalized through imagination and creativity. The suggestion here is that multitudes in religious festivals can be prone to such events and that their emerging sense of common purpose is akin to an assemblage of those events that can be grasped aesthetically—at the level of affect and sensibility—rather than conceptually. Mariátegui's socialism as configurative of liberatory collective agencies could be grounded in such an aesthetic assemblage, and there are aspects in it that attest to this. Flores Galindo states, "There is a correspondence between Mariátegui's defense of creative spontaneity in syndicalism, and the enthusiasm that he felt for the surrealist movement and for European avant-garde literature, which broke away from established norms, and vindicated the imagination, and recognized all the jurisdictions of the imagination." Flores Galindo's analysis (anticipating and echoing Beigel's) embeds Mariátegui's liberatory theory and method in a kind of surrealist aesthetics: his own writings should be engaged as multitudinal festive events and assemblages. Moreover, this kind of writing would correspond to the complex, heterogeneous, unbridled character of Peruvian reality. Reflecting on Mariátegui's preference for the essay form, he finds it to be the best way to conceptualize a country like Peru, where "reality itself appears a barely structured." Among other things, here he points to Mariátegui's attentiveness to the temporal disjunctions, simultaneities, and parallelisms that define the Peruvian reality, disruptive temporal configurations that inform his articulation of socialism as carried by a multitudinal festive assemblage. The imagination seems to be the power through which such a reality could be known, creatively rather than analytically, by means of an aesthetic grasp of nontotalizing and fragmentary collective revolutionary projects assembled from the multitudes and incarnated in festivals. And here even indigenous lineages can ground critical perspectives that figure such assemblages in nonexclusionary ways. Mariátegui is the precursor to the aesthetic imagination of César Vallejo and José María Arguedas, where indigenous lineages are engaged as open structures of experience and meaning, but with liberatory intent.[45]

TOWARD AN ENGAGEMENT WITH ALEJANDRO VALLEGA'S AESTHETICS OF LIBERATION

At this juncture, it would be productive to envision Mariátegui's aesthetic footing as an aesthetics of liberation, especially in Alejandro Vallega's terms. In this sense, Mariátegui works from the recognition of an unbridled reality, from the affirmation of the lives of others without the totalizing expectations of identities, as well as from a sensibility informed by temporalities that configure liberatory communities of the oppressed outside singular and progressive temporal horizons. These are all elements of an aesthetics of liberation in Val-lega's sense. Vallega states, "It is an aesthetic sense of reality which presents a great challenge and fecund possibilities for aesthetics in general, as well as for the philosophies of liberation and decolonial projects in particular, those on their way and those yet to come." Mariátegui may even be one of those think-ers that Vallega believes are scarce: "I have found a few thinkers able to risk rational analysis, argumentation, theorizing, and—on the other side of the coin—faith and religiosity in order to engage the aesthetic dimension in its aesthetic coloniality and to make a much needed decolonial aesthetic turn." Here the opportunity for dialogue appears. Does Mariátegui fit in Vallega's rich aesthetic vision, or do his concerns with faith and religiosity disqualify him? Or, perhaps, does he complicate the sense of aesthetics of liberation opera-tive here? Let's just note that Vallega's powerful account of an aesthetics of liberation draws heavily from Quijano, who, early on, as I have noted, excises religiosity from Mariátegui and with it the ethos and discipline I have analyzed through Beigel and Flores Galindo—aspects of Mariátegui's thought that are both aesthetic and liberatory. This dialogue with Vallega is too substantial to undertake here.[46]

QUIJANO'S LATER AESTHETICS

I have discussed Quijano's early interpretation of Mariátegui (in 1979) in order to articulate a difference from Flores Galindo's and open an aesthetic dimen-sion in Mariátegui's thought connected to myth or utopia, one that I under-stand as a surrealist discipline and, more specifically, as an ethos. Later, Quijano wrote at least two texts in which aesthetics appears central to his decolonial project. Probably the best known of these, especially among English-speaking audiences, is "Modernidad, identidad y utopía en América latina" (1988). Here I will focus on a shorter essay that builds on this one: "Estética de la utopía" (1990).[47] In this essay, Quijano turns to Mariátegui's texts on aesthetics and myth published in El alma matinal.

At first, Quijano seems close to Flores Galindo's position. He begins by stating, "It is persistently proven that the transformation of the world hap-pens first as an aesthetic transfiguration." That is, utopian thinking seems con-nected to an aesthetic mode that sustains it. This leads Quijano to ask, "Why does utopia find a home, first, in the domain of aesthetics?" I am interested in the way Quijano elucidates the relationship between aesthetics and utopia as a response to this question. He states, "utopia seems to be constituted and consist of the same material as aesthetics," and gives an account of utopia: "If we admit that utopia . . . is a project for the re-constitution of the historical sense of a society . . . this does not only imply that it occupies the territory of the inter-subjective relations that we recognize as society's imaginary, which is the domain of aesthetics. What is at play here, above all, is that there is an aesthetic sense in all utopia, without which it would not be possible to turn the antennas of the imaginary of society toward another historical sense."[48]

This quote demands close attention. First, it is necessary to unpack the meaning of *imaginary* and *sense*. The former means the web of intersubjective relations, both material and symbolic relations, that is grasped not through reason's analytic, atomistic, conceptual, and instrumental forms, but through intuition, feeling, and imagination—that is, aesthetically. The latter means the way in which this web is given and grasped, both as meaningful and actual, and as in processes of redetermination. This last point is essential. To say that "there is an aesthetic sense in all utopia" means that utopia depends on the aesthetic power to grasp the imaginary of a society as potential, as able to be otherwise. Without this, utopia would not be able to ground the project of reconstituting the historical sense of a society. In other words, Quijano is interested in aesthetics here insofar as it enables the turn from one world to another, a turn that is necessary for dismantling of structures of oppression. My concern, then, is whether this turn in Quijano is related to an aesthetic discipline and ethos.[49]

How does Quijano understand this turn? He writes, "In colloquial terms, one could say that we search for another society, for another history, for another sense . . . not only because one materially suffers the reigning order but, above all, because one finds it distasteful [porque disgusta]. All utopias for the subversion of power imply, for this reason, an aesthetic subversion." This is a provocative statement, to say the least. Quijano's point seems to be that suffering leads to the negation of the system but not to the affirmation of an alternative. The latter is possible as an aesthetic turn, one that is always already enacted when a kind of judgment of taste is in play. To find something distasteful is to already be inclined, to be turned toward, in both intellectual and physical aspects of one's being, to the possibility of an alternative to it. Another way to express this could be that, without such an aesthetic sense, even those who are oppressed by society would engage their practical reason to challenge the system but not within a liberatory horizon that would overturn it in the affirmation of a radical alternative. As Quijano states, "It is not enough to fight against the oppressors."[50] Aesthetics, then, would be at the heart of utopian movements.

There are some important implications here. First, Quijano's thought seems to have developed since his early readings of Mariátegui. In this later text, he is concerned with the imaginative (nonrational) dimensions of revolutionary agency, bringing him close to Mariátegui's view of socialism as myth. In fact, in later texts, he undoes the separation of myth from the idea of socialism in Mariátegui (the one that I noted in his early *Reencuentro*) and understands myth in Mariátegui as a fundamental insight into socialism in the Latin American context. Second, Quijano finds in an aesthetic sense a turn of one's whole being, which leads to a radical transformation of society: "Utopia projects a liberatory alternative in both dimensions. Implies, that is, a subversion of the world, in its materiality as well as in its subjectivity." Both material conditions and conditions for the intelligibility of reality are open to transformation aesthetically. Third, not all aesthetics is utopian, but only aesthetic senses that are not "resigned to the commentary of what exists." Fourth, the scope of aesthetic horizons of liberation is wide: rather than focusing on one manifestation of a structure of power, one is given imaginatively, beyond immediate constraints, to the overturning of structures of reality as such, evoking a surrealist dimension. Quijano writes, "In order for [utopia] to be at play . . . the struggle against domination is needed against all forms of domination." This leads him to affirm: "The common material between utopia and aesthetics is the rebellion against power, against all power." This fourth implication is at the limit of Quijano's aesthetics of liberation.[51]

Does Quijano's later aesthetics conform to the surrealist, disciplined ethos I teased out from multitudes in festivals with the help of Flores Galindo? Quijano's later interest in utopia certainly brings him closer to Mariátegui than he was in the late 1970s. They now share an appreciation for aesthetics as a ground for revolutionary agency and for the radicality of the liberatory horizon that is possible only as given aesthetically (rather than through practical reasoning, for example). Furthermore, they both find in the aesthetic ground of liberation not only the option of affirming an alternative order but also the turning away from the dominant one toward it. It is with respect to this turning, however, that Quijano and Mariátegui remain apart.

Quijano sees the turn as the result of distaste, that is, of a judgment of taste constitutive of a moment in which the current order is negated and an alternative one is affirmed with one's whole being. Mariátegui, as a disciplined surrealist, does not seem invested in such a judgment, or in such a moment, as the aesthetic ground of revolutionary agency. Rather, for him, such definitive valuations would themselves be grounded in a destabilizing surrealist discipline involved in community making beyond the restrictions of the real. One could issue a critique of Quijano from a surrealist perspective like Mariátegui's: Isn't the control of taste part of the coloniality of power? And aren't investments in a definitive moment of aesthetic judgment tethered to coloniality, especially in its temporal constructions of homogeneous presents and single futural horizons? Quijano would probably answer that this is why one should distinguish between liberatory and reactionary art. The former implies a prior commitment to liberation, to the struggle against all domination, to the rebellion against power that he finds to be the common material shared by utopia and aesthetics.

It seems that Mariátegui, and here I am elaborating on Flores Galindo's reading of him, understands the aesthetic ground and the turn operative here differently. Underneath valuative moments of judgment, he endorses an aesthetic, imaginative disposition toward the affirmation of the permanent release from structures that order realities, a disposition that, more than by judgment, is sustained by a commitment to a practice that preserves it, an aesthetic discipline cultivated in multitudinal events of community making. This discipline maintains itself in the turn between worlds rather than being tethered to worlds to be overturned and to redemptive worlds to come. Mariátegui finds this in surrealism, as well as in festivals to which multitudes return, with discipline, year after year. Yet it seems that Quijano's main concern in his later texts can be sustained only through such a discipline: "the rebellion against power, against all power."[52]

Just when one would think that the difference I noted early on between Quijano and Mariátegui as a disciplined surrealist is still operative, Quijano states, in this later thought-provoking text,

> What the dominant culture dishonors, blocks or hides, above all in cultures with a colonial origin, trapped in the labyrinth of an uncertain identity is, most of the time, what the oppressed speak, dream or love; their ways of relating to forms, to color, to sound; to their bodies and their worlds; everything that they do or omit in order to satisfy or realize themselves without the permission or the resources of the oppressors; their ways of liberating themselves from the patterns of forgetfulness or memory that are imposed on them as the lock to the cage of domination. And, above all, the splendor of the festival up against instrumental reason.[53]

This quote not only complicates the difference between Quijano's and Flores Galindo's approach to Mariátegui. It also turns to the central issue of the determination of identities, the Indian identity in particular, and to how they can come to exceed the single futural horizons of redemptive myths when they are incarnated in multitudinal assemblages that can be aesthetically grasped in their festive, disciplined, surrealist determinations.

NOTES

1. This discussion of a libetratory praxis that exceeds the sense of dominant worlds is related to María Lugones's essay "From within Germinative Stasis: Creating Active Subjectivity, Resistant Agency."

2. Mariátegui, *Escena contemporánea*, 11.

3. For an analysis parallel to that of this chapter, one that focuses on Mariátegui's surrealism, see O. Rivera, "Mariátegui's Avant-Garde." For an account of Mariátegui's avant-garde situated in Latin America, see Unruh, "Mariátegui's Aesthetic," and Unruh, *Latin American Vanguards*. For an account of Mariátegui's relationship to romanticism, see Löwy, *Morning Star*, 56–57. Some of the relevant texts by Mariátegui here are "Art, Revolution and Decadence," "Balance Sheet of Surrealism," "Creative and Heroic Meaning of Socialism," "Man and Myth," Materialist Idealism," "Nationalism and Vanguardism," "Reality and Fiction," "Two Conceptions of Life," all in José Carlos Mariátegui, *Heroic and Creative Meaning of Socialism*. See also Mariátegui, "Lucha final," in *Invitación a la vida heroíca*. For a thorough account of Quijano's reading of Mariátegui throughout the arch of his thought, see Germaná, "Epistemología otra."

4. See Quijano, *Reencuentro y debate*, 60.

5. For an account of Sorel's influence on Mariátegui, see Vanden, *Mariátegui*, 63–67. Ciccariello-Maher, *Decolonizing Dialectics*, 23–45, has an innovative reading of Sorel in relation to decolonial thought that, in my view, elucidates aspects of Mariátegui's appreciation for him.

6. Unless specifically noted otherwise, page numbers in this section refer to pages in Quijano, *Reencuentro y debate*. Quijano, *Reencuentro y debate*, 36.

7. Quijano, *Reencuentro y debate*, 36.

8. Quijano recognizes this, pointing out that Mariátgeui had limited access to texts by Marx. Melis quoted in Quijano, *Reencuentro y debate*, 58. See also 59. Here Mariátegui reveals the resonances between Marxism and the Latin American philosophical tradition, incipiently at play in Martí. See the determination of Latin American philosophy by Martín Alcoff in chapter 1 in this volume.

9. Quijano, Reencuentro y debate, 63.

10. See Tucker, *Marx-Engels Reader*, 143–45. This approach to Marxism also corresponds to Dussel, *Ethics of Liberation*, 218–34.

11. Quijano, *Reencuentro y debate*, 64, 28.

12. Quijano, *Reencuentro y debate*, 65. Quijano, *Reencuentro y debate*, 65, 66, quote Mariátegui. See also 67.

13. Quijano, *Reencuentro y debate*, 68, quoted by Quijano.

14. Quijano, *Reencuentro y debate*, 69, Italics mine. See also 68.

15. See especially book 6 of Aristotle, *Nicomachean Ethics*. Heidegger's *Being and Time* as a meditation on Aristotle is almost contemporary with Mariátegui's stay in Europe. This "hermeneutic philosophy" also resonates with Martín Alcoff's account of Latin American philosophy.

16. Quijano, *Reencuentro y debate*, 64.

17. Quijano, *Reencuentro y debate*, 70. See also O. Rivera, "Mariátegui's Avant-Garde."

18. Quijano, *Reencuentro y debate*, 71.

19. Quijano, *Reencuentro y debate*, 69.

20. See Vallega, *Latin American Philosophy*, 196–217.

21. There has been important work on the relationship between Mariátegui and Gramsci. See Fernández Díaz, "Gramsci y Mariátegui"; Roncagliolo "Gramsci, marxista"; and Mignolo, "Mariátegui and Gramsci."

22. Quijano, *Reencuentro y debate*, 72, 73, 76. In a later text, Quijano interprets Sorel's influence on Mariátgeui as an indication of a non-Eurocentric rationality situated in Latin America and grounded in myth. See Quijano, "Marxismo en Mariátegui." Quijano compares him to Gramsci, who was able to have a more critical relationship with Sorel.

23. Quijano gives support to his view by pointing to the fact that Mariátegui ultimately could not have agreed with Sorel's overall project, namely, the use of the class struggle to galvanize the bourgeoisie.

24. Quijano, *Reencuentro y debate*, 76, 77, 78.

25. Quijano, *Reencuentro y debate*, 82.

26. And Guibal; see Guibal, *Vigencia de Mariátegui*. Quijano, *Reencuentro y debate*, 82, 84. The engagement with global capital as the dominant economic form leads Mariátegui, according to Quijano, to understand the revolution always from a transnational perspective, which puts him at odds with strictly nationalist political projects, such as fascism. See Mariátegui, *Escena Contemporánea*. Quijano, *Reencuentro y debate*, 85. Mariátegui's influence on Quijano is evident in the latter's famous essay, "Coloniality of Power." Quijano, *Reencuentro y debate*, 84.

27. See Quijano, *Reencuentro y debate*, 86.

28. I have articulated this valence of indigenous economic forms in Mariátegui's *Seven Essays* (Quijano, *Reencuentro y debate*, 88).

29. Later, though, the first point will ground some of his important contributions to decolonial thought (Quijano, *Reencuentro y debate*, 108, 109).

30. In addition to Beigel's essential text, there has been important recent work that explores Mariátegui's relationship to the avant-garde and surrealism in particular. See Moore, *José Carlos Mariátegui's Unfinished Revolution*, and

Campuzano Arteta, *Modernidad imaginada*. See also Beigel, *Itinerario y la brújula*, 204. Quijano falls into this category in Quijano, *Reencuentro y debate*.

31. Beigel, *Itinerario y la brújula*, 94, 96.

32. Beigel, *Itinerario y la brújula*, 101.

33. Beigel, *Itinerario y la brújula*, 100.

34. Beigel, *Itinerario y la brújula*, 111, 114, 115.

35. See Mariátegui's account of discipline in Mariátegui, *Defensa del Marxismo*, 55–64.

36. Flores Galindo, *Obras completas*, 6: 197.

37. Flores Galindo, *Obras completas*, 4: 281, 214. Flores Galindo, *Obras completas*, 2: 55.

38. Flores Galindo, *Obras completas*, 6: 558; italics mine.

39. See Flores Galindo, *In Search of an Inca*. Rumi Maqui (1915–16) was an indigenous activist. See Flores Galindo, *Obras completas*, 6: 194, 2: 423, 6: 207.

40. Flores Galindo, *Buscando un Inca*, 275, 276.

41. Flores Galindo, *Obras completas*, 2: 545, 554; italics mine.

42. Flores Galindo, *Obras completas*, 2: 545; italics mine. It would be productive to start a dialogue with Gadamer here, especially on the relationship between festivals and hermeneutics. See Gadamer, *Truth and Method*, 121–22, and the complementary essays by Gadamer, "Relevance of the Beautiful" and "Festive Character." Flores Galindo, like Quijano, is critical of a metaphysical reading of Mariátegui.

43. There is an intersection here between Dussel and Mariátegui's works on the theme of festivals or feasts. See Dussel, *Filosofía de la liberación*, 167–68; Flores Galindo, *Buscando un Inca*; Flores Galindo, *Obras completas*, 2: 545.

44. Flores Galindo, *Obras completas*, 2: 495,

45. Flores Galindo, *Obras completas*, 2: 568. I am borrowing the term *unbridled* to describe a Latin American experience from Vallega, *Latin American Philosophy*. See also Flores Galindo, *Obras completas*, 6: 99, Flores Galindo, *Buscando un Inca*, 282. See II.

46. See Vallega, "Exordio/Exordium"; Vallega, *Latin American Philosophy*, 199. See also his account of a Latin American aesthetics of liberation in Vallega, "Exordio/Exordium," 125–42.

47. See Quijano, "Modernity."

48. Quijano, "Estética," 733–34.

49. See Quijano, "Estética"; Quijano, *Cuestiones y horizontes*, 733–42. Quijano, "Estética," 733–34. I connect the turn here to my discussion of Pachakuti in the introduction to this volume.

50. Quijano, "Estética," 734.

51. I am referring here to the text "El Marxismo en Mariátegui." In this text, Quijano focuses on Mariátegui's myth, differentiating it from Sorel's, and finds

in it a necessary aspect of revolutionary subjectivity and praxis, especially in the heterogeneous political and economic conditions of Latin America. See Quijano, *Marxismo de José Carlos Mariátegui*, 43–47. See my discussion of Mariátegui's account of Italian futurism in O. Rivera, "Mariátegui's avant-garde," 117–19. Quijano, "Estética," 735.

52. Quijano, "Estética," 735.

53. Quijano, "Estética," 740.

—ᴍ—

CONCLUSION

Delimitations

THERE ARE MANY WAYS to look back at the trajectory of this book. It weaves studies of key figures and texts in Latin American philosophy and, in the case of Mariátegui, it offers insight into interpretations of some of his most important readers. The trajectory also traces the themes of redemption, and of the possibility to move beyond it, as shedding light on main issues in philosophies of liberation, like the relationship between cultural identity and liberation, the epistemological dimension of decolonial movements, the role aesthetics plays in the articulation of liberatory praxis, and the temporal and spatial determinations that sustain such a praxis. Furthermore, it makes explicit three delimitations of Latin American philosophy emerging from seminal texts in this tradition. It begins with Martín Alcoff's contextual delimitation, moves to a transcultural one (gathered from Schutte's reading of Mariátegui), and ends with an aesthetic one (suggested by Flores Galindo's utopianism in particular). This conclusion offers a more thorough study of this third, aesthetic, delimitation of Latin American philosophy by turning first to Mariátegui's interpretation of José Vasconcelos (recalling some of the points made throughout this book) and then to Gloria Anzaldúa's text "Border Arte."

PHILOSOPHY, UTOPIA, AND TRANSCULTURALITY

Mariátegui gives a delimitation of philosophy by interpreting Vasconcelos's book: "Indología overflows . . . the limits of an "interpretation of ibero-american culture . . . in order to touch those of utopia. . . . And for this reason it is not the book of a sociologist, a historian, a politician; being, however, at the same time, history, sociology, politics . . . it is the book of a philosopher." Vasconcelos, as a philosopher, has a particular approach to the analysis of culture, one that transgresses the objective interpretation of culture in order to touch utopias. In this way, he mobilizes cultural determinations for the articulation of critical projects that elicit the commitment of the oppressed. Philosophy in this sense is not mainly characterized by its content, nor by its critical power, but, above all, by its ability to effect a turn toward the affirmation of alternative realities, which is the meaning behind the statement that Vasconcelos "returns to a tradition in which we find Plato and his Republic in order to apply all the accomplishments of the understanding to the conception of an archetype or superior plan of society and civilization." Mariátegui's characterization of philosophy is complicated further by its difficult positioning. It transgresses the *limits* of cultural interpretations in order to touch the *limits* of utopias. In other words, philosophy sustains a turn toward utopias, one between critique and liberatory affirmations, and in excess of definitive cultural determinations of identities.[1]

At this juncture, I recall two earlier points. First, on the basis of my reading of Quijano and Flores Galindo, Mariátegui's account of philosophy as stretching between cultural determinations and utopias points to a turn within an aesthetic plane of sensibilities and affects, which would give philosophy an aesthetic grounding, or, more specifically, assign to liberatory philosophy the role of effecting an aesthetic turn. Second, in terms of invisibilities in Mariátegui's indigenismo and in the work of Lugones, this turn can happen in the border between irreducible cultural positionalities that are in conflict. In this regard, crossing cultural differences can be destabilizing so as to unsettle dominant structures from subaltern positionalities and can work through liberatory, utopic sensibilities (in terms of chapter 4, for example, one can think of here of nostalgia, memory, and non-linear temporalities) in excess of particular worlds of sense. This is a way of shedding light on Mariátegui's indigenous socialism as a liberatory philosophy enunciated between European and indigenous social and cultural referents.[2]

CHALLENGING LIFE

The aesthetic-philosophical turn toward utopias does not happen in the abstract but at the level of one's whole being in the crossing of cultures. Philosophy in this sense involves an embodied, affective, poetic, and creative disposition that is oriented to the possibility of transforming reality. Mariátegui is explicit about this: "Philosophy recovers here its classical function of a universal science, that dominates and contains all the other ones and feels itself destined, not only to explain and illuminate life, but to create it, challenging life with goals for an incessant overcoming." Philosophical mastery does not consist in the systematic subsuming of the other sciences under it. Their domination and containment, rather, exposes them to transgressive conceptual movements that free them from demands for universality and objectivity and, specifically, from an objectifying relationship to cultural formations. Thus, the illumination and explanation of life ceases to be their aim and, through the disruption of the difference between subject and object, the sciences under the reign of philosophy become poetic, transformative of reality and culture—in Mariátegui's and Flores Galindo's terms, they are subjected to myths or utopias. Here the influence not only of Nietzsche, but also of Bergson and Marx, are evident. We can recall the latter's well-known thesis: "The philosophers have only interpreted the world, in various ways; the point is however to change it." Mariátegui seeks the vindication of philosophy in response to Marx's thesis.[3]

How does this "philosophical creation of life" take place? How does knowledge become poetic under the influence of philosophy?—through utopian goals as new determinations of reality that are held open in transcultural present possibilities rather than being posited futurally as single, final, and closed. Mariátegui seems unclear about this process in particular, and his thinking reaches a limit here. Sometimes he seems to believe in the finality of liberatory goals. But in other instances, especially when thinking from a surrealist disposition, he seems to conceive of the projected goals as themselves indeterminate, eliciting a faith without investments in some finality. It is this latter disposition that is pursued here in order to dislodge from a progressive temporality and a futural horizon, like the ones that determine Bolívar's thought. In this case, the lack of finality challenges life in its incessant overcoming. Holding utopias as possibilities without closure is part of the philosophical function elucidated here, which is connected to the surrealist discipline and ethos in Flores Galindo's interpretations of Mariátegui. It also echoes Mariátegui's own understanding of political deeds as indeterminate events, unpredictable within the comprehensive expectations of linear and finite thinking.[4]

TEMPORAL AND SPATIAL DISSEMINATIONS

Mariátegui's reflection on the aesthetic and utopian function of philosophy continues with reference, again, to Vasconcelos: "This conception, due to the liberty and to the audacity with which it moves in time, places itself beyond the reach of criticism, which is forced to be content with the analysis of its historical and scientific materials. The secret of the architecture imagined with these materials is not given but in a partial and fragmentary way. It is the secret of a creative spirit." The last two sentences of this statement refer to my last point: imagined utopias can be effective without closure, as open architectures or assemblages that give themselves only partially or in fragments. This kind of aesthetic presentation that appeals to the whole of one's being is, in Mariátegui's view, the "secret of a creative spirit" that challenges life to incessant overcoming. The first sentence, however, adds to my analysis thus far, with regard to the relationship between the utopian function of philosophy and time. Philosophical thinking moves in time. The movement of philosophy has two aspects: it destabilizes its own temporal positioning and its imagined architectures do not abide by single temporal horizons. This echoes one of Mariátegui's central insights: Peruvian reality, and Latin America's, do not abide by a consistent temporality, but is layered by multiple temporalities attached to heterogeneous realities; simultaneous, parallel, asymmetric temporalities—like those of the *costa* and the *sierra*.[5]

The philosophical function here includes a basic temporal sensibility informed by the exposure to this polymorphous reality disseminated by, and disseminating, time; which enables philosophy to open architectural utopias freed from single determinations of time and to resist definitive temporal frames, futural ones in particular. Recalling the earlier analysis of Mariátegui's "internationalism" and Lugones' invisibilities, this dissemination of time corresponds to disseminations of space. The proliferation of spatial determinations, especially within the colonial difference, disrupts temporalities through the layering of reality spatially, where even the present can be given to a sudden interruption by a hidden spatiality within it: like the space of the indigenous communities or *ayllus* making itself manifest transculturally in the postcolonial city without defining temporal mediations.

PHILOSOPHY AS "AUTO-HISTORIA"

Mariátegui describes Vasconcelos's "method":

> Every idea reveals to us, at once, in Vasconcelos, his roots, his process—I am almost about to say, his biography. For this reason, the great Mexican never offers us cold theses, congealed ideas; but a thought in motion, alive, warm, expressed with fluidity and movement. And for this reason, his work has, in part, a markedly autobiographic character ... that comes from a profound attachment, more than to the concept to the perceptions that nourish it, to the nature that gives it nuances and emotion, to the deed that communicates dynamism to it and gives an object to it.

The function of ideas is remarkable here: rather than being sedimented in conceptual structures, they expose the roots, process, and biography of the philosopher who generates them. That is, ideas reveal the philosopher's experiences and positionality, as well as the reflection upon them, as the sources of utopian imaginaries. The philosophical architecture of utopias makes manifest the singularity of the lives that express them, their cultural, historical, and geopolitical loci, and their transcultural reach. In the case of the oppressed within the colonial difference, utopian philosophy includes the critique of dominant systems and the affirmation of alternative, liberatory options, and it also incarnates the fractured loci from which they are articulated, including cultural identities. This undermines modern Western configurations of universal rationality by positing philosophy as a draw toward intimacy—an elusive operation that undermines the hierarchy of rationalities and knowledge production enforced by the entanglement between racism and philosophy within the coloniality of power.[6]

The intimate exposure to the philosopher is fundamental: only on the basis of it, of being exposed through ideas to her biography, can utopian thinking appeal to one's whole being. What matters here is not the "truth" of ideas, but their ability to open oneself to fluid thoughts that reveal the philosopher's life in intimacy. This is the function, for example, of Anzaldúa's "auto-historias." An aesthetic dimension is operative here. Ideas bring us close to the perceptions, memories, emotions, temporalities and deeds that constitute their "lives." Recalling Flores Galindo, we could say that the power of utopian thinking is the exposure to its singularity and living enactments, a process that can make communities out of the intimacy within multitudes. This is connected to a movement of community making that is indifferent to futural projections of redemption. Yet utopian philosophy as community making is necessarily liberatory.[7]

Mariátegui's critique of Vasconcelos can be interpreted in terms of this utopian philosophical perspective. He turns to Vasconcelos's anticipation of a cosmopolitan, universal civilization arising in America and quotes his *Indología*: "I see the problem of the world as not anymore subdivided into partial missions that each race and each historical epoch have had to develop. Rather, I see it comprised in three great cycles, toward which history has been converging and whose realization we are not yet able to see." This is Vasconcelos's utopian architecture. On the one hand, his universalism dislodges Eurocentrism and attends to a temporal coevality between cultures that disrupts the linear, developmentalist conception of history enunciated from Europe. In this sense, a singular horizon of time is disseminated. At the same time, this utopian architecture brings with it a new spatial awareness: space is not anymore organized around a European axis but begins to be organized differently, recognizing a plurality of spatial axes. This temporal and spatial disseminations are, however, ultimately absorbed into a new universal temporal logic. This philosophical approach, then, transcends a differential perspective toward a new universality by means of a futural projection and established trajectory. Moreover, in this progressive *mestizaje*, Vasconcelos develops his own hierarchy of values from which to conceive of a return to a new universal history and to a new spatial axis: America, echoing here Bolívar's construction of the term.[8]

Mariátegui's critique is clear: "But these periods progress without a doubt parallel to one another." He is making two points here. First, a historical and factual one, that is, that effectively Vasconcelos temporal cycles occur concurrently without tendencies to converge toward a new single temporal horizon. Second, he is making a point about time, rejecting it as a sequence that implies that one epoch proceeds from, and replaces, the other, as if one historical epoch were the condition for another. Thus, Mariátegui recognizes the entanglement between universalism and the positing of singular, developmental historical horizons and detects in them both a philosophical disposition that does not fit within his conception of utopian and liberatory philosophy.[9]

He condenses his critique of Vasconcelos: "the absence that we spirits of the new generation must confirm, with a little sadness and disenchantment, *is the absence of a more acute sense of the present.* The epoch asks for a more practical idealism, a more belligerent attitude. Vasconcelos accompanies us, easily and generously, to condemn the present, but not to understand it and use it. Our destiny is struggle rather than contemplation." Mariátegui, then, emphasizes the ultimate failure of Vasconcelos theory as utopian. Vasconcelos lacks a proper engagement with the present, which means that the utopian architecture in Vasconcelos's theory fails to return to the intimacy of the present out of which it is enunciated, to intimacy with the life that conditions it—that is, it does not reveal the potencies already operative in the present out of which the urgency for an alternative reality is manifest. It, rather, reinscribes itself into a futural projection. It does not succeed as an autohistoria. His ideas do not return us to his complex, volatile, polymorphous present. Vasconcelos, then, is a limit figure for Mariátegui. He inspired in him perhaps his most comprehensive account of philosophy as utopia but, at the same time, showed him the difficulty of sustaining it. This led Mariátegui to construe the present as a spatio-temporal excess, as disseminative, layered, and fractured. Philosophy is a site of simultaneous temporalities where alternative spatialities break through, given to be engaged by an architectural (rather than strictly temporal) utopian sensibility that can be definitive in the lives of the oppressed.[10]

VASCONCELOS'S FORMULA "PESSIMISM OF THE REAL AND OPTIMISM OF THE IDEAL"

Yet Mariátegui reflects on this utopian sensibility through Vasconcelos's famous formula: "pessimism of the real, optimism of the ideal." He connects this formula to the power of liberatory myths, to "millions of people . . . working with a mystical courage and a religious passion to create a new world," echoing the aesthetic opening in Flores Galindo's texts. Mariátegui finds three aspects at the core of this formula: to be superior to the moment, to repudiate reality and seek to destroy it, and to act out of an excess of faith. He focuses on the relationship between the last two.[11]

While Vasconcelos finds in pessimism an imperative to destroy reality, Mariátegui finds in it protest and condemnation of the present. Mariátegui has a more open relationship with reality: it does not need to be destroyed, but "rectified." At first, this disagreement may seem small. It is, however, fundamental. For Vasconcelos, the alternative reality that he affirms is achieved only through the destruction of the current one, that is, the former replaces the latter in the future. For Mariátegui, the affirmed alternative reality is already operative in the present, and what he means by *utopia* is a turning within the present, an aesthetic exposure to its temporal and spatial disseminations. He counters Vasconcelos thus: "All the great human ideals have started with a negation, but all have also been an affirmation." He posits here the simultaneity of affirmation and negation, which attests to the polymorphous and utopic character of the present.[12]

Now I turn to optimism. Mariátegui describes the revolutionary subject: "he is an optimist regarding his hope for the future." In Spanish, the phrase reads "optimista en cuanto a su esperanza." The easy interpretation of this is that revolutionary hope is optimistic, which says hardly anything. But the phrase is, in fact, more complex: the revolutionary is an optimist in relation to, or about, his hope. In this sense, optimism is the affirmation of the possibility of hope, a state that antecedes hope and makes it possible in the first place. More important, this optimism does not draw its affirmative force from the future, or from what the future can be: it is not a futural projection, but futural projections can issue from it. It is not redemptive. This kind of affirmation of the present gives one to hope through utopian architectures that remain indeterminate and return one to the intimacy, urgency, and layering of one's present.[13]

Utopian gestures in this sense allow for the articulation of liberatory projects by remaining with the polymorphy of the present, including cultural identities, fractures and crossings, as it is taken up by the oppressed aesthetically, at the level of sensibilities and affects. This discussion of Mariátegui's reading of Vasconcelos is related to Flores Galindo's and Beigel's interpretation of Mariátegui, specifically to the aesthetic sensibility that grounds utopian thinking and to the surrealist discipline to affirm the release of dominant structures, structures that are always already exceeded in the present. And it also sheds light on philosophy as enabling processes of community making as exposures to the alterity of others prior to hope.

It seems that this discussion has moved away from the issue of the relationship between cultural identity and social liberation, as encountered in Schutte's reading of Mariátegui, for example. Yet utopian philosophy situates itself at the borders of cultural determinations. All this analysis hinges on this basic point. That is, cultural determinations are the element through which realities can be given in their oppressive and liberating possibilities. At the same time, utopian philosophy and its sensibilities situate themselves in the transgression of the fixity of cultural determinations, opening up a field of liberation in the present that suspends the *values* of continuous cultural projections and, with this suspension, culture recedes as a totalizing referent for philosophical and political engagements. Perhaps the main point here is that liberatory and utopian philosophies can be operative with the passing of cultural horizons but without transcending cultural formations, which is very different from liberatory projects that originate in the affirmation of a static cultural identity (as in Mariátegui's indigenista logic of redemption that I elucidated in an earlier chapter). This discussion makes contingent the apparent need to appeal to transhistorical Indian identities, for example, while it retains the efficacy of indigenous lineages as conditions for critiques and utopian philosophies. Moreover, through interpretations of Mariátegui's own texts, one can undo the temporal structure of logics of redemption. His analysis of the present, and of the relationship between optimism and hope, leads to a present that does not need to be redeemed because it does not draw value from the future, a present beyond redemption that nevertheless can be the spatio-temporal condition for philosophical liberatory utopias.

GLORIA ANZALDÚA'S "BORDER ARTE"

This aesthetic delimitation of philosophy can be connected to the way Anzaldúa captures the condition of the oppressed within the colonial difference: "La negación sistemática de la cultura Mexicana—chicana en los Estados Unidos impide su desarrollo, haciéndole este un acto de colonización. As a people who have been stripped of our history, language, identity, and pride, we attempt again and again to find what we have lost by digging into our cultural roots *imaginatively and making art from our findings.*" The similarities with Schutte's position are evident. The liberation of the colonized depends on the remembrance mediated by a cultural identity, without which projects of liberation cannot be articulated. This is also Mariátegui's fundamental insight that drove him to develop an indigenous socialism.[14]

Anzaldúa turns to two factors that affect the remembrance of cultural lineages. First, echoing Fanon, she emphasizes that coloniality leaves the colonized feeling stripped of defining features of her culture, and that "digging into one's cultural roots" is the response to counter this. That is, the colonized is detached from her culture and yet finds in its affirmation the conditions for her liberation. This is a complex process, to say the least, one that is never fulfilled because the detachment is never overcome: "we attempt again and again." Anzaldúa, then, shows that the colonized does not only find herself culturally positioned but is also exposed to a sense of detachment from her culture that becomes an irreducible, defining sensibility for her, situating her at the limits or borders of cultures. Her project is to understand the relationship between cultural identity and social liberation from this connected detachment, something that in my view Schutte—within the confines of her interpretation of Mariátegui—does not focus on. Yet my analysis of Mariátegui's surreal aesthetic grounds for revolutionary praxis does find the emergence of a revolutionary faith precisely at the limit, and in the release, of cultural determinations, showing an affinity between him and Anzaldúa. Second, within this connected detachment the practices of digging into one's own cultural roots toward social liberation take aesthetic forms ("imaginatively and making art") rather than yielding objectifying approaches to cultural legacies. Here, again, we see the affinity with Mariátegui's aesthetic/philosophical grounds for the generation of utopias.

Anzaldúa reflects on the dominant disposition toward the culture of the colonized: "The essence of colonization: rip off a culture, then regurgitate its white version to the 'natives.'" The denial of the humanity of the colonized, the racist belief in the dispensability of their lives, does not simply attempt to erase or empty out value from their culture. It also curbs the ability of the colonized to affirm and articulate their own culture because such processes must be allowed, mediated, and evaluated by the colonizer. That is, the colonizer issues an image of the colonized culture that becomes definitive for the expressions of it within the colonial difference. The colonized are, thus, stripped of their culture and of their ability to manifest it.[15]

This dynamic, however, is even more complex. The regurgitation of the white version of the colonized culture is performed by both colonizer and colonized.

Moreover, the "natives" who receive this white construction are themselves constituted *as natives* through the regurgitation. Anzaldúa puts "natives" in quotation marks because this category is given fixity and meaning through white regurgitations of colonized cultures—it echoes the term *Indian* that has haunted this whole book. It turns out, then, that colonization is not only the erasure of colonized cultures, but also a complex mechanism for the construction of colonized culture and of the cultural determinations of the colonized themselves, a mechanism that furthers the dehumanization of the colonized and to which the colonized are drawn in complicity. Moreover, and Anzaldúa is especially sensitive to this, liberatory projects of the oppressed can be such mechanisms. These insights bring Anzaldúa close to my critique of dynamics redemption, of the redemption of the Indian in particular.

The connected detachment of the colonized as a sensibility toward her own culture arises in the context of the colonial erasure and construction of her culture, and allows her to gain some critical distance from these processes. The urgency to affirm her culture as the positionality for the expression of her liberatory demands remains, but she can come to be attentive to the possibility that what she affirms as her culture is a colonizing construction, and, even more, that her own drive to appropriate her own culture—even for the sake of liberation—can't be simply disentangled from the interests of the white appropriation of it. Anzaldúa confides: "we often do misappropriate and collude with the Anglos' forms of misappropriation."[16]

An implicit insight defines her text "Border Arte" as a meditation on the dangers of cultural misappropriation: the colonized must at the same time seek cultural footing and let go of appropriative dispositions toward her culture. In this way, a new field for the operation of culture is opened up at the borders of culture; this is where liberatory or utopian philosophy begins. Anzaldúa's account of *mestizaje* as a border sensibility shows that this field does not transcend culture but takes place immanently in the borders between cultures. Within this sensibility, culture never happens in the singular but in plurality, in enactments of proliferations of identities. In this border space, or nepantla, cultures clash with one another, and colonizing and liberatory investments come to be at war yet enmeshed with one another, even within the colonized. Anzaldúa writes, "En este lugar entre medio, nepantla, two or more forces clash and are held teetering on the verge of chaos, a state of entreguerras. These tensions between extremes create cracks or tears in the membrane surrounding, protecting and containing the different cultures and their perspectives, Nepantla is the place where at once we are detached (separated) and attached (connected) to each of our several cultures."[17] As in the discussion of Lugones in an earlier chapter, spatial sensibilities are predominant here: Nepantla is a place more than a temporal determination or a spatialization that interrupts closed temporal horizons in which conflicts come to be resolved, singular narratives are consolidated, and identities constituted. Anzaldúa writes, "to be disoriented in space is the 'normal' way of being for us mestizos living in the borderlands. It's the sane way of coping with the accelerated pace of this complex, interdependent, and multicultural planet. To be disoriented in space is to be in nepantla. To be disoriented in space is to experience bouts of disassociation of identity, of identity breakdowns and buildups." Connected detachment is given to spatial, border sensibilities as a way of sustaining the coming to pass of cultural determinations and identities as they clash with others within the colonial difference, enactments where the erasure and construction of colonized cultures is part of a pernicious and dehumanizing white mechanism. This attests to the possibility of exceeding the defining force of these conflicts and power dynamics by disengaging from appropriative dispositions toward colonized cultures even if for the sake of liberation; a disengagement that is not only a political but also a philosophical opening.[18]

As Anzaldúa observes: "The border is the locus of resistance, of rupture, of implosion and explosion, and of putting together the fragments and creating a new assemblage. For me, this process is represented by Coatlicue's daughter, Coyolxauhqui, la diosa de la luna." The border is the place where the fragments of cultural identities, and the remnants of cultural determinations, are spread out in the aftermath of colonial conflicts. They are remainders of the entangled internal and external power struggles between colonizer and colonized that reveal the nonexhaustive character of colonial power. The possibility of engaging cultural positionalities from which to articulate projects of liberation does not lie in the entrenchment within these power struggles. Such an entrenchment, in fact, rigidifies cultural determinations in ways that further colonial racist interests. It lies, rather, on picking up what is left in the aftermath and creating, with the broken pieces, a utopian assemblage or architecture (in Mariátegui's terms), one that elicits liberatory commitments by bringing one back to the border positionality of the colonized in nepantla in the wake of violence. It is perhaps one of Anzaldúa's most helpful insights to posit this *after* (which in my view restricts the draw of futural temporalities) in its excess of colonial violence also as a spatial determination that interrupts temporal projections. In the terms of this book: nepantla as a place beyond redemption. From this viewpoint, liberation appears differently. It is not the single-minded affirmation of identities that becomes complicit with colonial interests nor the entrapment in oppositions that lead to conflicts with the expectation of overpowering the other. Picking up the pieces and creatively assembling them as a liberatory praxis (the process of Coyolxauhqui) enacts the turn from critique of the dominant order to the affirmation of alternative realities in a different plane, tapping on different sources. And all this is made possible by the auto-historias of the oppressed inscribed in nepantla. This is where Anzaldúa's Coyolxauhqui processes intersects with Mariátegui's utopian philosophical approach.[19]

An aesthetics of liberation and an aesthetic delimitation of philosophy are at stake here. Anzaldúa points to an aesthetic excess that the border artist works from, characterizing what *remains* after the operation of mechanisms of erasure and cultural appropriation, including redemptive ones: "The process of 'borrowing' is repeated until the images' original meanings are pushed into the unconscious, and images more significant to the prevailing culture and era surface. However, the artist on some level still connects to that unconscious reservoir of meaning, connects to the nepantla state of transition between time periods, connects to the border between cultures." The "process of borrowing" refers here to colonization's destruction and manufacturing of colonized cultures. Anzaldúa finds a reservoir of images that exceeds these processes, an unconscious, aesthetic reservoir of meanings that remain for the border artist to use but that cannot be contained within definite cultural loci. The border artist picks up the pieces, the fragments of cultural formations and identities, and deals with them as images, that is, offering options for transvaluations and of open meanings, options that the border artist takes up beyond appropriative dispositions, with connected detachment in nepantla. Just as in strains of Mariátegui's thought, Anzaldúa's practices of liberation are grounded in an aesthetic sensibility. And she also thinks of it as a practice, an ethos, a discipline that responds to the "Coyolxauhqui imperative." The connections with Mariátegui's view of surrealism as discipline suggest themselves here, except that Anzaldúa would object to them on the basis that they could erase indigenous cultures by evoking Eurocentered aesthetic practices.[20]

The connection between "border arte" and liberation is evident for Anzaldúa. Liberation here means building border communities. She writes, "The multi-subjectivity and split-subjectivity of border artists creating various counter-arts will continue, but with a parallel movement in which a polarized us/them, insiders/outsiders culture clash is not the main struggle, and a refusal to be split will be the norm. . . . Art makes a wider community, one that transcends the artists culture and lifetime." "Border arte" refers to artworks but also to an aesthetic ethos in nepantla. The artist taps into the reservoir of images that exceeds the ways in which coloniality erases and constructs culture yet produces artworks that can be brought into the purview of these mechanisms. Anzaldúa expresses this danger: "Appropriating these figures is part of the cultural 'recovery' and 'recuperation' work Chicana artists and writers have been doing for the past couple of decades, finally acknowledging and accepting our native origins. . . . Only now, we have gone to the other extreme, 'becoming,' claiming and acting as though we are more indigenous than Native Americans themselves—something that Native Americans rightfully resent." In the text "Border Arte," this danger never ceases and the whole text circles around it as an inevitable axis. Nevertheless, "border arte" not only makes artworks but also sets into play an ethos, a discipline, a practice that can come to inform communities in the aftermath, as it were, of the polarizing dynamics of power of coloniality; communities beyond redemption where "culture clash is not the main struggle" but where cultural loci continue to be at play in the articulation of liberatory options.[21]

This grounding operation of aesthetics does not erase philosophical reflection or "mestizaje theories" (as Anzaldúa puts it). In fact, it showcases their utopian function, in Mariátegui's terms. This is, then, drawing from both Anzaldúa and Mariátegui, an aesthetic delimitation of Latin American philosophy. Also, in view of the trajectory of this book, border artists appear here as collective agents of liberation configured in liberatory processes, eluding closures of identity formations, and without redemptive purpose.

NOTES

1. Mariátegui, "Indología," 78, 79.
2. See chapters 4, 5 and 6 in this volume.
3. By disposition, I mean here, drawing from Heidegger and Vallega, an affective attunement that prearticulates conceptual and rational modes of understanding. Mariátegui, "Indología," 79. See also Tucker, ed., *Marx and Engels Reader*, 145.
4. See Mariátegui, "Lucha final," for an analysis on the ambivalence about the finality of revolutionary myths. See also Mariátegui, "Final Struggle," 389–94. See further chapter 3 in this volume.
5. Mariátegui, "Indología," 78. This is a reference to Vallega's account of anachronic, temporal sensibilities of liberation. See Vallega, *Latin American Philosophy*, 196–208. See chapter 3 in this volume.
6. Mariátegui, "Indología," 79.
7. See Anzaldúa, *Light in the Dark*, 6.
8. See Mariátegui, "Indología," 78, 80.
9. Mariátegui, "Indología," 81.

10. Mariátegui, "Indología," 81; italics mine.

11. Mariátegui, "Pessimism," 146.

12. Mariátegui, "Pessimism," 146. Ibid. One could connect this sense of the present to Kusch's indigenous-influenced notion of "estar" (Kusch, *Indigenous and Popular Thinking*, 158–64).

13. Mariátegui, "Pesimismo," 36.

14. Anzaldúa, *Luz*, 48; italics mine.

15. Anzaldúa, *Luz*, 48.

16. Anzaldúa, *Luz*, 53.

17. Anzaldúa, *Luz*, 56. See my discussion of Lugones in chapter 5 for an account of a critique that remains at the borders between cultures.

18. Anzaldúa, *Luz*, 57.

19. Anzaldúa, *Luz*, 49.

20. Anzaldúa, *Luz*, 55.

21. Anzaldúa, *Luz*, 63, 53.

BIBLIOGRAPHY

Acosta López, María del Rosario. "Gramáticas de la escucha: decolonizar la historia y la memoria." In Moraña, *Sujeto, decolonización, transmodernidad*, 69–84.

Agamben, Giorgio. *Homo Sacer: Sovereign Power and Bare Life*. Translated by Daniel Heller-Roazen. Edited by Werner Hamacher and David E. Wellbery. Stanford, CA: Stanford University Press, 1998.

Aguilar Rivera, José Antonio. "Men or Citizens? The Making of Bolívar's Patria." In Gracia, *Forging People*, 57–84.

Al-Saji, Alia. "A Phenomenology of Hesitation: Interrupting Racializing Habits of Seeing." In *Living Alterities: Phenomenology, Embodiment and Race*. Edited by Emily Lee, 133–72. New York: SUNY Press, 2014.

———. "Too Late: Racialized Time and the Closure of the Past." *Insights* 6, 5 (2003): 1–13.

Anzaldúa, Gloria E. *The Gloria Anzaldúa Reader*. Edited by Analouise Keating. Durham, NC: Duke University Press, 2009.

———. *Light in the Dark/Luz en lo oscuro: Rewriting Identity, Spirituality, Reality*. Edited by Analouise Keating. Durham, NC: Duke University Press, 2015.

Arguedas, José María. *Deep Rivers*. Translated by Frances Horning Barraclough. Long Grove, IL: Waveland, 1978.

Aricó, José, ed. *Mariátegui y los orígenes del marxismo latinoamericano*. 2nd ed. México City: Cuadernos del Pasado y Presente, 1980.

Aristotle. *The Nicomachean Ethics*. Translated by Joe Sachs. Indianapolis: Focus, 2002.

Bartky, Sandra. "Toward a Phenomenology of a Feminist Consciousness." *Social Theory and Practice* 3, 4 (1975): 425–39.

Becker, Marc. *Mariátegui and Latin American Marxist Theory*. Athens: Center for International Studies, 1993.

Beigel, Fernanda. *El itinerario y la brújula: el vanguardismo estético-político de José Carlos Mariátegui*. Buenos Aires: Biblos, 2003.

————. "Mariátegui y las antinomías del indigenismo." *Utopía y Praxis Latinoamericana* 6, no. 13 (2001): 36–57.

Belaúnde, Víctor Andrés. *Bolívar and the Political Thought of Spanish America.* New York: Octagon, 1978.

Bernasconi, Robert. "Who Invented the Concept of Race? Kant's Role in the Enlightenment Construction of Race." In *Race: Blackwell Readings in Continental Philosophy.* Edited by Robert Bernasconi, 11–36. Oxford: Blackwell, 2001.

Bolívar, Simón. "The Jamaica Letter." In Bushnell, David, ed. *El Libertador: Writings of Simón Bolívar.* Oxford: Oxford University Press, 2003. 12–30.

————. "The Angostura Address." In Bushnell, David, ed. *El Libertador: Writings of Simón Bolívar.* Oxford: Oxford University Press, 2003. 31–53.

Bosteels, Bruno. *Marx and Freud in Latin America: Politics, Psychoanalysis, and Religion in Times of Terror.* London: Verso, 2012.

Bushnell, David, ed. *El Libertador: Writings of Simón Bolívar.* Oxford: Oxford University Press, 2003.

Cadena, Marisol de la. *Indígenas mestizos: raza y cultura en el Cusco.* Lima: IEP, 2004.

Campuzano Arteta, Alvaro. *La modernidad imaginada: arte y literatura en el pensamiento de José Carlos Mariátegui (1911–1930).* Madrid: Iberoamericana/ Vervuert, 2017.

Castro, Augusto. *Filosofía y política en el Perú.* Lima: Fondo Editorial de la Pontificia Universidad Católica del Perú, 2006.

Castro, Daniel. *Another Face of Empire.* Durham, NC: Duke University Press, 2007.

Castro-Gómez, Santiago. *Crítica de la razon latinoamericana.* Barcelona: Puvill, 1996.

————. *La hybris del punto cero: ciencia, raza e ilustración en la Nueva Granada (1750–1816).* Bogotá: Pontificia Universidad Javeriana, 2005.

————. "No Longer Broad but Still Alien Is the World: The End of Modernity and the Transformation of Culture in the Times of Globalization." In *Latin American Perspectives on Globalization.* Edited by Mario Sáenz, 25–39. Lanham, MD: Rowman and Littlefield, 2002.

————. "Qué hacer con los universalismos occidentales? Observaciones en torno al giro decolonial." In Moraña, *Sujeto, decolonización, transmodernidad.* 181-208

Castro-Klaren, Sara. "Framing Panamericanism: Simón Bolívar's Findings." *New Centennial Review* 3, no. 1 (2003): 35–44.

Chavarría, Jésus. *José Carlos Mariátegui and the Rise of Modern Peru.* Albuquerque: University of New Mexico Press, 1979.

Ciccariello-Maher, George. *Decolonizing Dialectics.* Durham, NC: Duke University Press, 2017.

Cornejo Polar, Antonio. *"Indigenismo* and Heterogeneous Literatures: Their Double Sociocultural Statue." In *The Latin American Cultural Studies Reader.* Edited by Ana del Sarto, Alicia Ríos, and Abril Trigo. Durham, NC: Duke University Press, 2004. 100-115

———. *"Mestizaje,* Transculturation, Heterogeneity." In *The Latin American Cultural Studies Reader.* Edited by Ana del Sarto, Alicia Ríos, and Abril Trigo. Durham, NC: Duke University Press, 2004. 116–19.

———. *Writing in the Air.* Durham, NC: Duke University Press, 2013.

Coronado, Jorge. *The Andes Imagined.* Pittsburgh, PA: Pittsburgh University Press, 2009.

———. "El periódico *Labor* (1928–29) entre indios y obreros: el indigenismo ante la prensa operaria." In Moraña and Podestá, *José Carlos Mariátegui.*

Coronil, Fernando. "Beyond Occidentalism: Toward Nonimperial Geohistorical Categories." *Cultural Anthropology* 11, no. 1, 1996: 51–87.

D'Altroy, Terence. *The Incas.* London: Blackwell, 2015.

Dean, Carolyn. *Inka Bodies and the Body of Christ: Corpus Christi and Colonial Cuzco, Peru.* Durham, NC: Duke University Press, 1999.

De Andrade, Oswald. *Escritos Antropófagos.* Buenos Aires: Corregidor, 2001.

De la Cadena, Marisol. *Indigenous Mestizos.* Durham, NC: Duke University Press, 2000.

De las Casas, Bartolomé. *A Short Account of the Destruction of the Indies.* London: Penguin, 1992.

De Soto, Hernando. *El misterio del capital: por qué el capitalismo triunfa en occidente y fracasa en el resto del mundo.* Translated by Mirko Lauer and Jessica McLauchlan. Lima: El Comercio, 2000.

De Sousa Santos, Boaventura. *Epistemologies of the South.* London: Paradigm, 2014.

Díaz, Kim. "Mariátegui's Myth." *Hispanic/Latino Issues in Philosophy* 13, 1 (2013):18–22.

DuBois, W. E. B. *W. E. B. Du Bois: A Reader.* Edited by David Levering Lewis. New York: Holt, 1995.

Dussel, Enrique. "Anti-Cartesian Meditations: On the Origin of the Philosophical Anti-discourse of Modernity." *Journal for Culture and Religious Theory* 13, no. 1 (2014): 11–52.

———. "Christian Art of the Oppressed in Latin America (Towards an Aesthetics of Liberation)." *Concilium* 152 (1980): 40–52.

———. *Ethics of Liberation.* Translated by Alejandro Vallega, Eduardo Mendieta, Camilo Pérez Bustillo, Yolanda Angulo, and Nelson Maldonado-Torres. Durham, NC: Duke University Press, 2013.

———. *Filosofía de la Liberación.* México: Edicol, 1977.

———. *The Invention of the Americas.* New York: Continuum, 1995.

————. *Philosophy of Liberation*. Translated by Aquilina Martínez and Christine Morkovsky. Eugene, OR: Orbis, 1985.

————. "Transmodernity and Interculturality: An Interpretation from the Perspective of the Philosophy of Liberation." *Transmodernity* 1, no. 3 (2012): 29–55.

————. "World System and Transmodernity." *Nepantla* 3, 2 (2002): 221–44.

Earle, Rebecca. *The Return of the Native: Indians and Myth-Making in Spanish America, 1810–1930*. Durham, NC: Duke University Press, 2007.

Escajadillo, Tomás G. *Mariátegui y la literatura peruana*. Lima: Amaru, 2004.

Estermann, Josef. *Filosofía andina*. Quito: Abya Yala, 1998.

Fanon, Frantz. *Black Skin, White Masks*. Translated by Richard Philcox. New York: Grove, 2008.

————. *The Wretched of the Earth*. Translated by Richard Philcox. New York: Grove, 2004.

Fernández Díaz, Osvaldo. "Gramsci y Mariátegui: frente a la ortodoxia." *Nueva Sociedad* 115 (1991): 135–44.

Flores, Juan. *From Bomba to Hip-Hop: Puerto Rican Culture and Latino Identity*. New York: Columbia University Press, 2000.

Flores Galindo, Alberto. *Buscando un Inca: identidad y utopía en los Andes*. Cuba, La Habana: Casa de las Américas, 1986.

————. *In Search of an Inca: Identity and Utopia in the Andes*. Edited and translated by Carlos Aguirre, Charles F. Walker, and Willie Hiatt. New York: Cambridge University Press, 2010.

————. *Obras completas*. Vols. 2, 4, and 6. Edited by Cecilia Rivera. Lima: SUR Casa de Estudios del Socialismo, 1993.

Forgues, Roland. "Mariátegui y lo negro: antecedentes de un malentendido." In Moraña and Podestá, *José Carlos Mariátegui*.

Fornet-Betancourt, Raúl. "An Alternative to Globalization: Theses for the Development of an Intercultural Philosophy." In *Latin American Perspectives on Globalization*. Edited by Mario Sáenz, 230–36. Lanham, MD: Rowman and Littlefield, 2002.

Fountain, Anne. *José Martí, the United States, and Race*. Miami: University of Florida Press, 2014.

Frye, Marilyn. *The Politics of Reality*. New York: Crossing, 1983.

Gadamer, Hans-Georg. "The Festive Character of Theater." In *The Relevance of the Beautiful and Other Essays*. Edited by Robert Bernasconi. Translated by Dan Tate. Cambridge: Cambridge University Press, 1998. 57–65.

————. "The Relevance of the Beautiful." In *The Relevance of the Beautiful and Other Essays*. Edited by Robert Bernasconi. Translated by Dan Tate. Cambridge: Cambridge University Press, 1998. 1–56.

————. *Truth and Method*. 2nd rev. ed. Translation revised by Joel Weinsheimer and Donald G. Marshall. London: Continuum, 2004.

Gallegos-Ordorica, Sergio Armando. "The Racial Legacy of the Enlightenment in Simón Bolívar's Political Thought." In *Critical Philosophy of Race* 1, no. 2 (2018): 198–215.

García-Bryce, Iñigo. *Haya de la Torre and the Pursuit of Power in Twentieth-Century Perú and Latin America.* Chapel Hill: University of North Carolina Press, 2018.

García Márquez, Gabriel. *Cien años de soledad.* Buenos Aires: Sudamericana, 1967.

———. *Leafstorm: And Other Stories.* New York: Harper and Row, 1990.

García Salvatecci, Hugo. *Georg Sorel y Mariátegui: ubicación ideológica del amauta.* Lima: Delgado Valenzuela, 1979.

Germaná, César. "Una epistemología otra: la contribución de Aníbal Quijano a la reestructuración de las ciencias sociales de América latina." In *Des/Colonialidad y bien vivir: un nuevo debate en América latina.* Edited by Aníbal Quijano, 73–101. Lima: Universidad Ricardo/Editorial Universitaria, 2014.

Gobat, Michel. "The Invention of Latin America: A Transnational History of Anti-imperialism, Democracy and Race." *American Historical Review* (2013): 1345–75.

González Prada, Manuel. *Pájinas libres.* Paris: Paul Dupont, 1922.

Gracia, Jorge J. E. *Forging People.* Notre Dame, IN: University of Notre Dame Press, 2011.

Gracia, Jorge J. E., and Elizabeth Millán Zaibert, eds. *Latin American Philosophy for the Twenty First Century: The Human Condition, Values and the Search for Identity.* New York: Prometheus, 2004.

Graham, Richard, ed. *The Idea of Race in Latin America, 1870–1940.* Austin: University of Texas Press, 2006.

Grosfoguel, Ramón. "The Epistemic Decolonial Turn: Beyond Political-Economy Paradigms." *Cultural Studies* 21, nos. 2–3 (2007): 211–23.

Guaman Poma de Ayala, Felipe. *The First New Cronicle and Good Government.* Translated by Ronald Hamilton.

Guibal, Francis. *Vigencia de Mariátegui.* Lima: Amauta, 1995.

Hanneken, Jamie. "José Carlos Mariátegui and the Time of Myth." *Cultural Critique* 81 (Spring 2012): 1–30.

Harstock, Nancy. "The Feminist Standpoint: Developing the Ground for a Specifically Feminist Historical Materialism." In *Discovering Reality.* Edited by Sandra Harding and Merrill Hintikka, 283–310. Boston: Reidel, 1983. Austin: University of Texas Press, 2009.

Heidegger, Martin. *Being and Time.* Translated by Joan Stambaugh. Albany: SUNY Press, 2010.

Helg, Aline. "Simón Bolívar's Republic: A Bulwark against the Tyranny of the Majority." *Revista de Sociología e Política* 42 (2012): 21–37.

Hooker, Juliette. *Theorizing Race in the Americas: Douglas, Sarmiento, Du Bois and Vasconcelos.* Oxford: Oxford University Press, 2017.

Kim, David. "José Mariátegui's East-South Decolonial Experiment."
    Comparative and Continental Philosophy 7, no. 2 (2015): 157–79.
Kusch, Rodolfo. *Indigenous and Popular Thinking in América.* Translated by María
    Lugones and Joshua M. Price. Durham, NC: Duke University Press, 2010.
Llorente, Renzo. "The Amauta's Ambivalence: Mariátegui on Race." In Gracia,
    Forging People. 228–47.
Lomas, Laura. *Translating Empire: José Martí, Migrant Latino Subjects, and
    American Modernities.* Durham, NC: Duke University Press, 2008.
López Albújar, Enrique. *Cuentos andinos.* Lima: Peisa, 1991.
Löwy, Michael. *Morning Star: Surrealism, Marxism, Anarchism, Situationism,
    Utopia.* Austin: University of Texas Press, 2009.
———. "Marxismo romántico." *Anuario Mariateguiano* 5 (1993): 155–59.
Lugones, María. "From within Germinative Stasis: Creating Active Subjectivity,
    Resistant Agency." In *Entre Mundos/among Worlds.* Edited by Analouise
    Keating. New York: Palgrave Macmillan, 2005.
———. "Heterosexualism and the Colonial/Modern Gender System." *Hypatia*
    22, no. 1 (2007): 186–209.
———. "Motion, Stasis, and Resistance to Interlocked Oppressions." In *Making
    Worlds: Gender, Metaphor, Materiality.* Edited by Susan Hardy Aiken, Ann
    Brigham, Sallie A. Marston, and Penny Waterstone, 49–52. Tucson: University
    of Arizona Press, 1998.
———. *Pilgrimages/Peregrinajes.* Lanham, MD: Rowman and Littlefield, 2003.
———. "Toward a Decolonial Feminism." *Hypatia* 25, no. 4 (2010): 742–59.
Maldonado Torres, Nelson. "On the Coloniality of Being: Contributions to the
    Development of a Concept." *Cultural Studies* 21, nos. 2–3 (March–May 2007):
    240–70.
Manrique, Nelson. *La piel y la pluma: escritos sobre literatura, etnicidad y racismo.*
    Lima: SUR Casa de Estudios del Socialismo, 1999.
Mariátegui, José Carlos. *El alma matinal.* Lima: Amauta, 1950.
———. *Defensa del Marxismo: polémica revolucionaria.* 14th ed. Lima: Amauta, 1988.
———. "El destino de Norteamérica." In *Invitación a la vida heroica: José Carlos
    Mariátegui; textos esenciales.* Edited by Alberto Flores Galindo and Ricardo
    Portocarrero Grados. Lima: Fondo Editorial del Congreso del Perú, 2005.
———. *La escena contemporánea.* 15th ed. Lima: Amauta, 1988.
———. "The Final Struggle." In *José Carlos Mariátegui. An Anthology,* edited by
    Harry Vanden and Marc Becker. New York: Monthly Review Press, 2011.
———. *The Heroic and Creative Meaning of Socialism: Selected Essays of José
    Carlos Mariátegui.* Edited and translated by Michael Pearlman. Amherst, NY:
    Humanity, 1996.
———. "Heterodoxia de la tradición." In *Invitación a la vida heroica: José Carlos
    Mariátegui; textos esenciales.* Edited by Alberto Flores Galindo and Ricardo
    Portocarrero Grados. Lima: Fondo Editorial del Congreso del Perú, 2005.

———. "El imperio y la democracia yanquis." In *La escena contemporánea*. Lima: Amauta, 1998.

———. "Indigenismo y socialismo." In *7 ensayos de interpretación de la realidad Peruana: ideología y política*. 2nd ed. Lima: Minerva, 2012.

———. "Indología de José Vasconcelos." In *Temas de nuestra América*. 10th ed. Lima: Amauta, 1988.

———. *Invitación a la vida heroica: José Carlos Mariátegui; textos esenciales*. Edited by Alberto Flores Galindo and Ricardo Portocarrero Grados. Lima: Fondo Editorial del Congreso del Perú, 2005.

———. "Man and Myth." In Mariátegui, *Heroic and Creative Meaning of Socialism*.

———. "Nacionalismo e internacionalismo." In *El alma matinal*. Lima: Amauta, 1950.

———. "Pesimismo de la realidad y optimismo del ideal." In *El alma matinal*. Lima: Amauta, 1950.

———. "Pessimism of the Real and Optimism of the Ideal." In Mariátegui, *Heroic and Creative Meaning of Socialism*.

———. *7 ensayos de interpretación de la realidad peruana: ideología y política*. 2nd ed. Lima: Minerva, 2012.

———. *Siete ensayos de interpretación de la realidad peruana*. Lima: Orbis Ventures, 2005.

———. *Temas de nuestra américa*. 10th ed. Lima: Amauta, 1988.

———. "The Unity of Indo-Spanish América." In *José Carlos Mariátegui: An Anthology*. Translated and edited by Harry E. Vanden and Marc Becker. New York: Monthly Review Press, 2011.

Martí, José. "Coney Island." In *José Martí: Selected Writings*. Translated by Esther Allen. New York: Penguin Books, 2002. 89–94.

———. "Our America." In *Latin American Philosophy for the 21st Century: The Human Condition, Values, and the Search for Identity*. Edited by Jorge J. E. Garcia and Elizabeth Millán-Zaibert, 245–52. Amherst, NY: Prometheus, 2004.

Martín Alcoff, Linda. "La cuestión del eurocentrismo: Žižek, Vallega, y la filosofía latinoamericana." In Moraña, *Sujeto, decolonización, transmodernidad*, 69–84.

———. "Educating with a (De)Colonial Consciousness." In *Latin American Philosophy of Education Journal* 1 (2014): 4–18.

———. "Enrique Dussel's Transmodernism." *Transmodernity* 1, no. 3 (2012): 60–68.

———. "An Epistemology for the Next Revolution." *Transmodernity* 1, no. 2 (2011): 67–78.

———. "Mignolo's Epistemology of Coloniality." *New Centennial Review* 7, no. 3 (2007): 79–101.

———. "Power/Knowledges in the Colonial Unconscious: A Dialogue between Dussel and Foucault." In *Thinking from the Underside of History: Enrique*

Dussel's Philosophy of Liberation. Edited by Linda Martín Alcoff and Eduardo Mendieta, 249–68. Lanham, MD: Rowman and Littlefield, 2000.

———. *Visible Identities: Race, Gender, and the Self*. New York: Oxford University Press, 2006.

Martín Alcoff, Linda, Michael Hames-García, Satya P. Mohanty, and Paula Moya, eds. *Identity Politics Reconsidered*. New York: Palgrave Macmillan, 2006.

Mazotti, José Antonio. "La fuerza del mito (andino): apunte sobre los *7 ensayos y la deconstrucción de Sorel* por Mariátegui." In Moraña and Podestá, *José Carlos Mariátegui*.

Melis, Antonio. *Leyendo Mariátegui: 1967–1998*. Lima: Amauta, 1999.

Melis, Antonio, Adalbert Dessau, and Manfred Kassok. *Mariátegui: tres estudios*. Lima: Amauta, 1971.

Méndez, Cecilia. "De indio a serrano: nociones de raza y geografía en el Perú (siglos XVIII–XXI)." In *Antología del pensamiento crítico peruano*. Edited by Martin Tanaka, 577–617. Buenos Aires: Consejo Latinoamericano de Ciencias Sociales, 2016.

Mendieta, Eduardo, ed. *Latin America and Postmodernity: A Contemporary Reader*. New York: Humanity, 2001.

———, ed. *Latin American Philosophy: Currents, Issues, Debates*. Bloomington: Indiana University Press, 2003.

———. "The Making of New Peoples: Hispanizing Race." In *Hispanics/Latinos in the United States*. Edited by Jorge J. E. Gracia and Pablo de Greiff. New York: Routledge, 2000.

Mignolo, Walter D. "Aisthesis decolonial: artículo de reflexión." *Calle 14*, no. 4 (2010): 13.

———. *The Darker Side of the Renaissance: Literacy, Territoriality, and Colonization*. Ann Arbor: University of Michigan Press, 1995.

———. *The Darker Side of Western Modernity*. Durham, NC: Duke University Press, 2011.

———. "Decolonizing Western Epistemology/Building Decolonial Epistemologies." In *Decolonizing Epistemologies: Latino/a Theology and Philosophy*. Edited by Ada María Isasi-Díaz and Eduardo Mendieta, 19–43. New York: Fordham University Press, 2012.

———. "De-linking: The Rhetoric of Modernity, the Logic of Coloniality, and the Grammar of Decoloniality." *Cultural Studies* 21, nos. 2–3 (2007): 449–514.

———. "The Geopolitics of Knowledge and the Colonial Difference." *South Atlantic Quarterly* 101, no. 1 (Winter 2002): 57–96.

———. *The Idea of Latin America*. Oxford, UK: Blackwell, 2005.

———. *Local Histories/Global Designs: Essays on the Coloniality of Power, Subaltern Knowledges and Border Thinking*. Princeton, NJ: Princeton University Press, 2000.

———. "Mariátegui and Gramsci in 'Latin' America: Between Revolution and Decoloniality." In *The Postcolonial Gramsci*. Edited by Neelam Srivastava and Braidick Battarcharya, 191–220. New York: Taylor and Francis, 2012.

Mills, Charles. "Materializing Race." In *Living Alterities: Phenomenology, Embodiment and Race*. Edited by Emily Lee. New York: SUNY Press, 2014.

Moore, Melissa. *José Carlos Mariátegui's Unfinished Revolution: Politics, Poetics, and Change in 1920's Peru*. Baltimore: Bucknell University Press, 2014.

Moraña, Mabel. "Mariátegui en los nuevos debates: emancipación, (in)dependencia y colonialismo supérstite en América latina." In Moraña and Podestá, *José Carlos Mariátegui*.

———, ed. *Sujeto, decolonización, transmodernidad: debates filosóficos latinoamericanos*. Madrid: Iberoamericana/Vervuert, 2018.

Moraña, Mabel, and Guido Podestá, eds. *José Carlos Mariátegui y los estudios latinoamericanos*. Pittsburgh, PA: Instituto Internacional de Literatura Iberoamericana, 2009.

Ngo, Helen. *The Habits of Racism: A Phenomenology of Racism and Racialized Embodiment*. Lanham: Lexington, 2017.

Nietzsche, Friedrich. *Twilight of the Idols*. Translated by Duncan Large. Oxford: Oxford University Press, 1998.

Nuccetelli Susana. *Latin American Thought, Philosophical Problems, and Arguments*. New York: Routledge, 2018.

Nuccetelli, Susana, Ofelia Schutte, and Octavio Bueno, eds. *A Companion to Latin American Philosophy*. Singapore: Blackwell, 2010.

Nuccetelli, Susana, and Gary Seay, eds. *Latin American Philosophy: An Introduction with Readings*. Upper Saddle River, NJ: Pearson, 2003.

Oshiro Higa, Jorge. *Razón y mito en Mariátegui*. Lima: Fondo Editorial del Congreso del Perú, 2013.

Oyarzún, Pablo. "Memory, Moment and Tears: A Speculative Approach to the Problem of Latin American Singularities." *New Centennial Review* 7, no. 3 (2007): 1–20.

Pagden, Anthony. *Spanish Imperialism and the Political Imagination*. New Haven, CT: Yale University Press, 1990.

Paris, Robert. "Mariátegui: un sorelismo antiguo." In *Mariátegui y los orígenes del marxismo latinoamericano*. Edited by José Aricó. México City: Pasado y Presente, 1978.

Podestá, Guido. "El indigenismo y la estrategias de la modernidad." In Moraña and Podestá, *José Carlos Mariátegui*.

Quijano, Aníbal. "Colonialidad del poder, eurocentrismo y América latina." In *La colonialidad del saber, eurocentrismo y ciencias sociales*. Edited by Edgardo Lander. Buenos Aires: Consejo Americano de Ciencias Sociales, 2000. 201–46.

————. "Coloniality of Power, Eurocentrism, and Latin America." In *Coloniality at Large: Latin America and the Postcolonial Debate*. Edited by Mabel Moraña, Enrique Dussel, and Carlos A. Jauregui, 181–224. Durham, NC: Duke University Press, 2008.

————. *Cuestiones y horizontes*. Edited by Danilo Assis Clímaco. Buenos Aires: Consejo Americano de Ciencias Sociales.

————. "Estética de la Utopía." In *Aníbal Quijano: cuestiones y horizontes*. Edited by Danilo Assis Clímaco. Buenos Aires: Consejo Latinoamericano de Ciencias Sociales, 2014. 733–42.

————. "El marxismo en Mariátegui: una propuesta de racionalidad alternativa." In *El marxismo de José Carlos Mariátegui*. Lima: Amauta, 1995.

————. "Modernity, Identity and Utopia in Latin America." *Boundary* 2, 20, no. 3 (1993): 140–55.

————. "Racionalidad alternativa." In *El marxismo de José Carlos Mariátegui*. Lima: Amauta, 1995.

————. "'Raza,' 'etnia' y 'nación' en Mariátegui." In *Aníbal Quijano: cuestiones y horizontes*. Edited by Danilo Assis Clímaco. Buenos Aires: Consejo Latinoamericano de Ciencias Sociales, 2014. 757–76.

————. *Reencuentro y debate: una introducción a Mariátegui*. Lima: Mosca Azul, 1979.

Quijano, Aníbal, and Immanuel Wallerstein. "Americanity as a Concept, or the Americas in the Modern World-System." *International Social Science Journal* XLIV, 4 (1992): 549–57.

Quintero, Pablo. "Notas sobre la teoría de la colonialidad del poder y la estructuración de la sociedad en América latina." In *Des/Colonialidad y bien vivir: un nuevo debate en América latina*. Edited by Aníbal Quijano, 193–216. Lima: Universidad Ricardo/Editorial Universitaria, 2014.

Quiroz Rojas, Rodolfo. "Otra modernidad, otra geografía: una interpretación crítica de las influencias y orientaciones geográficas de José Carlos Mariátegui. *Investigaciones Geográficas* 94 (2017): 1–12.

Rama, Ángel. *Transculturación narrativa en América latina*. México City: Siglo Veintiuno, 2004.

————. *Writing across Cultures: Narrative Transculturation in Latin America*. Edited and translated by David Frye. Durham, NC: Duke University Press, 2012.

Ramos, Julio. *Divergent Modernities: Culture and Politics in Nineteenth-Century Latin America*. Translated by John D. Blanco. Durham, NC: Duke University Press, 2001.

Rivera, Fernando. "Mariátegui: la escritura de la travesía." In Moraña and Podestá, *José Carlos Mariátegui*, 268–74.

Rivera, Omar. "Epistemological and Aesthetic Aspects of Transmodernism: Linda Martín Alcoff's and Alejandro Vallega's Readings of Enrique Dussel." *Interamerican Journal of Philosophy* 8, no. 2 (2017): 42–57.

————. "From Revolving Time to the Time of Revolution: Mariátegui's Encounter with Nietzsche." *APA Newsletter on Hispanic/Latino Issues in Philosophy* 8, no. 1 (2008): 22–26.

————. "Hermenéutica, representatividad y espacio en filosofías de la liberación social: una perspectiva latinoamericana." In Moraña, *Sujeto, decolonización, transmodernidad*, 69–84.

————. "The Image of the "Indio" in a Non-representative Economy: Meditations on Peruvian Marxism." *New Centennial Review* 7, no. 3 (2007): 131–48.

————. "Mariátegui's Avant-Garde and Surrealism as Discipline." *Symposium* 18, no. 1 (2014): 102–24.

————. "Reading Alejandro Vallega toward a Decolonial Aesthetics." *Comparative and Continental Philosophy* 9, no. 2 (2017): 162–73.

Rivera Berruz, Stephanie, and Leah Kalmanson, eds. *Comparative Studies in Asian and Latin American Philosophies: Cross-Cultural Theories and Methodologies*. London: Bloomsbury, 2018.

Rodó, José Enrique. *Ariel*. Columbia: Internacional, 2015.

Roncagliolo, Rafael. "Gramsci, marxista y nacional." *Quehacer* 3 (1980): 118–28.

Rotker, Susana. "The (Political) Exile Gaze in Martí's Writing on the United States." *José Martí's "Our America": From National to Hemispheric Cultural Studies*. Edited by Jeffrey Belnap and Raúl Fernández, 58–76. Durham, NC: Duke University Press, 1998.

Ruiz, Antonio. "Mariátegui y el factor geográfico." *Symposio intenacional: 7 ensayos, 80 años; mi sangre en mis ideas*, 141–47. Lima: Ministerio de Cultura del Perú, 2011.

Ruiz Zevallos, Augusto. "Mariátegui, historia y verdad." In Moraña and Podestá, *José Carlos Mariátegui*.

Salazar Bondy, Augusto. *Dominación y liberación: escritos 1966–1974*. Lima: Fondo Editorial de la Facultad de Letras y Ciencias Humanas/Universidad Nacional Mayor de San Marcos, 1995.

————. *Historia de las ideas en el Perú contemporáneo*. Lima: Fondo Editorial del Congreso del Perú, 2013.

Saldívar, José David. *Trans-Americanity: Subaltern Modernities, Global Coloniality, and the Cultures of Greater Mexico*. Durham, NC: Duke University Press, 2012.

Sánchez, Luis Alberto. *Indianismo e indigenismo en la literatura peruana*. Lima: Mosca Azul, 1981.

Sandoval, Chela. *Methodology of the Oppressed*. Minneapolis: University of Minnesota Press, 2000.

San Jinés, Javier. "Between Doubt and Hope: The Religious Disjunction of José Carlos Mariátegui." In Moraña and Podestá, *José Carlos Mariátegui*, 115–38.

————. *Mestizaje Upside Down: Aesthetic Politics in Modern Bolivia*. Pittsburgh, PA: Pittsburgh University Press, 2004.

Sarmiento, Domingo Faustino. *Facundo*. Berkeley: University of California Press, 2003.

Schutte, Ofelia. "Cultural Alterity: "Cross-Cultural Communication and Feminist Theory in North-South Contexts." *Hypatia* 13, 2 (1998): 53–72.

———. *Cultural Identity and Social Liberation in Latin American Thought*. Albany: State University of New York Press, 1993.

———. "De la colonialidad del poder al feminismo decolonial en América Latina." In Moraña, *Sujeto, decolonización, transmodernidad*, 137–58.

———. "Negotiating Latina Identities." In *Hispanics/Latinos in the United States*. Edited by Jorge J. E. Gracia and Pablo de Greiff. New York: Routledge, 2000.

———. "Nietzsche, Mariátegui and Socialism: A Case of 'Nietzschean Marxism' in Peru?" *Social Theory and Practice* 14 (1990): 71–85.

Scott, Charles E. *Living with Indifference*. Bloomington: Indiana University Press, 2007.

Silva Gruesz, Kirsten. *Ambassadors of Culture: The Transamerican Origins of Latino Culture*. Princeton, NJ: Princeton University Press, 2002.

Sobrevilla, David. *El marxismo de Mariátegui y su aplicación a los 7 ensayos*. Lima: Universidad de Lima/Fondo de Desarrollo Editorial, 2005.

Tirres, Christopher D. "At the Crossroads of Liberation Theology and Liberation Philosophy: Mariátegui's "New Sense" of Religion." *Interamerican Journal of Philosophy* 8, no. 1. (2017): 1-16

Tucker, Robert C., ed. *The Marx-Engels Reader*. 2nd ed. New York: Norton, 1978.

Unamuno, Miguel (personal communication). de. *The Agony of Christianity and Essays on Faith: Selected Works of Miguel de Unamuno*. Edited by Martin Nozick. Translated by Anthony Kerrigan. Princeton, NJ: Princeton University Press, 1974.

Unruh, Vicky. *Latin American Vanguards: The Art of Contentious Encounters*. Berkeley: University of California Press, 1994.

———. "Mariátegui's Aesthetic Thought: A Critical Reading of the Avant-Gardes." *Latin American Research Review* 24, no. 3 (1989): 45–69.

Valcárcel, Luis E. *Tempestad en los Andes*. Lima: Editora Universitaria Latina, 2006.

Vallega, Alejandro A. "Exordio/Exordium: For an Aesthetics of Liberation out of Latin American Experience." *Symposium* 18, no. 1 (Spring 2014): 125–40.

———. "Exterioridad radical, estética y liberación decolonial." In Moraña, *Sujeto, decolonización, transmodernidad*, 121–36.

———. *Latin American Philosophy from Identity to Radical Exteriority*. Bloomington: Indiana University Press, 2014.

———. "Out of Latin American Thought from Radical Exteriority: Philosophy after the Age of Pernicious Knowledge." In *The Gift of Logos: Essays in Continental Philosophy*. Edited by David Jones, Jason Wirth, and Michael Schwartz. Tyne, UK: Cambridge Scholars, 2010.

————. "Radical Intelligibility and the Limit of Philosophy in Latin America."
Interamerican Journal of Philosophy 8, no. 2 (Fall 2017): 33–41.

Vallejo, César. *César Vallejo: The Complete Poetry*. Edited and Translated by
Clayton Eshleman. Berkeley: University of California Press, 2007.

Vanden, Harry. *Mariátegui: influencias en su formación ideológica*. Lima: Amauta,
1975.

Vargas Llosa, Mario. *La utopía arcaíca*. México City: Fondo de Cultura
Económica, 1996.

Vasconcelos, José. *The Cosmic Race/La raza cósmica*. 2nd English ed. Translated
by Didier T. Jaén. Baltimore, MD: Johns Hopkins University Press, 1979.

Winter, Sylvia. "The Ceremony Must Be Found: After Humanism." *Boundary 2*,
12, 3 (1984): 19–70.

Zea, Leopoldo. *Simón Bolívar, integración en la libertad*. Caracas: Monte Avila
Latinoamericana, 1993.

INDEX

aesthetic delimitations of Latin American philosophy, 2, 137, 141–42, 182. *See also* Anzaldúa, Gloria; Coronado, Jorge; Flores Galindo, Alberto; López Albújar, Enrique; Lugones, María; Mariátegui, José Carlos; Quijano, Aníbal; representational aesthetics; Sanchez, Luis Alberto; Vasconcelos, José

aesthetic discipline, 141, 164, 166. *See also* Flores Galindo, Alberto; Quijano, Aníbal

aesthetics and politics. *See* Beigel, Fernanda, *El itinerario y la brújula*

aesthetics of liberation, 1, 7, 10, 149, 162–63, 165, 182

Agamben, Giorgio, 118n30

Alberdí, Juan Bautista, 16

America: fragmentation of, 40; political and philosophical significance of, 1; village space and, 39–40. *See also* indigenous peoples

American identity: as anchored in oppressed peoples, 9; articulated through liberatory philosophers, 17; determination by spatiality, 48; duality in "Our America," 50–51; effect of second colonization on, 73; and equal rights, 25–26; formation through shared threat, 41; inclusion of indigenous people within, 20–21; process of anthropophagy in, 61–62; progressively unfolding process of formation, 51–52; and search for authenticity, 29; in terms of

mestizaje, 22, 23–25; Zea's Bolivarianism, 28–30. *See also* cultural identity; Indian identity; indigenismo; lettered class; natural man; oppressed peoples

"Angostura Address" (Bolívar), 14, 18–19, 23, 24–25, 26–27, 51

anthropophagy, 61–62, 103

anticolonialism, 15, 46, 47, 52–53, 56–57, 62, 63

Anzaldúa, Gloria, 2, 109–10, 113, 175; "Border Arte," 10, 171, 178–83

Arguedas, José María, 162

Aristotle, 146

art, revolutionary power of, 116, 182–83

art and artists, 154–55

auto-historias, 174–76, 182

avant-garde aesthetic practices, 154–55

baroque ethos, 61, 65n52, 65n54

Beard, Charles A., 69

Beigel, Fernanda, *El itinerario y la brújula*, 153–56

Belaúnde, Víctor Andrés, 35n16

Bello, Andrés, 30

Bergson, Henri, 113, 145, 149

"beyond redemption," 1, 2, 5, 8, 9, 10, 52–53. *See also* community making; invisibilities, aesthetics of; nepantla; Schutte, Ofelia, *Cultural Identity and Social Liberation in Latin American Thought*

black resistance to oppression, 101

OMAR RIVERA is Associate Professor of philosophy at Southwestern University in Georgetown, Texas.

Lightning Source UK Ltd.
Milton Keynes UK
UKHW011835151021
392281UK00002B/792